MANUEL DE FALLA

MANUEL DE FALLA

Drawing by Larionow
Original engraving by Dumser

MANUEL DE FALLA

BY SUZANNE DEMARQUEZ

Translated from the French
by Salvator Attanasio

CHILTON BOOK COMPANY
Philadelphia   New York   London

INTRODUCTION

"Slightly built, dark-complexioned, nervous, with a penetrating look and piercing eyes under a resolute forehead, an Andalusian face that showed Arab traces, a face in which Spain was strongly reflected, while his brief and rare utterances, from the beginning, gave me the feeling of a man who was simultaneously passionate and meditative. . . ."

These were the impressions of the critic G. Jean Aubry upon meeting Manuel de Falla who had just arrived in Paris. The encounter took place as they were leaving a concert given by the composer Joaquin Nin in 1909, shortly before the death of Albéniz. Later, after he got to know Falla better, Aubry added: "His artistic life is an example of meticulous choice and firm will, of considered prudence and prompt resolution."

This judgment also applies to his daily life. Indeed, these two reflections wonderfully evoke the personality, the work, the charming and mysterious being that Manuel de Falla was for his contemporaries, friends, critics, and public. And this description of the great composer, who continued the tradition of Moralès and Victoria and plumbed to its depths and synthesized the proud and remote soul of his country, still is meaningful for posterity. Can we preserve the aura of mystery which envelops and protects this being with the "piercing eyes under a resolute forehead," and still bring to life the artist, and, above all, can we understand this lofty soul whose music was to stir so many hearts and one day attain such a degree of purity? We shall try to do this by telling what we know about the man and the work he has left us, but also, and especially, through examining the songs, diaries, and music of his native land.

But Spain alone was not responsible for the molding of the master. Long and varied sojourns abroad, as well as in his homeland, mark the stages of his life and work. We can distinguish five principal periods: youth in Cádiz; musical studies pursued in Madrid and the meeting with Felipe Pedrell; first stay in France; return to Spain, principally to Granada, concert tours, numerous changes of place; and finally, the retreat to Argentina, from 1939 to his death in 1946.

We could also add to these the journey to Catalonia and to the Balearics, where the musician's presence left fond and abiding memories.

These are the diverse places that formed the withdrawn and changeable composer whose evolution began with the *zarzuelas*, written in Madrid, and ended with *Atlántida,* that strange monument—the culmination of the dream of a lifetime—which has aroused and attracted our impatient curiosity for so long.

TABLE OF CONTENTS

Introduction v

I. Childhood and Adolescence 1

II. In Madrid 12

III. Two Encounters—Two Competitions 20

IV. Paris—Maturity 36

V. Return to Spain 67

VI. *Nights in the Gardens of Spain* 85

VII. *The Corregidor and the Miller's Wife,*
and *The Three-Cornered Hat* 93

VIII. *Fantasia Baetica* 109

IX. *Master Peter's Puppet Show* 119

X. La Orquesta Bética de Cámara 137

XI. The *Cante Jondo* Competition 143

XII. *Psyché* 152

XIII. The Harpsichord Concerto 157

XIV. The *Sonnet to Córdoba* and the Origin
of *Atlántida* 170

XV. *Homenajes* 187

XVI. In Argentina 193

XVII. *Atlántida* 201

Bibliography 238

The Works of Manuel de Falla 242

Index 247

MANUEL DE FALLA

CHAPTER I / Childhood and Adolescence

Manuel Maria de Falla y Matheu (customarily Spaniards add their mother's maiden name to their surname) was born in Cádiz on November 23, 1876, the day after the feast of St. Cecilia. "An Andalusian face . . ." and Cádiz is unmistakably Andalusian. Yet Falla's parents did not come from the extreme south of the peninsula: his father was a native of Valencia, the eastern Spanish province that is rich in the influences of the eastern Mediterranean; and his mother was a northerner from Catalonia, a province tempered by the cool breezes of the Pyrenees and the nearness of France. This diversity of origin should be noted because it explains and symbolizes the slow development of an idea that had utterly fascinated him during his childhood and that was to find its ultimate realization in *Atlántida,* the work of his maturity. It is a work permeated with the atmosphere of both Cádiz, with its associations with Christopher Columbus, and Catalonia, the birthplace of Jacinto Verdaguer, *Atlántida's* poet. The musician, in his last years and up to the day of his death, was to be obsessed, as he had been as a child, with the idea of Christopher Columbus and his discoveries.

For the future composer of *Atlántida,* Cádiz truly represented a predestined birthplace. All writers describe it as a beautiful seaside city; the port in which the galleons unloaded their precious cargoes of gold from the West Indies. But we must go even further into the mists of prehistoric time, because Falla's aim in his last work was to celebrate the mystical origin of his native land by using an epic theme that would carry universality in terms of his musical thought. Actually, the whole extreme south of Spain breathes a legendary atmosphere that made a deep impression on Falla as a child —that he was to preserve unbroken throughout his life: grandiose landscapes, mystic settings, memories of past glories. Cádiz is close to the Pillars of Hercules, and, according to mythology, the two huge, curiously profiled limestone promontories at the western end of the Mediterranean, Abila (in Africa) and Calpe (in Europe), had been sundered by a mighty blow from the club of Hercules when he opened

1

the straits to the waters of the Atlantic. The ebb tide reveals the meadows where Geryon grazed his oxen. Calypso practiced her sorcery on navigators from her grotto on her nearby island. Undoubtedly, the name of the city comes from ancient Gadir, the last port of call of ancient shipping that came past the low-lying islands of the sand-covered coast by way of the estuary of the Guadalquivir. Here the waves of the Atlantic swell to stormy heights, while the Mediterranean, which bathes the enchanted lands bordering it, remains calm.

But is not Gadir the city of the country of Guderirus, named after its ruler Gadeirus, one of the kings of Atlantis, son of the god Poseidon and the mortal Cleito?[1] May we hazard the thought that the nine-year-old Falla steeped himself in the marvelous descriptions of Atlantis that Plato puts into the mouth of Critias? According to his friend and biographer Jaime Pahissa,[2] the child Manuel created in his imagination a city to which he gave the name Colón (Columbus) and where everything imaginable was provided—the plan of the city's construction, its organization, and the routines of its daily life, just as in the capital of exotic Atlantis. This game lasted six years, and young Manuel shared its excitements with his brothers and sisters but kept it a big secret from the rest of his family. Nothing was lacking in this invented Atlantis, not even newspapers or periodicals: *El Mes Colombino, El Burlón, El Cascabel,* with its serial explaining how pupils could avoid the terrors of examination time. The formula turned out to be eminently useful because Falla followed it himself, and to the great satisfaction of his family, successfully passed his entrance examinations for the *bachillerato.* In his imagination, Falla transcended daily the real life of his native city. Fantastic vehicles (at a time when there were no automobiles or airplanes) instantly transmitted messages; elections and even revolutionary upheavals were as common in this imaginary city as in reality. A theater occupied the place of honor in the boy's utopia. It was a marionette theater in which plays, characters, and sets were conceived, written, composed, painted, and fashioned by little Manuel

[1] Plato, *Critias.*
[2] Jaime Pahissa, *Manuel de Falla: His Life and Works.* Trans. by Jean Wagstaff. London: Museum Press Limited, 1954.

himself. His parents, thinking to delight the boy, bought him a magnificent marionette theater that was perfectly equipped, but the boy soon cast it aside because nothing suited his own creations better than the theater he had fashioned himself. A play about Don Quixote was the first one staged in the tiny theater. Can his future achievements be seen in these pastimes of childhood? The creative imagination of children disappears with the age of reason; only the artist knows how to preserve its incantational power, by transposing and imposing his dream upon reality. In fact, the childish plays about Don Quixote and the imaginary city of Colón were to materialize one day in the musical compositions of *Master Peter's Puppet Show* and *Atlántida*. The artist in the child was awaiting his hour.

Let us now go back to the real city and to its history, so suitable for providing nourishment for a receptive and magnifying imagination. After the Atlanteans (how can we not believe in such a beautiful legend!), who perhaps are meant to symbolize the Tartesians, came the equally famous Phoenicians, who, it seems, had "commercial relations" with the Greeks of Delos. They girded the city with ramparts and called it Gadir. They were followed by the Carthagenians (a Punic necropolis was discovered near the Puerta de Tierra at the beginning of our century) and finally by the Romans. Under Caesar, in fact, the dignity of Roman citizenship was conferred upon its inhabitants. (One day Falla was to celebrate Roman Spain in his *Fantasia Baetica*.) The Romans were replaced by the Visigoths, who predominated until April 30, 711, when the Berber chieftan Jebel Tarik took the rock that thereafter was to bear a corruption of his name (Gibraltar). Three years later Gadir also fell to the Moslems and had to wait until 1262 for its deliverance by Alfonso the Wise. But the neighboring Moslem kingdom of Granada still had to be reconquered before the city could start on the commercial development that would begin with Columbus and the discovery of America. We do not know whether the child Manuel ever made an excursion with his parents to La Rábida, Palos, and Moguer, near the estuary of the Rio Tinto from where the three caravels had set out to sea. Later, he did plan a journey of this kind. Although as a child Falla had no opportunity to see the statue of his hero that was erected by the American nations on the four hundredth

3

anniversary of his discoveries and that faces the immense seascape, and although he did not visit the replica of the Santa Maria, he was to meditate one day before the Fontanilla and pray at the monastery of La Rábida where Columbus heard Mass on the morning of his departure. Falla wanted, in short, "to listen to the sea," as he confided to his friend, the poet José Maria Pemán.

Théophile Gautier has described his arrival in Cádiz by steamship in 1840. From the deck, one could see the city rising gradually from its bay of low-lying pasture islands and salt marshes, blinding in the glare of the sun. The *"tacita de plata"* (its poetic sobriquet which means "the little silver cup") earned from Gautier a delightful description that painted Cádiz as Falla himself must have seen it, because the ramparts that had enclosed it since the reign of Philip IV were not torn down until the beginning of this century. Except for this, Gautier's description retains its validity to this day. "There are no colors or tints on the painter's or writer's palette that are bright or luminous enough to convey the striking impression that Cádiz made on us on this glorious morning. Two unique tints of blue and white catch your eye; the blue is as vivid as turquoise, sapphire, cobalt, or whatever you can imagine as being extravagantly azure, and the white is as pure as silver, milk, snow, marble, and the best crystallized sugar of the islands! The blue was the sky, mirrored by the sea; the white was the city itself." Elsewhere, Gautier describes how on this "narrow island linked to the continent by a slender thread of earth . . . every house curiously rises on tiptoe in order to lift its head above the thick belt of ramparts." How many times did young Manuel make a tour of the city along the Camino de Ronda or Vuelta Gaditara, from where he could imagine the fleets cutting their way through the waves en route to New Spain, protected by their *Virgencita Galeona*? "It was a rare family that did not wind up its promenade on a sunny winter Sunday afternoon with a luncheon along the coasts."[3] Toward evening people left their highly perched houses and climbed the terraces to enjoy the coolness of the sea breezes. From here they

[3] Jean Sermet, *Espagne du Sud*. Paris, 1953.

could look down on the maze of old streets and Moorish towers now dominated by the white mass of the cathedral. If the wharves no longer swarmed with the same hustle and bustle as before, the liners and freighters continued to unload and add colors that contrasted vividly with the quiet green and white touches of the town's patios, enclosed by spotless columns.

For a long time, this was the setting for a refined society that lived in beautiful salons furnished with massive mahogany pieces and that gathered in the patios to enjoy the cool of the evening. The old aristocratic families, the descendants of the rich privateers, the dealers in precious woods, mother-of-pearl, hemp, or tobacco from the Philippines, used to meet at *sobremesas,* after-dinner gatherings in winter and at *tertulias,* conversational groups in summer. But the Gaditanians, thanks to their active life and international trade, have always preserved an open mind to advanced ideas. From 1810 to 1812, while the French were laying siege to Cádiz, an insurrectional junta was set up in the church of Santiago, proclaimed a model constitution, and assembled the first *Cortès.* This liberalism later was to characterize Falla, who became a friend of Federico Garcia Lorca (it has been asserted that this was not an irrelevant factor in his exile overseas).

The straight streets cut at right angles and the grand plazas with their flower beds and palm trees were started in the eighteenth century and laid out bit by bit. The Plaza de Mina was named after Espoz y Mina, a hero of the Peninsular War; the Falla family lived at No. 3. Now it is called Plaza del Generalissimo Franco, and the number on the house has been changed to 37. It is a charming house with large windows and the high glass-enclosed balconies, customary in that region. The Fallas occupied an apartment on the first floor with an inner balcony that looked out on a beautiful patio paved with marble and bordered with glazed tiles, *azulejos.* The future musician was born here, and a bronze plaque now informs passers-by of the date of this event. A *templete de la música* or bandstand rises from the flower beds in the middle of the plaza, swarming with children, and it is circled by a palm-lined walk. This wholly modern plaza may look banal by itself, but "the waves embellish Cádiz by envelop-

5

ing it from all sides, surrounding all the streets with patches of sky and stretches of sea."[4]

As in most ports, people from all countries are mixed with the natives. The activity of the Gaditanians and their unbroken contacts with the former American colonies attracted foreigners and many provincial merchants. It has already been mentioned that Falla's parents came from Valencia and Catalonia. In Cádiz they established themselves in the export trade. Being well-to-do, they could afford to give their children a particularly good education. Of the five children born to them, only three survived: Manuel, his sister, Maria del Carmen, and the youngest, German. They were not sent to a boarding school for their elementary studies, but were tutored at home each day by Don Clemente Parodi, a man of Italian origin. One of the most lasting impressions made on Manuel, as a child, was caused by a cholera epidemic that killed an aunt whom he particularly loved. The epidemic forced the immediate transfer of the children, still wearing their school uniforms, to the neighboring town of El Puerto (the El Puerto of Albéniz) and a sojourn in Seville, which also made a deep impression on him. He kept a vivid memory of his stay in this city because it coincided with the birth of the future Alfonso XIII. The child never took his eyes from the Giralda, where the Spanish flag was to be raised for a male heir to the Spanish throne or a white banner in the event that the royal infant was a girl. He was so delighted with this shining city that he begged his parents to settle there permanently. Of course, this was out of the question, and on his return, to console himself, he created his imaginary city, the famous, previously mentioned Colón. His love for the piano started in Seville; he practiced with such ardor that the neighbors of the Fonda de Madrid, where his parents were staying, complained constantly. Manuel's musical studies had begun and seemed full of promise.

What was the musical atmosphere of the city of Cádiz, and more particularly, of the Falla family at this time (around 1880)? The father, entirely wrapped up in his business, was not a musician, but he left complete freedom to his wife, an excellent pianist who had

---

[4] A. T'Serstevens, *Le Nouvel Itinéraire Espagnol.* Paris, 1951.

6

inherited a very keen taste for music from her father, a merchant like her husband. "Heavenly Bellini" was the musical idol of the city, the salons, and the theater. *Señoras* and *señoritas* passionately listened, sang, and played the operas, transcriptions, and inspired moonlit melodies of the composer of *Norma* and *La Sonnambula*. On the evening that Manuel was to attend the opera for the first time, a performance of *Faust* was announced. Unfortunately, in a last minute change of program, *Faust* was replaced by *Lucia di Lammermoor*. Manuel was greatly disappointed, and he developed a distaste for Donizetti that was to last a lifetime. Several days later *Faust* reappeared on the program and Falla, at last, could see the opera. Everything filled him with a sense of wonder, not only the stage spectacle, but the music, its varied character, and its dramatic effects. On this occasion he staged a childish tantrum when, because of the late hour, his parents decided to take him home despite his indignant protests.

The *zarzuela* was at this time the prevailing theatrical entertainment in Cádiz, as in all other Spanish cities. Falla must have heard a certain number of them when he became old enough to be taken to the theater. We do not know what impression they made on him at that time, but later we shall find him struggling with the composition of *zarzuelas,* and we shall examine more closely this national, albeit superficial, form of Spanish music.

Meanwhile the future maestro, under his mother's direction, worked assiduously at his piano. He stood at her side as she played transcriptions from the operas (very much in vogue at that time), pieces by Chopin, and Beethoven's sonatas—the *Pathétique* and the *Moonlight*. Mother and child also played piano pieces for four hands, not only the usual transcriptions, but also Mozart, Beethoven, and Grieg, who was then at the peak of his glory. Falla used to go to the house of his maternal grandfather, the merchant Matheu, a chain smoker of cigarillos who owned a harmonium whose keys had turned yellow under the constant barrage of tobacco fumes. The old man played Bellini, and Manuel joyfully improvised. One day—he was then eleven—he was allowed to take part with his mother in a performance of Haydn's *The Seven Last Words of Christ*. It was an old tradition in the city to give this oratorio on Good Friday under

7

the direction of a canon of the church of La Cueva in the Calle del Rosario. We can imagine the vivid and deep impression that the dark and enormous chapel on the "Street of the Rosary," with its flickering yellow glow of the candles, must have made on young Manuel. Another impressive experience occurred later—he was then seventeen—when a symphony orchestra came to Cádiz on tour and played works of Beethoven and Grieg among the paintings by Zurbarán hanging in the museum.

Recognizing her son's musical gifts, Señora de Falla entrusted him to the best teacher in the city, Eloisa Galluzzo. This woman, who later became a Sister of Charity, passed her pupil on to her former teacher, Alejandro Odero, a very accomplished musician, who introduced the boy to the study of solfeggio and harmony.

Odero's death soon thereafter led to a new change of teachers, and Falla furthered his studies of harmony and counterpoint with Enrico Broca, a composer who enjoyed a moderate reputation. Falla himself says that from this time on he analyzed every musical work that fell into his hands with avid curiosity, especially those of Wagner and those that seemed to present an affinity with his secret aspirations. At this time, needless to say, he wanted to compose. He had already written for the theater of his imaginary city a "serious opera," *The Count of Villamediana,* based on the poems and ballads of Duque de Rivas. But his first real work was a *Gavotte et Musette,* inspired by a piece by Bach that had been published as an insert in a Paris fashion magazine to which his mother subscribed. He wrote it secretly, during his recreation periods, being too shy to show it to anybody. But as the work progressed, he grew bolder and worked openly on the composition. In this he was warmly encouraged by a friend of the family, Don Salvador Viniegra, an enthusiastic music lover and friend of Camille Saint–Saëns, who never failed to pay Viniegra a visit when he passed through Cádiz on his trips to the Canary Islands. Later, in Paris, Falla was to avail himself of his connection and call on the old French master. Viniegra had a library well stocked with scores and a veritable museum of musical instruments and he gave memorable chamber music concerts in his house. He played the cello in quartets and naturally played sonatas with young Falla. At that time Falla wrote a piece for cello and piano, which he dedicated to his friend, and Viniegra, with the enthusiasm peculiar to the Andalusian character, hailed it as a magnificent piece of work.

The young pianist–composer had entré to the house of another musical family, that of Señor Quirell, a piano dealer. He was a passionate admirer of Gounod and particularly of *Faust*. At Quirell's house Falla gave concerts for some relatives and close friends, consisting exclusively of his own works: the piece for cello and piano dedicated to Señor Viniegra, which he later called a sonata; an andante and scherzo for a piano quartet; and a fantasy quintet in two movements for violin, viola, cello, flute, and piano, inspired by *Mireio,* the fifth section of Mistral's poem about the Rhone, a work that Falla had discovered as a child and devoured with passion. Its impact on young Manuel had been so great that he carefully preserved the Provençal poet's work with the intention of setting it to music, which he soon did. The first hearing took place, amid great pomp, at Señor Quirell's house, with formal invitations accompanied by printed programs. The subject of this impressionistic composition, which could be called program music, was described as follows: The Rhone; the Night of St. Médard; The Procession of the Drowned Along the River Banks; The Sinking of Elzear's Boat; Dance of the Ghosts on the Bridge of Trinquetaille. Falla was to see this old wooden bridge in person later, on his return from a journey to Italy, before it was replaced by a modern stone bridge that would be less beautiful and less picturesque, but obviously more solid. The sight of this bridge would evoke a moving remembrance of the work of his first youth, which described the sinking of the boat, the ghosts of the drowned, and their fantastic dance. The music must have been marked by lively orchestration, to judge from the remark made by a lady who was sitting in the first row during the performance: "One would think that one were at the opera!" Falla never forgot these words. The success of this private concert was so great that it was repeated the following year, and this time in public. Subsequently, whenever anyone talked with Falla about his first youthful musical exploits, he would answer, with a faint touch of irony, "After all, they weren't so bad."

Such was the musical atmosphere of the salons in which

Falla made his debut as a composer. But we must not forget, nor, above all, underestimate the atmosphere of the street, of the life of the people whose influence left an indelible mark on the artist's sensibility and which was to inspire his most beautiful songs. In his own home, young Falla could hear Morilla, a domestic whose name indicates her Moorish origin, sing the *cante jondo*.

During his childhood, Carnival was still the great festivity for which everybody in Cádiz waited impatiently. All social classes mingled freely at Carnival behind masks that hid their identities. Every street corner echoed to *viejas ricas,* accompanied by *guarijas* and other habaneras. This is not yet the place to study the role of folk music in the inspiration of the future composer of *El Amor Brujo* and of the *Seven Popular Songs,* but its first traces go back to those weeks when Carnival was celebrated with the aid of *manzanilla* and *jerez* coming from the nearby vineyards of San Lucar, and when one could watch the procession of the "Giants," all that remained of the famous *Corpus Christi* procession of before.

The famous festivals of the Corpus Gaditan, which drew enormous crowds in June at the time of Calderón, date from the seventeenth or possibly the sixteenth century. At the head of the parade were the *danzantes,* Gypsies or girls of Valencia preceding the soldiers. After them came the Tarasaque, the giant effigies of Don Alfonso X the Wise, liberator of the city, and of his wife Doña Violanta. Immense *pasos* laden with flowers and *candils* made their way through the kneeling crowd. People jammed the balconies, which were hung with elaborately designed shawls and tapestries, and candles burned everywhere. The shouts of children merged with the music of bands, hymns, and *saetas* (literally "arrows of music" aimed at the procession).

A woman dancer tried an *alegría,* in which the movements of the body, the facial expression, the clicking of the heels on the ground, and the twisting of the arms all have a special significance. It is a provocative dance, sustained by the *"Olés"* of the people. The dancer, by a sudden relaxation of her leg, unfurls and flings back her yellow dress with its long train and frills.

It is believed that the *alegría,* a peculiarly Gaditan dance, goes back to an ancient dance of India, the Gypsies' country of origin.

10

The train of the dress is like that of the peacock, the royal bird, symbol of splendor. The music, the lights, the cheers of the crowd, the beat of the drums, and the firecrackers weave a spell around the dancer, who twists to the short strophes of the *alegría* as though possessed by demons.

"In Spain (as among all the peoples of the Orient, where dance is a religious expression)," wrote Federico Garcia Lorca, "the demon (*duende:* demon, elf, hobgoblin) exercises a limitless authority over the bodies of the women dancers of Cádiz (whom Martial praised), over the throats of those who sing (whom Juvenal praised), and over the entire liturgy of the bulls. It is an authentic religious drama, in which, in the same manner as at the Mass, a god is worshipped and sacrificed."

Unfortunately, the oldest traditions gradually fade away or are corrupted, and Manuel de Falla has not included such colorful scenes in his remembrances of childhood. It has even been said that he shunned them and preferred his marionettes or his invented city of Colón. But no matter how they were softened and distorted, these sights and sounds could not have failed to make a striking impression on him, and one day they were to lead him to undertake those ethnological studies that marked a long period of his life. But this time was still a long way off, and despite Carnival, the processions, the drawing-room concerts, Falla had to pursue his studies of musical notation and especially of the piano. Now, in addition to taking lessons in harmony from the composer Broca, he began to study with José Tragó, a famous piano teacher at the Real Conservatorio de Música y Declamación of Madrid, which Manuel frequently attended.

CHAPTER II / In Madrid

When Falla reached his twentieth year, his family decided to move to Madrid. Once the family had arrived in the Spanish capital, young Falla called on Count de Morphy with a letter of introduction signed by his friend Viniegra. Count Morphy had introduced Pablo Casals to Queen Maria Christina and had obtained a stipend for the cellist which had enabled him to continue his studies in Paris. This same financial aid had made it possible for Albéniz to enroll in a piano class at the Brussels Conservatory. Did Viniegra hope that the same favor would be accorded to his protégé? At any rate it was not forthcoming, and Falla had to give up the idea of a trip to Paris for the time being.

Meanwhile he enrolled at the Conservatory as a pupil of Tragó and vigorously continued his piano studies. He went through the seven-year course in two years. In the first year, despite his teacher's opposition, he took and successfully passed the final examinations for the first five sessions. He finished the program for the two other sessions in the second year, 1899. His aim was to obtain a certificate of graduation as quickly as possible, for his major concerns were to earn a living and possibly go to Paris, a dream he had cherished for a long time. At the same time, he in no sense had given up composing, and he decided to try his luck in the theater, specifically by composing *zarzuelas*. This was the only door open to composers in search of success, money, and reputation, since at the end of the nineteenth century, the Spanish musical renaissance had hardly begun. Albéniz and Granados had not yet produced the works that were to make them famous, and Pedrell's fervent exhortations for a return to Spain's high musical tradition, that of the polyphonists of the sixteenth century, as well as to the deep wells of national folk art, had fallen on deaf ears. The European musical scene, with its lyric drama and great symphonic forms, then dominating Germany, France, and Russia, had no prospects of being repeated in Spain. Any composer who hoped for the performance or publication of a symphony for a large orchestra found doors shut in his face. Aside

12

from Italian opera (Verdi, Rossini, Bellini), whose popularity in Cádiz has already been noted, there was only the *zarzuela,* a purely national product that theater-lovers had absolutely no intention of giving up.

What was the *zarzuela*? What was the origin of this operatic form which was then so much in vogue? Its beginnings go back to the reign of Philip IV, King of Spain in 1621. When Philip ordered his son to build an amusement pavilion in the gardens of the Prado at a place called La Zarzuela (named after *zarzas,* the blackberry bushes that grew wild there), he never dreamed that he was baptizing a musical form that was to enjoy a tremendous popularity in his native country. Musicians, actors, singers, and dancers came nightly to this tiny rustic retreat to give command performances before the pleasure-loving monarch, who was also passionately fond of music. At first they were only *villancicos, cantarillos* (eclogues with mostly spoken dialogue), *tonadillos,* and *ensaladas,*[1] intermezzi inserted between lyrical dramas in the Italian manner, pastimes whose sole purpose was to amuse the king. Gradually, the form became more precisely defined, and, in 1629, in a ceremony before Philip and Queen Elizabeth de Bourbon, a pastoral eclogue by Lope de Vega was presented, *La Selva sin Amor* (The Forest Without Love), staged by the Florentine engineer Cosmo Lotti. According to Rafael Mitjana[2] it was the first *zarzuela* recognized as such. Unfortunately, we do not know the name of the composer of the music. But we do have the *zarzuela* for a mythological comedy by Calderón (performed in 1637), based on the fable of Psyche, *Ni Amor se Libra de Amor* (Love Frees Not Itself from Love), composed by Juan Hidalgo, the harpist of the Royal Chapel and composer of secular and sacred songs. It reveals the style of the lute players of the sixteenth century. The impetus had been given, and a fantastic number of *zarzuelas* were suddenly to appear and subsequently disappear just as suddenly. It was amusement meant to last a day, to be replaced on the next by another bit of whimsy. Any theme was good enough for the librettist and the

[1] Religious and popular canticles; canzonets for four voices; drawing room comedies; interludes.

[2] Rafael Mitjana, "La Musique en Espagne" in *Encyclopédie de la Musique.* Paris, p. 2003–4.

composer of this brand of comic opera, this operetta in miniature with its innumerable introductory dances, the *bailes cantados,* mimes, *coplas de caballo,*[3] comic interludes by the buffoon, and its improvised *saynètes,* more or less imported from the American possessions. In short, the *zarzuela* was an expanded and elaborated version of the *cuadros de empezar,*[4] the *tonadillas,*[5] and the *entremesas* (interludes), even the *autos sacramentales*[6] of the processions in Seville, and the spoken or sung *danzas.* It excelled, above all, in the portrayal of the folkways of Madrid and of Andalusia. Romantic or realistic, witty, and at times coarse, these *zarzuelas* were written by great authors such as Tirso de Molina, Alarcón, Rojas, Guillen de Castro, later Ramón de la Cruz, and Blas de Laserna, who did not disdain to acknowledge their offspring. Ramón de la Cruz was the first to replace mythological heroes by ordinary people's familiar backgrounds. His *zarzuela, Segadores de Vallecas* (Reapers of Vallecas), 1771, enjoyed a great success.

The reactionary character of the reign of Philip V and the advent of Italian opera eclipsed somewhat the vogue for *zarzuelas.* They enjoyed a rebirth around the end of the eighteenth century, and a real "golden age" was ushered in for the *zarzuela* with Francesco Aseajo Barbieri. This was the time when it assumed its distinctive character—a combination of a spirited comedy of manners and uniquely Spanish comic opera with an array of popular songs and dances. Its enormous success led to the opening of a dozen theaters reserved exclusively for the performance of *zarzuelas,* and no one knows the number of *saynètes* that had been created by the end of the nineteenth century. Naturally, there was bound to be much sheer trash in such an enormous production. Some *zarzuelas,* nevertheless, have preserved a certain fame, and some fragments are still taken from them, for example, *Il Barberillo de Lavapiés* (The Little Barber of Lavapiés) by Barbieri (1874), *Agua, Azucarillos y Aguardiente* (Water, Sugar, and Brandy) by Chueca (1897), and, above all, the celebrated *Verbena de la Paloma* (The Feast of Our Lady of the Dove) by Bretón (1894).

[3] Trooper's song.
[4] Pieces for four voices serving as prologue.
[5] *Saynètes,* intermezzos.
[6] Dramatic composition in one act in honor of the Blessed Sacrament.

Some *zarzuelas grandes* aspired to operatic stature. Bretón, among others, tried this with *Los Amantes de Teruel* (The Lovers of Teruel), but this genre could not compete with Italian opera, and in these attempts the *zarzuela* lost its lively and characteristic attraction. Falla appreciated the *zarzuela,* and in one of his essays he pays sincere homage to Barbieri's culture and talents.

Although the music composed for the *zarzuela* for a long time had been "graceful, brilliant, and enjoyable,"[7] it was usually shallow, trivial, all too often vulgar (if not actually base), technically weak, and devoid of any artistic pretensions. At any rate it could not satisfy the lofty aspirations and the sense of refinement of a composer of Falla's caliber. Unfortunately, there was no living to be made, no royalties to be had outside the field of the *zarzuela.* Consequently, he wrote five of them, but in his opinion only *La Casa de Tócame Roque* seemed worthy of his efforts. He hoped that someday he would have the time to rearrange the prelude, with its characteristic syncopations and its marked Scarlattian second theme, with an eye to its performance. According to Pahissa, he used part of it for the "Dance of the Corregidor" in *The Three-Cornered Hat.* But he was not satisfied with *Limosna de Amor,* with a libretto by Jackson Veyán, nor with the *zarzuelas* he wrote in collaboration with his colleague and friend Amadeo Vivès, *El Corneta de Ordenes* and *La Cruz de Malta,* although he did not set aside his sense of artistic integrity when he composed them. This is true, even of *Los Amores de la Inès* (The Loves of Inez), the only *zarzuela* of the five that was staged.

The libretto of *Los Amores de la Inès* was written by the journalist Emilio Dugi. It is a one-act play, divided into two parts, and the action takes place in an inn owned by a Madrilenian named Lucas. In the second part Lucas gives a little party to celebrate the opening of his inn, an episode that lends itself to singing in chorus, songs, and dances. It ends with a marriage, or rather two marriages, consummating the loves of Inès and Juan, and of Felipe and Fatigas, more or less through a series of mistakes and misunderstandings.

Although the critics almost unanimously, and rightly, recognized that the libretto was well written, they deplored its hackneyed

---

[7] J. Pahissa, *op. cit.,* p. 27.

subject matter. One newspaper criticized "the excessive use of the dramatic note." Another found the libretto "inferior to the music, as is the case with a great number of works in our lyric theater."

The score contains six numbers, two for the orchestra, four for voices. There is a typical Madrilenian flavor about the beginning bars of the prelude, which includes the Inès theme. It suggests the influence of the principal motif of a *zarzuela* by Albéniz, *San Antonio de la Florida,* which had been performed eight years before. The music becomes very banal and sentimental in the second number, in which Juan and a chorus appear, although it is quite representative of the state of mind of the character, who has just been released from prison. In contrast, the third number is a passionate duet between Inès and Juan, offering a curious alternation of binary and ternary rhythms, varying 3/4 time with 6/8, as in a number of Andalusian songs, such as the *petenera.* Falla was to utilize this later in *The Three-Cornered Hat* and in the finale of *Nights in the Gardens of Spain.* The duet is followed by a joyous folk dance, the *zapateado.*[8] The last part, an ensemble with chorus, is less successful in terms of style and invention.

But the newspaper critics did not fail to recognize the merits of the score of *Los Amores de la Inès,* singling out for special mention Juan's ballad, "which was admirably sung by Señor Rodondo." Falla was praised for his exceptional talents as a composer for the theater and for his particular talent for orchestration, which had enabled him to avoid the "calamity" inherent in a shallow and banal libretto of this kind. In fact, the anonymous critic of *La Correspondencia de España* added, "In his first work for the theater the composer of the music, Señor Falla, reveals an exceptional talent for composition, and there is reason to believe that these happy faculties will have an important development in his subsequent works."[9]

The premiere of *Los Amores de la Inès* took place at the Teatro Comico of Madrid on April 12, 1902, and was performed by the cast of the famous company of Loreto Padro and Enrique

[8] From *zapato* (shoe).
[9] Cited by Angel Sagardia, *Manuel de Falla*. Madrid, 1946, p. 13.

Chicote. The work went through about twenty performances and must have taxed the composer's patience often, for if we are to go by his remembrances, as reported by Pahissa, the orchestra played very badly. It had no oboe, only one violist, and a double bass player who constantly had to be dragged out of a bar around the corner.

At the same time as he began composing *zarzuelas,* Falla continued to try his hand at different compositions, which he later disowned. Thus it was without his consent that the Unión Musical Española, in 1940, republished—during the war and the composer's exile in Argentina—some of his pieces for piano: *Serenata Andaluza, Vals-Capricho, Nocturno,* which he wrote about 1900, and the melody *Tus Ojillos Negros* (Your Little Black Eyes). The last was based on a play by Cristóbal de Castro, a well-known poet whose authorization he obtained by an amusing subterfuge, according to his biographer Sagardia.[10] Should we deplore this indiscreet publication? Manuel de Falla's reputation rests on work of sufficiently high value, so that it cannot be diminished by juvenilia, no matter how weak. Actually, these pieces enable us to admire the surprising evolution of a career marked by the simultaneous development of gifts of the rarest quality and of a technique that was polished to absolute perfection by constant application and hard work.

But if we glance at these early pages, we will note the fine sensibility that already shows through the sentimental motifs, which are too close to the "zarzuelesque" ballad. But they are relieved by a remarkably instinctive ease in the modulations and, here and there, by an accent, a thrust toward a refinement that presages the *Four Spanish Pieces,* published later in Paris.

La Serenata Andaluza has the flavor of a folk song that is closer to a Madrid street tune than to an authentic *cantar andalou,* but the light accompaniment of the opening bar lends it a certain charm and a captivating beauty. The *Vals Capricho* would not be out of place in a *zarzuela.* The chromaticisms of the *Nocturno* betray the good pupil enamored of Chopin. An intermediary motif, based on the dominant, with rapid accents on the first beat, suddenly con-

[10] *Ibid.,* p. 8.

tributes a touch of unexpected local color (measures 29 to 34).[11] As to general form, in the *Nocturno* Falla seemingly was content with a development based exclusively on changes of tonality, but he used an A-B-A treatment of two themes for the other two pieces. The notation is of the most simple variety: slightly varied arpeggios in the bass, pivoted now on the dominant, now on the tonic. We are correct in perceiving in the *Nocturno* the embryo of one of those contrapuntal battles in which Albéniz enthusiastically engaged during the composition of *Ibéria* and that Falla himself was to win with infinite tact in his future *Four Spanish Pieces* (p. 4).

The melody *Tus Ojillos Negros,* an Andalusian song dedicated *"A Los Excomos, Sres, Marquesas de Alta Villa,"* promises much thanks to its *appassionato* and charming beginning:

Yo no sé qué tienen tus ojillos negros que me dán pesares y me gusta verlos.[12]

But the mysterious accompaniment of adroit, persistent arpeggios subsequently lapses into an ordinary Madrid street tune.

Contemporary with these juvenile works, we find an unpublished *Allegro de Concert*. It had been written for the Madrid Conservatory, which had sponsored a competition in order to obtain a modern unpublished piece to serve as a set subject for the year-end examination for the piano. Falla's *Allegro* won the honor of being *significado,* that is, favorably mentioned by a jury made up of teachers of composition and piano at the Conservatory, including José Tragó. But the prize was awarded to the *Allegro de Concert* by Granados. A little later, Falla himself performed his *Allegro* at a memorable competition, which was sponsored by the firm of Ortiz y Cussó and which definitely decided his career.

In regard to this *Allegro,* the famous critic of *La Epoca,* Cecilio de Roda, wrote that "the tendencies of and the love for Grieg and Chopin, the great favorites of the majority of pianists," predominated in the work.[13] Roda, a concert critic, gave only slight

[11] Edition Unión Musical Española, Madrid.
[12] I don't know what it is about your little eyes that worries me and enchants me so.
[13] A. Sagardia, *op. cit.,* p. 9.

recognition to young Falla's gifts as a composer, despite the *zarzuela* that had already been performed. Nevertheless, these gifts were soon to attract general attention thanks to two crucial events in the great artist's life. The age of "Premanuel de Antefalla," to cite the witticism of the critic Gerardo Diego,[14] was to give way to that of Manuel de Falla.

[14] *Ibid.*, p. 13.

CHAPTER III / Two Encounters—Two Competitions

Two chance encounters were enough to set this magnificently endowed young musician on his true path. A "logical and natural progress in technique and perfection, achieved step by step, which with any man of talent is the fruit of constant study and hard and persistent work, did the rest."[1]

The first encounter was with a book he came upon in one of the secondhand bookstalls along the iron fence of the Madrid Botanical Gardens. This book, by Louis Lucas, entitled *L'Acoustique Nouvelle,* written in the middle of the nineteenth century, discussed the phenomena of natural resonance. Lucas can be said to have anticipated and heralded the forms of modern harmony, going considerably beyond the principles of Rameau. The full title of the book reads: *The New Acoustics—A Revolution in Music—An Attempt to Apply a Philosophical Theory to Music—Preceded by a Preface by Théodore de Banville and Followed by a Treatise by Euclid and by Plutarch's Dialogue on Music.* Paris. Published by the Author, 1854.

L'Acoustique Nouvelle contains bold statements like the following: "For a long time, from the melodic point of view, we have adhered to two series called the major mode and the minor mode. Without discussing either the beauty of this formula or the utility of its exclusive use, I shall merely observe that by this single fact alone, we break with all originality, all foreign resources. . . . We have built an impassable barrier between ourselves and the entire Orient and many other peoples too numerous to list."

Further, Lucas discusses enharmony as the Greeks understood it, and after them, the anonymous folk singers. He sees "in the mobile, voluntary division of tone, in this infinite decomposition of sound, the application of the phenomenon of attraction pushed to its extreme limits. . . . Nature has placed therein the most complete force for expressing our instincts and passions." He counsels the

[1] A. Sagardia, *op. cit.,* p. 13.

20

reader to listen to a young peasant girl "with a pure and naive voice . . . and you will have the most complete representation of an element that you believe to have been lost for two thousand years, the enharmonic genre in its purity! The motif turns on such a small number of actual notes that we can often enclose them in a single tetrachord. But they are overloaded with embellishments and especially with enharmonics and enharmonic modulations. . . . Some of those ancient ballads . . . use all subtle variations to create an amorous murmur, a sentimental lament, or, sometimes, erotic or even hysterical ardor." Lucas, at random, takes as an example a young girl from Brittany, but this study in folklore really describes the *cante jondo* as it was sung by the *cantaores famosos* of Andalusia in the caves of Sacro Monte. While reading it, Falla must have recalled the Morilla of his childhood. Moreover, asks Lucas, have not the bayadères of Egypt—ancestors of the Gypsies, according to many ethnologists—"preserved the custom of expressing all the events of a love story through music, thanks to enharmony?"

Lucas was indeed anticipating the novelties of the following century when he recommended, as did Messiaen one hundred years later, "taking over the limited vocabulary of the birds, which, if studied from the point of view of melodic combinations, could be made as exact as many others . . . !" And when he declares that "tonality is not the delimitation of a typical, absolute series, but is the admission, more or less persistent, of any formula to which one refers or submits everything through a law of comparison and equilibration," he sounds like a pupil of Schönberg!

These long quotations had a terrific impact on Falla, who recognized that this reading was to influence deeply his conception and execution of harmony and orchestration and, in consequence, endow his style with a new and personal character. Thereafter he never passed the old secondhand bookstall without an appreciative recollection of the great discovery he had made there.

In the remarkable work—one of the first—that he devoted to his friend Falla,[2] Roland-Manuel asserts that Louis Lucas gave Falla the idea that "the arrangement of internal rhythm . . . of the

---

[2] Roland-Manuel, *Manuel de Falla.* Paris, 1930.

harmony born of the dynamic equilibrium of phrases, depends on the judicious placement of related sounds." Later, Falla learned to apply these discoveries with a mastery that was to be revealed principally in the works after *El Amor Brujo*.

The other fateful encounter resulted from the chance reading of a copy of the *Revista Musical Catalana,* organ of the famous choral group Orfeo Catalá of Barcelona. This issue contained an excerpt from the opera *Los Pireneos* by Felipe Pedrell, the premiere of which had just taken place in Barcelona's Teatro del Liceo. Writing later about his teacher, Falla declared "To find finally in Spain something which I had had only the illusion of knowing since the beginning of my studies, I went to Pedrell's house to beg him to be my guide. It is to his teaching (much better than it was said to be by those who took his classes without the necessary technical preparation) that I owe the clearest and strongest direction of my work."

Pedrell did not conduct his classes along formal academic lines but conversed with his pupils on esthetics and on the analyses of musical compositions, doubtless in the manner of Balakirev with his group known as "The Five," with the difference that the Spaniard's intuition and knowledge were to prove more authentic and solid than the Russian's, although he was not able to apply them to his own works. At that time Pedrell was exchanging letters with the famous group which it might be said he had joined, as it were, through the works of Glinka, who had spent several lengthy visits in Spain.

In 1920 Adolfo Salazar,[3] the distinguished music critic of the Madrid newspaper *El Sol,* an authority on Spanish music and especially on that of his teacher Falla, surveyed contemporary Spanish music in an article which appeared in *La Revue Musicale*.[4] After pointing out the decadence of his country's music in the nineteenth century after the invasion of Italianism with the Bourbons, the end of the flowering of polyphonic religious music, the triumph of the lowest style along with a mixture of Wagnerism, Franckism, and

[3] Salazar was born in Madrid in 1890, and was a pupil of Pérez-Casas and Falla. He was associated with Ravel and a number of French musicians. He was a founding member of the Société Française de Musicologie.

[4] November 1, 1920. *La Musique Espagnole Contemporaine.*

other "isms," he wrote: "The voice of Felipe Pedrell rose when the confusion was at its peak. . . . He preached a return to tradition and to a national art." This took place about 1891. The notion of folklore had gradually taken shape during the nineteenth century, after the flowering of romanticism, which brought about the investigation throughout Europe of national differences in the world of ideas and forms. Glinka was one of the first to set the example by utilizing Spanish local color, which he discovered with delight on his journey to Spain and his stay in Granada (1845–47). His *Caprice Brillant on the Theme of the Jota Aragonesa* and his *Summer Night in Madrid* with its seguidilla and *jota* motifs did little to imbue musical Russia with enthusiasm for the Spanish musical idiom, but it was not to forget the road that Glinka had opened up.

Liszt's *Spanish Rhapsody* (1844–45) and Rimski-Korsakov's *Capriccio Espagnol* (1887) encouraged a degree of emulation in Spain, to which was added the influence spread by the romantic accounts of their travels in Spain written by Mérimée, Théophile Gautier, and Dumas, and the appearance of numerous collections of ancient music, among them Barbieri's *Cancionero*. "It was Pedrell especially who galvanized and coordinated the isolated initiatives."[5]

Felipe Pedrell, a Catalan, was born in Tortosa in 1841. In addition to being a composer, he was a student of folklore and an eminent musicographer. Pedrell issued his manifesto *Por Nuestra Música* on September 1, 1891, in which he exhorted composers to look for the subject matter of their inspiration in the unbroken connection with the past and to enrich it with national folk traditions. "Let us aspire to the essence of an ideal and purely human form," proclaimed Pedrell, "but seated in the shade of our southern gardens."

In Pedrell's view the musician should steep himself in two inexhaustible sources: the lofty Spanish polyphonic tradition, going back to the thirteenth century, and the immense riches of Spanish folklore, which inspired the folk *cantaores bailadores,* and *guitarreros.* Already in 1774, Eximeno, in his *Origins and Rules of Music,* had asserted that each people should construct its artistic system on

[5] Gabriel Laplane, *Albéniz*. Geneva, 1956.

the basis of its national folk songs.[6] Although Pedrell applied his musical conceptions to operas, his influence and his great reputation are due more to his editions of the great Spanish polyphonists: Victoria, Moralès, Cabezón, and Villalonga, and to his vast musicological and folkloristic works, the most famous of which are: *Hispaniae Scholae Musica Sacra, Thomae Ludovico Victoria, Abulensis, Opera Ommia,* and the *Canicionero Musical Popular Español.* His monumental edition of the works of Victoria threw a flood of light on one who, in his last years, was among the greatest masters of the Renaissance. The *Hispaniae Scholae Musica Sacra* (unfinished) takes up the subject of religious music from the fifteenth to the eighteenth century. The preface deals with the activity of the collegiate churches, cathedrals, and convents where music was taught and performed from the fourteenth century. Kings and princes surrounded themselves with poets and musicians. Thus there developed a musical art that simultaneously served the court and the church, linked to the prosody of the language and related to folk dances and folk songs, as was then the custom. Confused with them we find some *cantarcillos,* or canzonets, subtly harmonized for three or four voices, in which the music, while remaining technically proficient, is subordinated to poetry. The learning of the professional musicians enabled a Ramos de Pareja to criticize the hexachord system of Guido d'Arezzo and to anticipate the laws of temperament. The Masses, responses, and motets composed by Moralès and his pupil Guerrero, and especially those composed by the admirable Ludovico da Victoria, provide enough well-known examples to prove his point. In connection with the mingling of the sacred and the profane, Pedrell comments on the custom of the *Autos Sacramentales,* comparable to the French mysteries, on the *villancicos,* which were dances performed during the Octaves of Corpus Christi, the Immaculate Conception, or the three days of Carnival by the *seises,* the choirboys of the Seville Cathedral. The choirboys were trained in a special school in Seville for these performances, which the Pope wanted to bring to an end. But the *seises* went to Rome, danced before His Holiness, and won their case. As a result, the custom was continued until the nineteenth cen-

[6] H. Collet, *Essor de la Musique Espagnole au XXe Siècle.* Paris, 1929.

24

tury.[7] We find elements of this tradition at certain places where religious festivals are held, such as the pilgrimage of Rocio in honor of the Blanca Paloma (the holy image that was hidden in the trunk of a tree during the Moorish invasion) and that of the Morenita of Andújar, or the Virgin of Guadalupe, *Hispaniarum Regina*. There are also the aforementioned Corpus Christi procession in Cádiz, the mystery at Elche on the Feast of the Assumption, and finally the extraordinary beauty of Holy Week in Seville, which draws throngs of tourists every year.

The preface and the numerous commentaries contained in the *Hispaniae Scholae Musica* and other works attest to Pedrell's enormous erudition and to his capacity for enthusiasm. He praises "the magnificent art of the Masses to the *Beata Virgine*" composed by Cristóbal Moralès and the refinement and the outflow of feeling from the genius of Antonio de Cabezón. This blind organist and clavichordist in the service of Philip II toured Europe in the entourage of his royal patron and knew how to express in music "the vision of a beauty never before enjoyed." Pedrell's writing also reflects his lively and passionate personality. He was capable along with his enthusiasm of enormous contempt, of astonished indignation at the ignorance, the inaccuracy, the indifference of the ages and, especially, of his contemporaries toward the lofty form of art to which he had dedicated all his energies.

In an article published in *La Revue Musicale*[8] one year before his death, Pedrell recounted the phases of his apostleship, from the time in his childhood when he first heard his mother sing a lullaby or the blind beggar on the street corner voice his complaint, until the publication of his *Cancionero Musical Popular Español*. "A fundamental work, representing the synthesis of all his musical labor," wrote Manuel de Falla in an article that he dedicated to his teacher in the same magazine,[9] shortly after Pedrell's death in Barcelona in 1922. He added, "He shows us the development of the folk song and its technical function in our primitive and classical art

---

[7] This charming tradition is said to have been resumed in our day.
[8] *La Revue Musicale*, Paris, October 1, 1921.
[9] *Ibid.*, February 1, 1923.

25

from the thirteenth to the seventeenth century." Pedrell saw the origins of folk songs and their constituent elements in the ancient Greek modes, either authentic or modified by the liturgical influences of the two great reforms, the Ambrosian and the Gregorian in the orientalism of St. Eugene of Seville, who was reared in Constantinople and was a great friend of St. Gregory; in the Celtic modes and the influences that came down from the north: troubador recitative chants (melopoeia), which were distorted at the time of the Crusades by the musical systems of other races; and, naturally, in the immense influence of the Arabs. Was not Abd-er-Rahman II, the famous *emir* of Córdoba, a composer? We know that the teaching of music was established very early in the madrasahs of Córdoba, Seville, and Toledo. In 822, under the same prince, the Syrian musician Ziryab, very celebrated at the time, came to the court of Córdoba. He introduced the lute—*el aloud*—in Andalusia, and is said to have added a fifth string. According to Ziryab, the five strings possessed a symbolic power. He improved the wooden plectra, going so far as to replace them with eagle's claws! He had an immense repertory of songs, more than a thousand according to commentators, and the origin of some of these songs is lost in the mists of time. Naturally, he composed and sang his own songs while accompanying himself on the lute. Moslem poets also used the *rebec* and the *quitar,* ancestor of the guitar, while Arab dancing girls, the *troteras,* performed in the streets. In the twelfth century Islamic Spain already had produced *cantaras para danzar.* Moreover, we know the names of numerous musicians from the times of the Omayyads to those of the Nasrides. It is sufficient to mention the names of Averroës and Maimonides among the theorists of music to get an idea of the high level of musical development.

The Mozarab[10] influence is found in some Andalucisms which, although not completely Arab, at least have a Moorish tendency. In this connection, what about the origin of the flamenco song, whose character seems to have been preserved exclusively in Andalusia? Pedrell recognized that it had been the object of innumerable discussions, from which no definite proof had ever emerged. With

[10] The name given to Spanish Christians under Moorish rule.

26

his usual vigor he thunders against these authors of "veritable musical infamies" who talk of the flamenco song and who harmonize it without knowing its structure, its proper rhythm, or its modality. According to Pedrell—and several others also—its origin goes back to the arrival in Europe of Moorish, Syrian, and Egyptian tribes (from which comes the name Gypsies). Charles V and Philip II imposed laws on these nomads, most of whom, driven out by war and famine, settled in the south of the peninsula, which had scarcely yet been reconquered, and where they found Oriental customs still very much in use. After hearing Russian choruses at the Paris international exposition in 1878, and after making a study of Tunisian songs, Pedrell was struck by their similarity to the art of the *cantaores,* particularly that of the famous Juan Breva.

But let us go back to the *Cancionero,* so fervently admired by Pedrell's former pupil Manuel de Falla. Pedrell starts with the famous *Cantigas de Santa Maria*[11] composed by Alfonso the Wise (1252–1284), which are preserved in the Escorial and which contain more than four hundred pieces, stanzas, distichs, or refrains in the form of the Arab *zéjel.*[12] He cites the numerous *cantigas, romanceros,* and *cancioneros,*[13] which, since then, have multiplied

---

[11] *Codice de los Cantares y Loores de la Virgin Santa Maria,* better known under the title *Las Cantigas del Rey Sabio.* Two copies are preserved in the library of the Escorial. The most beautiful of the two must have been written and illuminated in Seville between 1275 and 1284. The music of the canticles, in square notation, occupies half of one page, the other half being reserved for the verses. The opposite page contains miniatures inscribed in different squares illustrating the life of the Virgin. They have the lightness of a water-color with harmonious tones dominated by a transparent gray-blue, with pinkish whites relieved here and there by a touch of red. They are framed by a delightful floral pattern. "Christian and Moslem Spain of the late thirteenth century lives again in this manuscript. The architecture is Mudejar (the name given to Moslems living in Christian territory), the ogive being connected to the arc of the overpassing circle and bearing Arab inscriptions and the sacramental formulas of Islam." (M. Dieulafoy, *Espagne et Portugal.* Paris, 1926.)

[12] An Arab poetic composition in the form of a distich or refrain with stanzas of three plus one verse.

[13] *Cantigas:* Poetic compositions divided into stanzas that end in a refrain, related to the *zéjel.*

Romanceros: Collections of romances, or ballads. A very special type of Spanish poetry, including a series of octosyllables, the even verse lines of which

rapidly. Some of these are anonymous and some are signed by illustrious names such as those of Juan Ruiz (ca. 1283) with his *Libro de Buen Amor,* Mendoza (1398–1488), Guzman (1376?–1460?), Lope de Vega (1562–1635), author of *La Filomena,* Luis de Góngora, who lived in Córdoba (1561–1627), and the zarzuelist Barbieri. It was he who in 1870 compiled the *Cancionero de Palacio,* already mentioned, a collection of court pieces of the fifteenth and sixteenth centuries.

Pedrell tried to introduce some order into this immense epic and lyric production, a typical example of Spanish genius and its history, in which appear Charlemagne, the Cid, and the reconquest. He classified it by popular songs of domestic and public life and then by songs of technical proficiency bearing the stamp of *l'escuela musical española.*

The study of these national riches was to make a more or less profound impression on Pedrell's principal pupils: Albéniz, Granados, Vives, and Pérez-Casas, conductor of the Orquesta Filarmonica, although Salazar claims that Falla alone profited from it. It is true that Albéniz had achieved a certain amount of fame without Pedrell. But the fact remains that his *Ibéria* and the *Maria del Carmen* of Granados, dated 1898, belong to the line of thought so vigorously emphasized by their teacher. Be that as it may, one must return to Pedrell in order to trace the decent of Falla's great works, which are related either to Andalusian folklore—*Seven Spanish Songs, El Amor Brujo, Nights in the Gardens of Spain, The Three-Cornered Hat*—or to Castilian folklore—*Master Peter's Puppet Show* —or to certain religious themes, as in the harpsichord concerto.

In his manifesto *Por Nuestra Música* Pedrell, addressing himself to operatic composers, advises them to give to each character "his own special melodic-harmonic quality." Each quality must be developed in changing themes that follow the general and expressive situations of the drama, but interest should never be con-

are assonant, the odd lines being free. The first romances are of Arab origin.
   Cancioneros: Collections of *canziones,* a kind of ode celebrating an historical event or the fame of a great man. An anthology of compositions nearly always of a lyrical character. (From R. Larrieu and R. Thomas, *Histoire Illustrée de la Littérature Espagnole.* Paris, 1952.)

centrated in the orchestra if this detracts from the importance of the vocal part, which should have musical supremacy. The composer should get his nourishment from this quintessence (of folk song, of the voice of the peoples), should assimilate it, and should invest it with a refined appearance and with a richness of form. From this will grow local color and the color of the period.

We may naturally presume that Pedrell began by developing his precepts in his own theatrical works. His main ones are *Los Pireneos,* a lyrical trilogy in three scenes and a prologue, based on a poem by Victor Balaguer (1894); *La Celestina,* a musical tragicomedy based on Fernando de Rojas and dealing with the love of Calisto and Melibea; and *La Vision de Rauda* (Ramon Lull). All three were based on thoroughly Spanish subjects and were inspired respectively by the sentiments of homeland, love, and fidelity. How are we to explain that of these operas only one, *Los Pireneos,* was performed publicly—and with little success? The other two were not even able to interest a producer. Unfortunately, the composer's ambitious concepts, namely "the profound grasp of the genius of the race which makes it possible to bring to life particular customs, to recast them, to integrate them into a homogeneous whole, and indeed to reinvent them"[14] were not accompanied by the necessary creative or recreative force. The realization is laborious and cold; the harmony weighed down by misuse of the pedal and of emphasis; the motifs are juxtaposed and not "refined"; the whole is monotonous, in short, boring.

In the article that we have previously mentioned,[15] Falla expressed regret and even indignation over the general lack of understanding of his teacher. After dwelling at length on Pedrell's efforts in the field of folklore, he recalls that Pedrell himself rejected the "qualification of scholar with which some critics diverted attention from his musical compositions while concentrating on his work as a musicologist." Falla himself claims to have been "stimulated and guided by Pedrell's compositions" and declares categorically that "they alone would have been enough to bring about the rebirth of

[14] G. Laplane, *op. cit.*
[15] *La Revue Musicale, op. cit.*

29

Spanish musical art." He recognizes in Pedrell's works, subsequent to *Los Pireneos,* an individuality in the means of expression, a serene power of emotion, and an extraordinary evocative force that only ignorance or bad faith could deny. Falla admits a certain quite natural fondness for *Celestina* and *El Conde Arnau,* which date from the decisive period in his own life when he was taking lessons from Pedrell.

About the lessons he gives hardly any details. At that time Pedrell was giving courses in the history and esthetics of music at the Royal Conservatory and at the Madrid Athenaeum, where according to Salazar, Falla probably found his road to Damascus. Pahissa relates that the master was extremely demanding and strict about the correction and perfection of musical notation. According to an article published some years ago in the review *Música,* Pedrell at first gave the young man a rather cool reception when he arrived, probably because he came at a moment when the maestro was in a bad humor or depressed. He did not recognize Falla's originality and never understood it.[16] Yet Pedrell himself told the musicologist Edgar Istel that Falla never wrote to his teacher without preceding his signature with the words "your grateful student."[17]

Falla testified at length to his appreciation in his obituary article for his mentor. After a detailed discussion of the different works of the composer-musicologist, he dwelt in particular on the value of Pedrell's realizations of ancient music based on the modality of the period. He deplored the hostility that surrounded his teacher, exemplified by the haste with which some of his academic colleagues declared Pedrell's chair vacant when he had to leave Madrid for reasons of health, and by the fact that the theater directors refused his operas or, after attempting them, never put them on the stage. He expresses pleasure at the high esteem that his beloved teacher enjoyed abroad and ended his article with the hope that the future would blot out so much "guilty silence" and "senseless injustice." Finally, he paid respectful homage "to the memory of the man whose work and message enabled Spain to resume her place among the musical nations of Europe."

[16] Esther Van Loo, "Manuel de Falla" in *Música,* August, 1959.
[17] Edgar Istel, "A Study" in *Musical Quarterly,* October, 1926.

Two Competitions

The place that Manuel de Falla himself would occupy among the great European musicians still rested with the future. An occurrence, however, was to bring fame closer to the young composer. In 1899, the award to him of a first prize freed him from giving piano lessons. Since then his various compositions, including the *Allegro de Concert,* and the performances of *Los Amores de la Inès* had hardly enriched him, and, Pedrell having left Madrid in 1904 to live in Barcelona, the young man must have found himself quite without resources. But just at this time, in the same year, 1904, his prospects suddenly brightened. At the end of spring the Academia de Bellas Artes of San Fernando held a competition for a one-act opera and a symphonic work. The scores had to be handed in on March 31 of the following year "before sunset." Falla immediately decided to compete for the opera which was to be performed (supposedly!) at the Teatro Real. A national competition for pianists was also announced during that summer. The firm of Ortiz y Cussó, piano manufacturers, was offering one of their grand pianos as a prize. The competition was a regular concert recital and was to include a Bach fugue, a Beethoven sonata, and pieces by Chopin, Schumann, Liszt, and Saint-Saëns. The day fixed for the competition was April 1, 1905, the day after the decision concerning the opera. On Tragó's advice Falla signed up, thinking that he had nothing to lose, but with very little confidence of success. He worked particularly hard on the opera.

The libretto was written by Carlos Fernández Shaw, a poet and a well-known supplier of *zarzuelas* for composers. One day, while leafing through a Madrid review, *Blanco y Negro,* Falla came across a poem by Shaw entitled *El Chavalillo,* which he thought might be the basis for a theatrical production. The story, a contemporary one, is an elaboration of an Andalusian couplet on the following theme:

> *Malhaya la jembra pobre, que nace con negro sino;*
> *Malhaya quien nace yunque, en vez de nacer martillo.*

(Woe to the poor man who is born under an evil star;
Woe to him who is born an anvil instead of a hammer.)

This couplet serves as a leitmotif, creating the poetic atmosphere, rather than as a musical element. Summarized, the plot is as follows:

A gypsy girl, Salud, lives with her grandfather and her aunt in the Albaïcin quarter of Granada. She has been seduced by a certain Paco, a fashionable young fellow. Both have sworn eternal love, but Paco has deserted Salud for a rich *novia,* Carmela, whom he plans to marry. On the day of the wedding Salud, followed by her relations, appears in the middle of the wedding feast, reproaches her lover for his unscrupulous conduct and falls dead at his feet.

Such a plot contains very little action and even less of a dramatic theme. Fernández Shaw was too much accustomed to dashing off librettos for *zarzuelas* to worry very much about the authenticity of the psychology of his characters, not to mention simple probability. Some critics justifiably asked whether Salud died so suddenly of love or from a stroke. Be that as it may, Falla was inspired by the libretto, whose author had entitled it *La Vida Breve,* and he worked on it most ardently and enthusiastically.

April 1, the day of the piano competition, arrived, and Falla, as can be imagined, had had little time to prepare for such a heavy program. Fortunately, the competitors had to play in the order of their enrollment, and Falla's was the last place. This gave him about two weeks for some intensive practice. He threw himself into it like a madman, and Tragó did not spare either advice or encouragement.

The jury was composed of Tomas Bretón, chairman, Joaquin Malats, the pianist, well known at the time, José Pellicer from the Barcelona Municipal School of Music, Maria Cervantes, representing the firm of Ortiz y Cussó, and Pilar Mora and José Tragó, both teachers at the Conservatory. Among the contestants was the young pianist Frank Marshall, the favorite pupil of Granados, whom he was to succeed as head of the Academia Granados after his teacher disappeared at sea when the *Sussex* was torpedoed in 1916. Already famous, Marshall drew a large audience for his performance, which he executed with exceptional brilliance. Hearing him, Falla admitted to himself that it would be impossible to outclass him. He was, however, among the first to congratulate him.

His turn came the next morning. There were only a few people in the hall. Falla was tired because of the intensive work of the past weeks, but he was buoyed up by an intense desire to succeed. He put his whole soul into his interpretation, thereby making up for the weaknesses in his technique. "The impression he made was tremendous," says one of his biographers. Bretón and the members of the jury were surprised, and Pilar Mora was moved to tears. Falla won the prize, and it was Marshall's turn to congratulate him. That day marked the beginning of a close friendship between the two artists, which does honor to the character of both, for Marshall followed a career as a pianist, something that could not appeal to Falla's tastes or aptitudes. Falla, who had put forth an effort beyond his capacities, could not keep it up, and the recital he was asked to give at the Ateneo in Madrid, where he repeated the contest program, was a disappointment. The excitement of the first performance had subsided. In truth, Falla's technique was not that of a virtuoso, and when one heard him play, it was primarily his qualities as an artist that were appreciated. Shortly after winning the piano prize, Falla won the opera award, and Pérez-Casas was given the prize for his symphonic suite *A Mi Tierra.* Falla's triumphs had begun, but at first they seemed to lead nowhere.

As mentioned, the opera prize included acceptance of the work by the Teatro Real. But it turned out that this promise had not been official, and the Real refused to honor it despite the librettist's reputation. Nor did any other theater want to accept the score even as a "grand" *zarzuela.* Admittedly, the plot left much to be desired and required major changes, and the two authors accepted the situation. Later, the composer reworked the orchestration according to advice he received in Paris, and it was after this that the work could be performed. We shall discuss it in greater detail in a later chapter.

Disappointment or no disappointment, Falla still had to earn a living. He gave lessons in piano and harmony and continued to compose. He began the *Four Spanish Pieces* for piano, which were to have their premiere in Paris, and his strongest, his most persistent, desire was to go to that city. To understand, we need only to recall the prestige of the musical life in Paris of that time; the stir caused by *Pelléas,* the first successes of Dukas, Ravel, Fauré, the rule of Vincent d'Indy, lord and master of the Schola Cantorum, over a whole band of composers then at the peak of their reputation. "Without Paris," said Falla, "I would have remained buried in Madrid, done for and forgotten, laboriously leading an obscure existence, living miserably and keeping my first prize in a frame, like in a family album, with the score of my opera in a cupboard." And he added: "To be published in Spain is worse than not being published at all. It's like throwing the music into a well."

Nevertheless youth did not lose its privileges. Gatherings of young people came together at his house on Saturdays and Sundays for noisy and musical *tertulias,* sustained by a barrel of beer, cakes, and ham supplied by one or another of the group. One day they were joined by the secretary of the Bilbao philharmonic Juan Carlos Gortazar, who organized a concert for Falla in that city.

According to Pahissa, this concert was the entirely unexpected basis of Falla's departure for Paris. Some of his biographers relate that having had a chance to accompany a friend to the resort of Vichy, he continued on to Paris, expecting to return at once . . . but he stayed seven years! The sequence of events reported by Pahissa seems less romantic but more probable. Nevertheless, Vichy did play a part.

Upon arriving in Bilbao, Falla was told by Gortazar that he was to accompany the cellist Kochansky. This was a disappointment because he had expected to read only his own name on the program, but how could he refuse? After the concert Kochansky suggested that he go to supper with his "impresario from Paris." Suddenly full of hope, Falla accepted. Was this not an open door? During the meeting, Falla told the impresario of his great desire and heard him reply, "I'll arrange it and organize a series of concerts for you next summer at the watering places." The young man could hardly believe his ears and returned to Madrid with new hope. But time passed without bringing the expected news. Falla decided to write, and the reply was that "things are not so easy." A new disappointment. He wrote again, insisting, suggesting dates. He finally received word: "Come, I shall meet you at the station." He departed, "in his heart enough enthusiasm for a lifetime, in his purse enough money for a few days."

This took place at the beginning of summer, 1907. Falla was thirty-one. He traveled with a friend who, before stopping at Vichy, gave him a message for the brother of the pianist Ricardo Viñes, Pepe, an engineer in an aircraft factory.

CHAPTER IV / Paris—Maturity

As with many artists arriving in Paris, Falla's beginnings were difficult. Needless to say, the "impresario" whom he had met in Bilbao did not meet him at the station. It was only after a great deal of difficulty that Falla found him in a more than modest house in the vicinity of the Place Clichy. It turned out that the self-styled impresario was merely an ordinary employee of the firm whose director he had impersonated. The only job he could find for the needy Falla was that of pianist-conductor for the small orchestra of a company of pantomimists preparing to go on tour. They were to present the work of a wholly unknown composer—albeit a winner of the Prix de Rome—who was exceedingly demanding and inspired terror in the heart of the unhappy pianist. The tour ended in financial disaster, and the performances had to be stopped. But Falla preserved a fond memory of the tour as much because of the trip through the Vosges, the north of France, and Belgium as for the kindness of the troupe, which became very friendly toward him.

Upon returning to Paris he took lodgings at the Hotel Kléber, rue de Belloy, where his friend Joaquin Turina was living. But soon he had to leave this place because the two artists disturbed each other with their playing. The writer Melchor de Almagro San Martin, in an article cited by Angel Sagarda,[1] describes how, one day in the middle of winter, he went to see Falla at this modest hotel where he was living on the very top floor for a franc a day, which seemed very little even then. At this time, Falla was living on only five francs a day, and took his meals in the Restaurant Chartier on the Avenue de la Grande-Armée. "He looked like a monk, with his short stature, his threadbare but impeccably neat black suit, completed by an equally black tie. During our dinner, speaking little and smiling from time to time, he told me—without any apparent enthusiasm—of his preference for French composers, especially Debussy, to the Germans and also told me that he had a strong desire

[1] A. Sagardia, *op. cit.,* p. 18.

36

to live until the end of his days in a *carmen,* a country house in Granada. After we left the restaurant, he distributed, as he did every day, crumbs of bread to the sparrows and blackbirds shivering in the snow. Then, surrounded by the hopping birds, chirping and quarreling over the crumbs, his face, which had been impassive until then, lit up with an indescribably radiant smile. . . . At this moment, he expressed the same sweetness we see reflected in some of the saints painted by the divine Fra Angelico. He looked to me like the "poor man of Assisi" reincarnated. And in a few years this saint was to be revealed as one of the greatest composers of the world."[2]

We are all too familiar with the propensity of journalists to embellish reality in order to stir the imagination of the reader, but Falla's life and character have sufficiently confirmed such traits and others like them.

With work his only aim, Falla was able to endure a difficult life of this kind. As we recall, he had begun his *Four Pieces for Piano* in Madrid. Since the first and the second were almost finished, and the third was in an advanced stage, he set to work on the fourth and dedicated them to his illustrious compatriot, the bohemian, Isaac Albéniz, the Spanish Chabrier. We can also see in these pieces homage, in the form of musical portraits, to the most typical characteristics of Spain, which the titles—*Andaluza, Cubana, Aragonesa, Montañesa*—suffice to indicate. Although the influence of Albéniz is detectable throughout, in his melodic sweep and especially in his way of modulating, these pieces also disclose Falla's personal style, now unmistakable and assured. There are as many observable differences between the styles of the two masters as there are between etching and engraving, to say nothing of watercolor. Albéniz emphasizes extreme brilliance of line by applying his burin with all his might, whereas Falla discreetly suggests it. Albéniz accumulates themes, demanding almost three hands of his interpreter, imposing an arduous mechanical job on him, if not the rewriting of entire passages in order to make them playable. Falla's counterpoint is more subtle, and his linear juxtapositions and ornaments contrast

[2] M. de Almagro San Martin, *"Silueta de Falla"* in *A.B.C.,* Madrid, August 6, 1929.

modestly with Albéniz's "explosion which is more plateresque than baroque."[3] Albéniz offers a real geographical representation, Falla an impression—a word that suggests another influence, that of Debussy of whom, as we know, Falla was a great admirer. There is nothing surprising in this double influence, which may be said to be unique, for Debussy's tonal ambiguity and modal feeling are closely related to the characteristics of Spanish folklore, which Falla possessed as a birthright. We may add to them also the frequent use of false relations, the parallelism of certain intervals (fifths in particular), the unresolved appoggiaturas, the metric complexity of the melodic structure, and the great rhythmic freedom.

Falla perfected himself in Paris mainly through hard work. What he particularly retained from the French composers who were his friends were techniques of orchestration, which, for that matter, confirmed his own. At this time, how far had folklore, real or imaginary, already penetrated Falla's style, which it was soon to take over completely? Before proceeding further in a more detailed study of the *Four Spanish Pieces,* it would seem necessary to shed a little more light on this ancient expression of the Spanish soul.

After Pedrell many musicologists devoted themselves to the research, study, and classification of a folklore whose richness easily matched that of the Slavs and the peoples of the Near East and whose close connections in origin there is no point in underlining since they are sufficiently explained by history and ethnography. These scholars based their studies on regional differences and outward expression as represented by song and dance and their instrumental and rhythmic accompaniment—guitar, castanets, *zapateado* (stamping and tapping of the feet), and *palmas* (clapping of the hands to encourage the dancers).

In his important study of the music of his country, the eminent Spanish musicologist Rafael Mitjana,[4] like Pedrell, links the origin of folklore to Arab music and to the *cancioneros,* as liturgical as they are secular. From them gradually emerged the characteristic dances and songs imputable to the different regions of the peninsula,

[3] Joaquin Rodrigo, cited by Sagardia, p. 16.
[4] *Encyclopédie de la Musique,* part one.

38

not forgetting, of course, the fact of their inevitable interpenetration. From these collections or transmissions, which were more or less oral or in the form of stage performances, came the previously mentioned *danzas habladas* (spoken dances) and *bailes cantados* (sung dances) and the pieces for the Arabian lute, the *vihuela,* the ancestor of the guitar.

Among the *danzas* were the *zarabanda,* popularized by the *troteras,* the street-dancers of very ancient origin, who had an important role in the processions and *autos sacramentales,* the *chaconne,* soon forgotten in favor of the seguidillas and fandangos, and the *pasacalle* or *passacaille* (from *pasar,* "to pass," and *calle,* "street"), a march tune that was sung with guitar accompaniment. Most of these popular motifs exhibit the intervals of Arab modes, the melismas of plainsong, rhythmic combinations in quintuple time, and a constant mingling of 3/4 and 3/8 time. The contribution of the American colonies is seen in the tango, a primitive Andalusian dance modified in Mexico, the habanera, and the *guarija,* with alternating 6/8, 3/4 or 6/8, 3/8 rhythms, and harmonies based on the open chord of the guitar, E, A, D, G, B, E, which soon became a part of primitive songs.

In the same work Raoul Laparra and Julien Tiersot classify the songs by region, beginning with the nineteenth century, emphasizing the peculiarities natural to the Spanish character, which virtually place their stamp on the rhythm. The well-known *jota* in 3/8 time belongs preeminently to Aragon; it is an important dance which was invented apparently by an Arab musician exiled to Calatayud. There are several genres or *estilos* of this dance, *ravaleras, zaragonazas,* and *femateras.* The *coplas de jota* (sung quatrains) are accompanied on the guitar. There are the *cantares de labrador* which are found in the environs of Murcia. We shall see how Falla used them in his *Seven Songs.* The hostile grandeur of Castile also gave birth to the *jota castillana,* to the *rueda,* a round dance in which the participants alternately dance and walk without touching each other, to a kind of seguidilla-bolero, and to various *canciónes de cuna,*[5] which are accompanied on the tamboril or small drum and also on

[5] Lullaby. (*Cuna:* cradle.)

the *dulziana,* a primitive oboe with a double reed and a shrill tone (the *douçaine* of the *chansons de geste*).

But it is in the south of Spain, in Andalusia, that the folklore harvest is particularly abundant. It is from Andalusia that folklore composers have made most of their borrowings, including Falla, who was himself almost an Andalusian. There more than elsewhere we find a mingling of songs and dances accompanied by the guitar, these three offspring seemingly inseparable from the country which gave them birth. Andalusian folklore, more than any other in Spain, bears the stamp of the East, for the Arabs remained in the country until the conquest of Granada and the surrender of Boabdil in 1492. We are aware of the Moslem liking for ornamentation: the arabesque of stucco and tile has a parallel in their vocal and instrumental art. Following their example, the Mozarabs introduced these Oriental melismas even into the liturgy.

But the Arabs, or rather the Syrians, merely ornamented the songs borrowed from Persia, if not from the depths of Asia. This art is particularly *Mudejar* in its efflorescence, its repetition of motifs, its Moslem technique; it swings from a concern for realism to classic simplicity and baroque embroidery. Although protected by the mountains, Andalusia assimilated the Gypsy contributions of the fifteenth century, the *cante jondo,* the flamenco, and mingled lamentations from the depths of time with Byzantine liturgical melismas and the excesses of Oriental melody. Only the *cantaores,* anonymous or known by their surnames, their place of origin—Niña de los Peines, Chato de Jerez, and in our day Roque Montoya "Jarrito" and Tomás de Antequera—can reproduce the quarter-tone inflections, the portamenti of the enharmonic style which require special voice training and can hardly be acquired, except by birth.

Falla devoted a large part of his time to the *cante jondo,* a higher form of flamenco as we shall see when we study the work he did in Granada. Was the word "flamenco" formerly a term of contempt, applied to soldiers returning from the Low Countries who boasted about their exploits, or to Flemish nobles brought back by Charles V? Or does it stem from a deformity of Arabic or Semitic words, or, as Mérimée wrote, from a name the Gypsies gave themselves, *Flamencos de Roma,* that is, Flemings from the "tribe of the

40

Romans"? This question will be discussed for a long time. In any case, the *cante jondo,* or *hondo,* or big or little flamenco, is an Oriental and Occidental blend of an "unmistakable" character as Falla described it, inimitable and purely national. It is possible to distinguish the a capella forms: the *martinete,* a rhythm that Gypsy blacksmiths beat out with the blows of their hammers, which Falla was to utilize in *La Vida Breve;* the *saeta,* sung in religious processions, and its derivative, the *tona.* There are also the forms accompanied by guitars, castanets or by the clapping of hands, the *caña* (from the Arab *gannia*), whose prolonged stress runs the whole length of the tone-scale; the rough, poignant *polo* in D minor with its characteristic leitmotif—A, B flat, C, B flat, A—and its sighs; the soft *rasgado*[6] of the guitar, which gradually becomes inflamed to the point of ferocity; the *solea,* a song of loneliness and desertion, with its various tangos, *tientos, bulerias,* its gutteral lamentations with their raucous

and stifled sonorities, its endings on an ornamented dominant. Thus, for example, the Gypsy *siguiriya,* "the most celebrated of the great songs of the *cante jondo.*"[7] This song, with its strongly marked accents, rests, syncopations, and obsessive repetitions of an ornamented dominant or tonic, which is reminiscent of the call of the muezzin, seems to be shaken by hiccups. Finally, there is the *serrana,* a kind of fierce dirge, sung by the "bandits of the mountains for the repose of the souls of travelers whom they have stabbed to death!"

We have already mentioned the heady *alegrías* in 3/4 time of the Gaditan region, which in Madrid became the *caracoles.* Among the *cante pequeño* there are the *petenera,* the legend of a girl "who takes revenge on all men for her first misfortune in love" and of which Lorca made a song in his admirable *cancionero;*[8] the *Sevillanas,* graceful dances, *chispeante* (from *chispa:* spark); and the lively *bulerias* in 3/4 time.

[6] A special effect producing a more or less rapid arpeggio.
[7] Georges Hilaire, *Initiation Flamenca.* Paris, n.d. Prof. Andrade da Silva, *Anthologie du Cante Flamenco.* Paris, Madrid, 1954.
[8] Federico Garcia Lorca, *Romancero Gitano.* Paris, 1954–55.

From the flamenco as such there is derived the Andalusian fandango in 3/4 time, unfolding "from the major to the minor through successive stages of sustained notes and ending with a lively ornamentation." Also from the flamenco come the *granadina* and the *el vito* forms characteristic of Granada, and the sorrowful, sinuous, nostalgic *malagueña,* which was sung by the famous Juan Breva. Falla made use of these forms in his *Seven Songs.*

Many other titles could be cited. In Andalusia alone there are "up to five hundred kinds of dances of popular origin" which have been celebrated by famous writers from Lope de Vega to the modern Lorca and Montherlant, without forgetting Mérimée, Dumas, and Théophile Gautier. Understandably, we must limit ourselves to a small number, but we shall come upon them again, along with some others, as we find Falla introducing them into his compositions, because this poses a very perplexing problem.

The discovery of folklore, the large number of studies that it has produced, the abusive and often clumsy use that composers have made of it, and the awkward, flat, vulgar harmonizations that spread almost everywhere provoked an inevitable reaction. Folklore became an all too facile source. A composer no longer dared to confess a vocation for folklore. It could no longer be a question of only an "imaginary folklore," to use the happy expression of the late Serge Moreux.[9] With this purpose in mind, composers steeped themselves in the essence of the folksong, creating songs by making use of the classic forms and then modifying them to their liking, at the same time continuing to suggest their origin and perfume. Thus Pedrell's ideas were broadened if not surpassed. On this subject Falla, in an article in the Madrid review *Música,* declared:

"I modestly believe that in the folk song the spirit matters more than the letter. The rhythm, the modality, and the melodic intervals which determine its rise and fall and its cadences constitute the essential ingredient of these songs. . . . I am opposed to music which takes authentic folklore originals as its base. I believe, on the contrary, that it is necessary to start with hardy natural sources and to utilize the substance of their sonorities and rhythms, but not for

[9] Serge Moreux, *Bartók*. Paris, 1955.

the superficial effect."[10] Falla, however, admitted that there were exceptional and chance cases in which an original motif might be used.

Therefore, criticism, falling in step, praised the composer for having "extracted the juice, the perfume, the essence of the folk song while elaborating it in terms of his own *personality*."[11] Since then such praise has been bestowed, more or less frivolously, upon many others, including Bartók!

Salazar, who, after all, must have known his former teacher better than anyone, asserts: "The localized Spanish point disappeared to make way for the suggestion of highly simplified elements that might be called 'seeds of style,' brief details worked into the folk-song and subjected to an adequate harmonic treatment that contributes to the suggestion."[12]

In connection with *Nights in the Gardens of Spain* Pahissa writes: "The music possesses the Spanish character so typical of Falla's early style, or rather the typical Andalusian flavor, without being, as in any of his other compositions, a direct copy of the folksongs and themes, but having simply the spirit, the feeling, the aroma, the atmosphere of the music of his Andalusia."[13]

Pérez-Casas affirms that Falla "used popular themes, not that he had collected but that he had created for himself."[14]

We might multiply these quotations, nor would we omit those of Sagardia[15] and the musicologist Gilbert Chase,[16] who go so far as to claim that in the *Seven Songs,* with their rigorously authentic and well-known themes, Falla used only "the essence, the modality, and the melodic intervals" and not a literal transcription of the folk tunes.

Manuel Garcia Matos, a learned musicologist and Falla scholar, professor at the Madrid Conservatory and a member of

[10] *Música,* June 2, 1917. Article cited by Manuel Garcia Matos. Also cited in *Excelsior,* Paris, May 31, 1925.
[11] Rogelio Villar, in *Ritmo,* Madrid. Cited by Garcia Matos.
[12] Adolfo Salazar, *La Música Contemporánea en España.* Madrid, 1930.
[13] J. Pahissa, *op. cit.,* p. 101.
[14] *El Espanol,* November 30, 1946.
[15] A. Sagarda, *op. cit.,* pp. 25–26.
[16] Gilbert Chase, *The Music of Spain.* New York, 1941, p. 188.

the Spanish Institute of Musicology, put things in proper focus in two important studies published in 1953 in the review *Música.*[17] He admits that a procedure such as that employed by Rimski-Korsakov in his *Capriccio Espagnol,* consisting of a melodic structure strictly based on a simple succession of folk themes, is over-simple and sterile. Garcia Matos cites the collection, now no longer available, of José Inzenga, *Ecos de España* (Barcelona, n.d.), from which Rimski must have simply copied the elements of his *Capriccio.* Nevertheless, he thinks that the disdain shown by critics for the use of raw material stems from the erroneous idea that the composer would distinguish himself more by avoiding it, as if, he rightly adds, "the taste and felicitous instinct that preside over the selection of folk motifs that are useful to the work, the inspired wisdom that places them and develops them in its arrangement, the choice of an exquisite harmonization and of an original instrumentation suitable for framing the others with the maximum of relief and effectiveness—as if those were not already a high attainment."

In conclusion, Garcia Matos suggests that these various mistaken thoughts and laudatory statements stem from a "lack of seriousness in analysis and from an absence of precise and thorough observation, which such music demands." He asserts—and proves —that "actually, almost all of Falla's works, from *La Vida Breve* to *Master Peter's Puppet Show* and the harpsichord concerto are constructed on the solid basis of genuine folk originals, transcribed completely or lightly retouched, and not, more or less vaguely, on 'aromas' and 'essences.' "

Perhaps the *Four Spanish Pieces* should be excluded from this statement. A close study of them may decide the matter.

The Four Spanish Pieces

Since the *Four Pieces* were begun in 1906, they belong to the time of *La Vida Breve.* It is generally admitted that the opera and these *Four Pieces* are among Falla's first works of real value, and he always recognized them as such. Actually, they show a considerable technical improvement over the pieces for piano—*Vals*

---

[17] *Música,* Madrid, October–December, 1953.

Capricho, Nocturno, etc.—which they followed very closely, and indicate an incomparably more solid command of composition. Doubtless this is due to the intensive work that the musician put into his opera, to his reading, and constant analyzing and listening to the works of certain composers, Albéniz and Debussy, for example, whom the *Four Pieces* irresistibly bring to mind.

The first, *Aragonesa,* introduces a *jota* folk theme in the fourth measure, virile and clear, in keeping with the somewhat crude strength of the Aragonese character. This kind of *rondella,* brought forth twice alternately with both hands, ends with the characteristic triplet which produces a *copla* with a supple inflection in which one discerns the slightly troubled sensibility of the second theme of the *Evocation* of Albéniz (cf. *tranquillo,* p. 3). Skillful superpositions and falling arpeggios in the manner of Chabrier (whom Falla does not seem to have mentioned but whom he must have read) lead to an ample peroration in which the *jota* theme is repeated in its primitive essence. The piece ends on a diminuendo and an expressive ritenuto.

Cubana, the second piece, is completely different. The motif of *Aragonesa* is more or less personal, but that of *Cubana* is an authentic *guarija,* a Creole theme introduced in the eighteenth century into the flamenco repertory, which burdened it with numerous ornaments and variants that were added gradually by the *cantaores.* Falla strips it of all of these, leaving only its spontaneity and the languor of its rhythmic swaying in 3/4, 6/8 time, which he uses to good advantage. He uses the same methods of style and development as in the *Aragonesa:* a single theme whose undulating contours modify and interpenetrate each other, forming contrapuntal mazes of an exquisite refinement. The modulations prepared by altered chords in the manner of Albéniz, the rhythmic ambiguities that, without transition, pass from the ternary to the binary form with their syncopated stresses, all contribute to a sultry, languorous, sensual atmosphere which finally sinks into a pianissimo quadruplet.

The *Montañesa* is resolutely impressionistic. Falla, moreover, subtitles it "Landscape" and marks it for a sonority *quasi campani*—like bells. This landscape portrays the *Montaña,* that part of Castile which borders the Bay of Biscay and lies between the Basque country and the Asturias. We hear Debussyesque bells and also those of Ravel's *Vallée des Cloches,* which answer each other among the syncopations of the opening. "The sound of distant small bells carried on the evening air or rising suddenly from the nearby mountains like the peaceful smoke from a chimney."[18]

An authentic Asturian song (*piu animato,* p. 2) deals with the parish priest, who is very much at home in this landscape filled with bells. It murmurs:

> *La casa del señor cura*
> *nunca la vi como ahora;*
> *Ventana sobre ventana*
> *Y el comedor, a la moda.*[19]

This gay *cante* brightens the slightly melancholy painting a little. Falla develops it very curiously with descending chromatic scales, in the Russian manner.

Andaluza is the brilliant finale. Lively, with a pronounced rhythm and a feeling of wildness, it fades away, however, in a pianissimo quadruplet, as do its three sister pieces and, later, the *Nights in the Gardens of Spain.* This handling is quite in keeping with the modesty of Falla who had a horror of flashiness. Nevertheless the piece opens with the rhythm of an ancient *buleria de baile.*[20] The vigorous guitar, *ritimica y brava,* supplies a grating staccato in the *copla* which is sustained by the open strings—E, A (second line). The *malagueña de baile,* virile and expressive, seems to rise from a *punteado guitarristico*[21] that entwines itself around an A pedal point, with its groups of notes issuing from the throat of the *cantaor.* It spins wildly like the flying skirt of the *bailadora.* The *zapateado* (rhythmic stamping with the heels) accents the violence of the dance. We will find it again in the *Polo* of the *Seven Songs.* The modulations follow one another rapidly, using Albéniz-like chords. A change of mood follows: a beautiful *siguiriya-soleare* theme which gently dies

[18] J. Pahissa, *op. cit.,* p. 51.
[19] A. Sagardia, *op. cit.,* p. 17. (No one ever saw the curé's house as it is now; window after window and a stylish dining room.)
[20] T. A. de S. *"El Piano de M. de F.,"* in *Música.* Madrid, 1953, no. 3–4.
[21] Played note by note (point by point).

away on a distant echo of the guitar-like strains of the opening and of a syncopated *zapateado*.

The *Four Spanish Pieces* were first performed publicly by Ricardo Viñes at the Société Nationale de Musique in Paris on March 27, 1909, and by the same artist at the Sociedad Filarmónica de Madrid on November 30, 1912. By then Falla had met the most outstanding French musicians of the day.

His first visit was made to Debussy, with whom he had already corresponded. After Falla had won the award of the Academia de Bellas Artes, at the time that his eyes were turned longingly toward Paris, he took part in a concert at the Teatro de la Comedia in Madrid, where, under the direction of Tomas Bretón, he was to play, along with Bach's *Concerto in D minor,* the piano version of Debussy's *Danses Sacrées et Profanes.* He wrote to the French composer for some information. Debussy replied—somewhat tardily, but very politely—apologizing for the delay which was due to rehearsals for *Pelléas et Mélisande* at the Théâtre de la Monnaie in Brussels, and gave Falla the advice he had requested. On the strength of this first contact, Falla, toward the end of September, 1907, presented himself at the residence of Debussy, who at that time was at the peak of his glory. He was told that the maestro was still on vacation but that he would soon be back. From there he made his way to the home of Paul Dukas, but he too was away, spending the summer in Saint-Cloud, coming in to Paris only once a week. Falla left his card, announcing that he would be back the following week. This time he met the great musician, who at first received him with natural reserve. The young man was carrying under his arm the score of *La Vida Breve,* and Dukas resigned himself to hearing it. The scene is described with a touch of gentle humor by Pahissa,[22] who no doubt heard it recounted a number of years later. Falla sat down at the piano and began to play, not without first asking Dukas to interrupt him the moment he felt tired. Several times Falla wanted to stop, fearful that he was abusing the patience of his listener, but each time Dukas motioned him to continue. After the last bar, Dukas

[22] J. Pahissa, *op. cit.,* p. 42.

declared: "That's good enough to be put on at the Opéra Comique!" Falla could not believe his ears. There followed a series of comments on the score, its value, and on the modifications and retouches needed. Falla then told Dukas of his plan to go to the Schola Cantorum, like his friend Turina, and study under Vincent d'Indy.

"That would be useless," replied Dukas. "Work on your own, and I'll give you some advice on instrumentation." Dukas kept his word, and Falla profited greatly from his instruction. Then Dukas introduced him to Albéniz, whom Falla, because of Albéniz's nomadic life, knew only through his works. Albéniz, like Dukas, praised the composition at great length. The warm friendship that instantly developed between the two compatriots lasted only a short time, for Albéniz died soon afterward, in 1909. In the meantime Falla had finally met Debussy. According to the biographers the first meeting between these two was an awkward one. Both were distant, wrapped up in their private dream worlds, on the defensive, and both afflicted by shyness, which the Frenchman dissembled under a mask of irony. In order to break the ice, Falla amiably announced that he had always liked French music. "I don't!" replied Debussy.

Nevertheless, having already been informed of the value of Falla's score, Debussy expressed a desire to hear it. The same scene that had previously unfolded before Dukas and Albéniz was repeated to the last detail. Debussy listened to *La Vida Breve* through to the end and showered it with praise. From this day on, Falla was welcome inside the temple of French music. Ricardo Viñes, whose goodness equaled his talent, and to whom Falla had an introduction from his brother Pepe and another from Albéniz, received him with open arms. He remained one of his best friends and his favorite interpreter. Through Viñes, Falla made the acquaintance of Ravel, who at that time was living in a remote section of Paris, with an old piano and some old pieces of furniture and without a servant. Ravel himself had to open the door to the young Spaniard.[23]

At the home of Viñes, the devoted interpreter of the new French school, Falla also met Florent Schmitt and Roland-Manuel. We are indebted to the latter not only for the work already cited but

[23] J. Pahissa, *op. cit.*, p. 46.

for numerous critical articles inspired by the great Spanish composer. Falla also met there Maurice Delage and Gustave Samazeuilh, who dedicated a sensitive and moving essay to him in his memoirs, *Musiciens de Mon Temps*.[24] Through them Falla gained entry into the most enlightened musical circles of the day, the Godebski salon on the rue d'Athènes, where all French or foreign artists who really counted gathered on Sundays, and the famous Club des Apaches, to whose members Maurice Delage played host every Saturday night in his little hotel on the rue de Civry in Auteuil. Later on Stravinsky also became part of this group.

Although Falla was far from being a drawing-room type, he established many solid friendships among the French composers. His courtesy, his natural distinction, his discretion, combined with a lively intelligence, and his great nascent talent, inspired a sympathetic response in them that was translated into a helpfulness for which Falla was to be always appreciative. One day, to his great surprise, he received a note from the publisher Durand, requesting, on the recommendation of Dukas, Debussy, and Ravel, his *Four Spanish Pieces*. Not believing his eyes, he made haste to take the score to Durand, who paid him three hundred francs (a healthy sum!). Such generosity overwhelmed his friends, particularly Ravel, who had to wait until 1910 for the publication of his *Quartet*.

Meanwhile Falla worked steadily to earn a living. He gave lessons, accompanied singers, and even did translations. He went on tour with the cellist Miresky and the violinist Bordas, the future director of the Madrid Conservatory. But at the end of the tour, he rushed back to Paris, the city of his choice, in spite of the difficult life he was leading there.

His constant moving from one place to another hardly made it any easier. As mentioned, he had to leave the hotel where he lodged with Turina because they disturbed each other. The two musicians, although remaining good friends, nevertheless drifted apart, not so much because of the differences in their personal styles, as because of their circles of friends. Turina, a pupil at the Schola,

[24] Gustave Samazeuilh, *Musiciens de Mon Temps*. Paris, 1947, pp. 334–40, and appendix.

49

naturally belonged to the D'Indy circle, which, as we know, opposed the tendencies championed by Debussy and Ravel. Ironically, although Falla had a great need for quiet for his work, his piano aroused numerous complaints among his neighbors. He changed his address so often that Debussy joked that "he moved more often than Beethoven."

The *Three Songs,* based on poems by Théophile Gautier, date from this period.

The Three Songs

These compositions are to be viewed as Falla's homage to the new French music that he admires so much and whose influence on his own work is easily perceptible. The prosody of these pieces is skillfully handled; Falla took great care with accents, long or short syllables, and silent letters. The first, *The Doves,* is dedicated to Mme. Adiny-Milliet, the wife of the translator of *La Vida Breve,* a Wagnerian singer who had had some success in her performances of *Die Walküre.*

> *Sur le coteau là-bas où sont les tombes,*
> *Un beau palmier, comme un panache vert*
> *Dresse sa tête, où le soir les colombes*
> *Viennent nicher et se mettre à couvert*
> > From *La Comédie de la Mort* (1838)

On the hill yonder where the tombs are,
A beautiful palm tree, like a green plume,
Lifts its head. Here, in the evenings the doves
Come to nest and to seek shelter.

These doves draw their inspiration from Debussy's *Ariettes Oubliées, Proses Lyriques,* and *Poèmes de Baudelaire.* A G sharp pedal point strings out sextuplets in a melodic line that has the character of an expressive recitative. Deliberately vague and distant patterns are inlaid on the pianistic texture (p. 3, line 1). Adroit, supple modulations and certain ways of introducing ninths forcibly recall the *Il Pleure Dans Mon Coeur* . . . (*de Grève, Spleen*) of Debussy.

50

Chinoiserie, dedicated to a Mme. R. Brooks, seems to be the result of Falla's visits to the Musée Guimet, a museum of Oriental art that was near his lodging. Debussy thought the beginning was too encumbered and advised him "to try to find something else" for the initial recitative. Falla, after searching for a long time, could think of nothing better than to suppress all support for the voice so as to give full value to the poem's real beginning: "She whom I love now is in China." On the word "China" a percussion rhythm stresses an accompaniment based on the defective scale, called Chinese, with a dominant E, and with fourths which produce a very attractive effect.

The brilliant *Séguidille*—an extract from *España* (1845) —was dedicated to "Madame Claude Debussy."

Théophile Gautier's celebrated poetry, already responsible for passable *espagnolades,* must have reminded Falla of the period when he was writing *zarzuelas.* Perhaps he found it amusing to embellish this superficial poetry with the rhythm of a real seguidilla, with the inevitable final triplet which stresses the *vuelta* of a long swirling skirt. Falla's grace and finesse breathe the Spanish spirit of Chabrier and Albéniz. There is plenty of shouting of *"alza!"* and *"olé!"* And Falla rediscovered here the octosyllables of the *romancero.*

A clear C major, boldly colored modulations, much *brio,* elegance, and adroitness wittily color this charming little tableau, which, regrettably, is not seen on the programs of vocalists more often.

Paul Dukas, always at the service of his friends, had the *Three Songs* published by Rouart-Lerolle (Paris, 1910). The first performance was given at the Salle Gaveau in November, 1910, by Mme. Ada Adiny–Milliet, with Falla at the piano. It was the second concert of the Société Musicale Indépendante, which had been recently founded by Maurice Delage's circle of friends. Madrid heard them sung by Genevieve Vix on May 23, 1916, at a concert of the Sociedad Nacional de Música. The composer again was the accompanist.

While he was working on the *Songs,* Falla, on the advice of Dukas and Debussy, was making some important changes in the score of *La Vida Breve.* After having won the Madrid competition he had rearranged the opera in two acts in agreement with the librettist. Falla next elaborated the interlude considerably and undertook a detailed revision of the orchestration. A creator must have a deep faith and a keen desire for perfection to endure the fatigue and tedium involved in the work of revision. Falla himself told Pahissa that he was encouraged in an unexpected way by the example of Blériot, who was the first to cross the English Channel in a plane (1908). There was an airplane workship near his *pension*. When he heard the joyous shouts of the workers, mingled with those of the newspaper sellers, at the announcement of the great news, Falla was swept up in the general excitement and "saw clearly that man, with steady, daily toil and the unshakable will to advance, can overcome great difficulties and achieve his ideal."[25]

Applying Dukas' principles, Falla plunged deeply into a study of the technique of orchestral instrumentation. Without altering his original plan but by deleting useless details or substituting new ones, he strove to achieve the most exact expression of sound, the one best suited for rendering the orchestral impression he wanted. Following Debussy's advice, he tried to preserve a commendable restraint in his orchestration, even at the most dramatic moments. Falla detested intensifications. "Hace sucio" (that's nasty), he said to his pupil and friend Henri Collet while correcting compositions in which the latter had applied the textbook rules too scrupulously. "Obviously, these rules," Collet added, "were not very suited to southern music. Bizet clearly felt this because, in *Carmen,* he limits himself to some arabesques of pure timbre that circle freely above four equipollent voices of the classical quartet."[26]

It was after a visit to Debussy that Falla deleted the last bars of *La Vida Breve.* Originally, after Salud's collapse, her aged relatives overwhelm Paco with their curses, and then the curtain falls. Debussy thought that the intervention of the two Gypsies in the finale would spoil the effect of Salud's sudden death and instead advised Falla not to dwell on the dramatic effects and their consequences.

[25] Pahissa, *op. cit.,* p. 55.
[26] Henri Collet, article in *La Revue Musicale,* January, 1947.

"At this moment," he said, "the orchestra should use the utmost restraint. It should play 'I have some good tobacco' (and in a minor key, too!), and the audience won't even be aware of it because it will be taken up with the action."

Falla related this quip—quite in keeping with Debussy's temperament—to his sister Maria del Carmen, who in turn passed it on to the music critic André Gauthier when he was on a trip to Spain. In fact, she was so taken with this story that she even remembered the date of her brother's visit to Debussy: October 10, 1911.

But these were not the main problems. As always in such cases, the practical side produced even more. Before offering the work to the Opéra Comique, a translator had to be found. Albéniz suggested Paul Milliet, treasurer of the Société des Auteurs, which, he thought, might be of some help in the future. A contract was signed, with certain confusing clauses that could be interpreted to the benefit of the translator at the expense of the composer.[27] Then an audition was arranged before Albert Carré, at that time director of the Opéra Comique. Carré expressed admiration for the score and declared his readiness to stage the opera without, however, being able to fix a date, because his contract obliged him to limit the production of works by foreign composers.

Time passed without bringing a solution until Milliet managed to obtain another audition, this time before the director of the Nice Casino, who, after hearing it, indicated his willingness to accept the work. How to decide between the offer of the Opéra Comique, which was certainly the more flattering proposition but apparently would mean a postponement to a more or less distant future, and that of Nice, which carried the assurance of an immediate performance? At this very moment an offer arrived from the Ricordi music publishers, thanks to Gentien, director of the Ricordi branch in Paris. Falla was offered an audition in Milan, all expenses paid, before the managing director Tito Ricordi, to be followed no doubt by a duly drawn-up contract. Overjoyed at the prospect of a journey to Italy and of reading his name on a score published by this firm,

27 J. Pahissa, *op. cit.*, p. 51.

with its venerable and worldwide reputation, Falla set out for Milan full of hope. Again the music had its usual success, but Tito Ricordi, most surprisingly, judged the work to be more suitable for the concert hall than the stage! For the theater wanted a less national style, one that was more universal and appealing to the taste of a large international public. He concluded the interview by offering Falla a contract to write a score along the desired lines, based on *Anima Allegra,* a libretto taken from a comedy by the Quintero brothers and previously offered to Puccini. But Falla refused to force himself into a musical mold that was the opposite of his ideal and of his serious temperament. He felt that he would be wholly unable to bring it off. Discussion continued for two days, and to Tito Ricordi's great amazement and admiration, the young Spanish composer, poor and unknown, declined the brilliant and tangible prospects held out by the powerful firm of Ricordi. He preferred to return to Paris on his own terms.

Naturally, the return journey was less joyous than the departure. But once Falla was back in Paris, his translator Milliet took him to the music publisher Max Eschig. Another audition, another success, and this time there was a contract for the publication of *La Vida Breve* and of *Nights in the Gardens of Spain,* already in progress, as well as for any music which Falla would write during the term of the contract. Moreover, he received a monthly stipend, fixed and assured, drawn against future royalties. Thus he could devote himself completely to his work and give up the extraneous activities that took up so much of his time and energy.

He began by arranging for the reduction of his score for voice and piano and, then, at the advice of André Messager, he elaborated the second dance of the second act "to satisfy the subscribers." Finally, it was decided that the first performance would take place in Nice during the winter season. Falla spent three months there supervising the rehearsals and correcting proofs as he received them from Eschig. Remembering his first experience with his *zarzuela,* he was greatly worried about how his orchestra would sound, despite encouraging words from Debussy and Dukas. The latter recommended that he immediately assert his authority. At the first objection from the orchestra's conductor, he was to reply firmly that he wanted to hear "exactly what he had written," and that the conductor would have to begin over again from the beginning until the desired result was obtained.

Actually the rehearsals proceeded without a problem, to the general satisfaction of the conductor, the stage manager, the interpreters, and, above all, the composer, who was "delighted on hearing the wonderful reality of imagined sounds."

The premiere of *La Vida Breve* took place at the Nice Casino on April 1, 1913, under the direction of J. Miranne, with the soprano Lillian Grenville and the tenor David Devriès in the roles of Salud and Paco. It was staged by Streliski.

LA VIDA BREVE

We have already summarized the plot of *La Vida Breve* in an earlier chapter describing the competition sponsored by the San Fernando Academia. Within the broad frame of an opera, the composer for the first time grappled with the problem of painting a musical portrait of a region with which he was unfamiliar, although he already had a keen desire to live in Andalusia some day. He did not dare confess this deeply embarrassing ignorance to his French associates. Nevertheless, thanks to his powerful imagination and his wide knowledge of the ethnography, history, and folklore of Andalusia, Falla was able convincingly to evoke the region by blending his own musical nature with the declamation of flamenco song. The precise feeling of the countryside envelops the plot. Albaïcin, with its picturesque trades, and its blacksmiths singing about their sad lot, the young girls selling flowers and fruit, wandering gaily down the street with a song on their lips, and the final intermezzo of the first act where we see Granada colored with the twilight hues from the Sacro Monte—all are bathed in an atmosphere of poetry. The characters are stock portraits: Salud, the "Andalusian girl," so passionately in love that she will die of it; Tio Sarvaor, the old Gypsy uncle always ready to use his clasp knife; and the *abuela,* the fatalistic and despairing grandmother, are contrasted with *señorito* Paco, an odious member of the privileged classes, a pleasure-loving egoist, a ladies' man whose ostentatious vanity will break poor Salud's heart.

After three measures serving as an introduction, the curtain rises on the first scene. The program notes read as follows:[28]

"The courtyard of a house of Gypsies in the Albaïcin quarter of Granada. Large gate in the background with the perspective of a tiny but very lively street. To the right, the house, to the left, the entrance to a blacksmith's shop, lit up by the red glare of the fire. It is day, a beautiful day."

In the first scene the grandmother, who is alone on the stage, is feeding her birds. A theme of foreboding rises from the double basses; hammer blows resound—the exact evocation of a *martinete*,[29] which the blacksmiths, singing, beat rhythmically on their anvils. Tragic lamentation of a chorus of men, with its ejaculations of *"Ay!"* struck under the note of an appoggiatura taken within the chord. "Beat without letup, such is your fate. To some every good fortune, to others every hardship" (p. 5, measure 1). Suddenly, a playful *allegretto* in 3/8 time (p. 6), pivoted on a dominant-tonic in E minor, brings the joyous strains of a song echoing in the winding lane and the outlines of a dance tune. A young man (p. 8, *largamento e molto espr.*), while hammering the iron, breaks into an amorous *copla,* freely rhymed, with long sustained notes followed by a rapid vocalization of a modal character. The grandmother appears (p. 10, measure 1), carrying a cage "in which a poor bird is dying." The impression is one of great sadness but also of indifference, to which is added the irony of an orchestra whose pizzicatti stress the gaiety of the nearby street. Thus the whole scene offers a picturesque contrast of sorrow, misery, somber menace, and lighthearted, sunlit insouciance. A man sings (p. 10, measure 11) the despairing *copla* which is the basic theme. It will function as a kind of leitmotif symbolising the tragedy of life:

Malhaya el hombre, malhaya . . .

Distant sounds of the city, or even nearer, of Albaïcin; hammer blows, joyful shouts, lamentations, all merge in an ensemble

---

[28] According to the piano and vocal score (Max Eschig, Paris, 1913). The indications of pages and measures refer to this score.

[29] According to Chase, *op. cit.,* the *martinete* derives from the *siguiriya gitana* and is a prisoner's song, without accompaniment, in which the prisoner manifests his despair by beating against the bars.

which recalls the equivalent, and celebrated, scene of *Louise,* the opera by Gustave Charpentier.[30] Falla treats his own scene harmonically, using the same altered chords as the French musician. In view of the triumph enjoyed by *Louise,* we can suppose that Falla knew its score.

An agitated, steady mounting of the strings (p. 12, measure 10) climactically ushers in the second scene.

Salud enters. Desolate, she is waiting for her *novio,* who does not come. There is a duet between the two women in which Falla demonstrates his gifts as a melodist, as well as a certain undeniable quality of *verismo.* The grandmother tries to console her grandchild and with dramatic force seeks to convince her that it is wrong to succumb to such despair. (The expressive ninths which rise chromatically from the bass, the strings doubling the melody, and the appoggiatura effects clearly betray the Italian lyricism of the times.) Salud stops her and proclaims her intense feelings: "I have two loves in my soul, Paco's and yours" (p. 17, measure 6). She instinctively employs the melodic formulas of her race, the trills which burst forth from her throat in a raucous cry. But soon she lets herself be persuaded (p. 19). This is a very tender passage, suffused with sweetness, weariness, and an orchestral lullaby of muted strings.

In scene three the young girl is alone, her grandmother having departed. The song from the smithy resumes: "Beat without letup, such is your fate." Falla, who had not yet forgotten Wagner in favor of Debussy, here was thinking of the forge in *Siegfried.* An accompanying motif in ostinato, punctuated by the hammer, sustains the sad *siguiriya* that Salud sings and with which her mother used to rock her to sleep:

> *Vivan los que ríen!*
> *Mueran los que lloran* . . . (p. 22, measure 12)

> (Long live those who laugh!
> Death to those who weep.)

There follows a slow recitative derived from the Orient, with augmented intervals, its complicated ornamentations, its muted setting of the dominant that stamp it with an agonized tension. Its melismas

[30] Performed at the Opéra Comique on February 2, 1900.

offer a certain relationship to the future *Nana* of the *Seven Songs,* and its rhythmic balancing and pauses are on a raised note. The young girl interrupts herself at times for an examination of conscience, during which she recalls her dead mother, in the manner of Marguerite in *Faust* or the Willow Song in *Otello* (p. 23, *quasi recitativo*). When she arrives at the peak of her despair (p. 24) with the verse

> *Flor que nace con el alba*
> (The flower born at dawn)

the accompaniment becomes more intricate; it uses the same formulas as the song, the trills spread to the woodwinds, the chromaticism is intensified, and majestic unisons rise along with the song.

In the smithy the hammer blows and the chorus of *"Ays!"* resume, and the tenor recalls the misfortune promised to the man

> *que nace con negro sino* (p. 26, measure 14).
> (Who is born under an evil star).

The grandmother returns in scene four, and in an agitated recitative she announces the arrival of Paco, the lover. There is now a different harmonic character and theatrical *verismo* again, with the aid of diminished sevenths and spectacular sequences of dominant chords, boldly spread out along the whole orchestra.

A love duet in two parts for Salud and Paco occurs in the fifth scene. The first is composed of the despairing cries of the girl contrasted with the tender words of her lover. The very light orchestral support gradually warms up to the inflamed song of the lovers, which is accompanied by lyricism, ascending treble notes, agitation of arpeggios, tremolos, orchestral display of theatrical sixths and fourths such as we find in many scores of the time (p. 33, *poco animato*), especially in Massenet, Puccini, and Leoncavallo. According to Pahissa,[31] the deliberate, grandiloquent effects of Paco's phrases betray the duplicity, the hypocrisy of the young *señorito*.

The finale offers a rather unfortunate formula which certainly recalls Leoncavallo's *Pagliacci* (p. 42–43). The lovers sing

---

[31] J. Pahissa, *op. cit.*, p. 20.

their love in unison, fortissimo, in which (scene six) the grandmother, who comes to share their happiness, participates, despite the menacing noise of the hammer blows still surrounding them. The menace is more exactly defined by the arrival of the ominous uncle Sarvaor (p. 39), a wild old Gypsy with a wrinkled brow, who knows about Paco's betrayal and wants to kill him. In an aside, he tells the grandmother that Paco is preparing to marry a very rich *novia* of his own class (p. 40). She manages to calm him down and drags him into the house while the duet in which Paco and Salud swear to be "joined forever" sinks into a "dying" ecstasy (p. 43), underlined by the very beautiful introduction of a violin solo that gradually blends with the orchestral chromaticism.

Darkness suddenly envelops the scene (p. 47). A rapid crescendo leads to the interlude of the second intermezzo, flooded with a full light which the twilight will soften little by little. It intends to be a panoramic portrayal of Sacro Monte (p. 45) and uses intense atmospheric effects (p. 46 to 57). It includes the rhythm of distant seguidillas mixed with outbursts of laughter, vocalizations, and sobs, while the lights of the city slowly fade. The orchestra evokes several of the themes heard in the first act: the light *scherzando* of the beginning, fragments of the love duet. The voices of the flower vendors alternate with the "Ahs!" of the unaccompanied choir. This beautiful section reveals Falla's desire to describe a landscape, to give the primordial role to a corner of his native earth, to personalize a country and its people. After the performance at the Opéra Comique Pierre Lalo wrote in *Le Temps*:[32]

"The most felicitous passage is that at the end of the first act which describes twilight in Granada, a page of penetrating poetry that, in its sensitivity and melancholy accent, preserves something intimate and concentrated."

The first scene of act two shows a tiny street in Granada, including the house of Carmela and her brother Manuel. There are large windows through which one can see the patio and brilliant setting of a very gay party, the party celebrating the wedding of Paco and Carmela.

[32] March 6, 1914.

At the beginning of the first scene the orchestra sketches the *Jota,* the dance that has made *La Vida Breve* famous all over the world. The cries of *"Olé!"* in the house encourage the *cantaor* and guitarists. The latter are tuning their instruments to play the traditional harmonies in E minor. The *cantaor* steps forward and begins with interminable melismas. He announces that he will sing *soleares* in honor of the two young people, Paco and Carmela (p. 59). The *solea* unfolds its languorous melopoeia, ornamented with sudden grace notes, its raucous stifled finales on the ternary rhythm of the guitars, which persistently pursue their own movement without seeming to follow the song, nor to wait for it. The chorus, divided into two groups, excites the *cantaor* by clapping hands: "Sing, boy, keep it up, Pepe" (p. 61). But the girls want to dance and the violins strike up the famous *Jota.*

A theme sustained by the rhythmic stamping of feet (*zapateado*) begins in A minor, passes through different modulations, and is interrupted by a brief interlude (p. 67, measure 29) before leading to a second motif with a more powerful sonority and of a very distinct accentuation, somewhat in the manner of a *pantoum.*[33] It introduces a choreography based on the *taconeo*[34] (p. 69, *pesante ma con fuoco*).

Different shadings gradually tone down the fiery spirit of the scene up to the reprise marked *allegramente* (p. 71, measure 7). Salud appears shortly before the end of this scene. In the next she looks anxiously around the house, then begins a recitative and an aria of despair, expressing the confusion into which she has been plunged by the discovery of the betrayal. The expression is intense, once again markedly *verismo*. The theatrical effect climaxes in her bitter *"Qué ingrato!"* (p. 74, measure 10). But Salud calms down as she recalls the songs:

Flor que nace and *Un pájaro solo y triste*
(A flower born); (A bird, lonely and sad)

(p. 76, measure 10. Compare with p. 24 of the score).

[33] Piece of oriental origin in which the two melodies contrast while completing each other. The real *pantoum* is very short.
[34] Of the heel.

She wishes for death, which is better than this "horrible suffering" (p. 77, measure 10). The guitars and *soleares* are heard again (p. 77, measure 12). She rushes to the window singing: "He must hear me, the infamous one!" (p. 78, measure 6).

In scene three the grandmother and the uncle arrive. Salud falls into their arms. The two Gypsies hurl curses at the traitor: "At his life, his race, his mother." Salud adds her fury, her cries of sorrow, to the curses and approaches the window to sing the *copla* of the first act:

Malhaya la jembra pobre (p. 85).

The sounds of the party in the house taper off, as if all the guests were listening to the song. Salud continues:

"He no longer comes to Albaïcin" (p. 86, measure 7).

Darkness falls (p. 88). The setting is changed. An orchestral interlude blends the preceding motifs, Andalusian songs, dramatic effects of scene two and three with the theme of the *Jota*. The party continues, and the second scene discloses the patio of the house of Carmela and Manuel, where the wedding is to take place. Flowers are seen in the brilliant light. There is a marble fountain in the center, and in the background, an iron gate. Doors lead off both to the right and left.

It is a very animated tableau: well-to-do men and women form picturesque groups. They are dressed with great care: gaudy-colored suits, bright gowns, and lace shawls amid the profusion of flowers.

Carmela, her brother Manuel, and Paco are together on one side; on the other the *cantaor* and some young people with their guitars. Some couples are dancing, each showing excitement by voice and gesture. Paco feigns gaiety as Carmela watches him.

A second dance, based on an authentic *petenera* theme, mixes syncopations and rhythm in 3/4 and 2/4 time. It is punctuated by the cries of *"Olé!"* and the hand-clappings of the chorus. It is known that this dance was elaborated further at the request of the conductor Messager.[35] We discern in the dance a curious and very

[35] From pages 89 to 110, with the exception of pages 91 and 92.

brief polymodal passage between the orchestra in D major and the "Ah" of the chorus in D minor (p. 93, *piu animato*).

There is a short recitative between Carmela, her brother, and Paco, now obviously disturbed because he has heard Salud's voice (p. 109 to 112), and the last scene begins with a recitative trio for Salud, her uncle, and her grandmother. They claim to have come to dance and sing. But Salud cannot sustain the pretense for long (p. 115). Paco is stunned as she pours out her love and her despair in a recapitulation of the duet of the first act (*lento,* p. 118) and then falls dead at his feet. Pandemonium follows. The orchestration is marked by rapid arpeggios, vigorous chords, and tremolos in the double basses. Curtain.

Of course, this sudden ending, which raises doubts as to the real cause of the heroine's death, is not wholly satisfactory. The libretto was hastily put together. Fernández Shaw neglected the normal methods of lyric drama, the comic or dramatic secondary episodes preparatory to the main point of the plot, and Falla himself, a young novice at the time of the Madrid competition, did not have the experience or the necessary authority to express his own opinion. On the other hand, we must not forget that the rules of the competition compelled the authors to remain within the confines of a one-act play, which singularly restricted the possibilities open to the librettist.

Moreover, in the matter of the folklore theme of the *petenera* which served as a basis for the second dance of the second tableau, according to Pahissa,[36] the critic Edgar Istel contends that the leitmotif *Malhaya el Hombre, malhaya . . .* (the smithy's song, pp. 10 and 85) is an authentic *copla,* which he compares to some songs of Hungarian tziganes, close relatives of the Spanish Gypsies.[37]

On January 7, 1914, the Opéra Comique staged *La Vida Breve* with Mmes. Marguerite Carré and Brohly, Messrs. Francell, Vieuille, and Vigneau in the principal roles, under the direction of Franz Ruhlmann. The settings were created by Albert Carré.

---

[36] J. Pahissa, *op. cit.,* pp. 75 and 78.
[37] *Musical Quarterly,* vol. 12, no. 4, October, 1926, p. 497.

As often happens in such cases, difficulties and misunderstandings arose both before and after the premiere. Since no official certainty of performance had yet been obtained from Carré, the work was claimed by Astruc, who planned to include it in the opening season of the *Théâtre des Champs Elysées,* which had just been completed. This upset the director of the Opéra Comique and, even more, his wife, Marguerite Carré, who had already pictured herself as a Gypsy. Lillian Grenville, the creator of Salud, was desolate at the idea of losing such a role. All this was compounded by the uncertainty of the publisher Eschig and especially of the composer. The *Comoedia,* all too happy to print sensational news, announced that Mme. Marguerite Carré had ordered a beautiful lace shawl to wear in the role of the poor girl of the Albaïcin! Serious disagreement also arose with Paul Milliet, who demanded that the title page of the score for voice and piano carry the note: "Adaptation from the poem of Fernández Shaw by Paul Milliet," a credit line confusing enough to transform the translator into the librettist. Shaw had died in 1911, and Falla insisted that the name of his friend occupy a place on the score in keeping with his rank as author. A compromise was reached, and the translation was labeled "from a French adaptation."

Everything was happily settled, and despite these incidents, inseparable from the theater, the rehearsals continued to the satisfaction of all, not always including the composer. According to Henri Collet, he was terribly unhappy because of the cuts that were forced on him. "But where? Where?" he would protest. Several days later he was again heard to complain: "I still have to cut two minutes! They're killing me!" He confessed to a friend "his despair at an interpretation that would betray his conception."[38]

Falla and Ruhlmann became friends. They dined together often, and naturally they talked about music, discussing the details of instrumentation that are not mentioned in the manuals, for example that the spaced arrangement of chords is suitable for strings because the harmonics fill the blank spaces, but it is prejudicial to woodwinds whose harmonics are too weak.[39]

[38] Henri Collet, article in *La Revue Musicale,* Paris, January, 1947.
[39] J. Pahissa, *op. cit.,* p. 63.

All Paris attended the dress rehearsal and hailed the work as a triumph for the composer. The Paris press ratified this judgment. A last-minute difficulty cropped up thanks to the famous Spanish painter José Maria Sert, who had married the beautiful Misia, eager patron of the Ballet Russe and sister of Cipa Godebski. To celebrate the success of his compatriot, an occasional guest at the fashionable and very influential Godebski salon, Sert gave a dinner to which neither M. Carré nor his wife was invited. Mme. Carré, deeply piqued, refused to appear at the second performance, and this required a frantic change of posters. Fortunately, this fit of peevishness had no serious consequences.[40]

As for the critics, we have already read Pierre Lalo's opinion of the intermezzo. He wrote: "The score has qualities of charm and beauty; it is one of the most pleasing things of its kind that we have heard at the Opéra Comique for many years. Not everything in it is good, and I should like first to discuss what I enjoyed least, that is, the love scenes, or at least part of them. In expansive sentimental moments it would seem that Manuel de Falla has been unable to free himself completely from that Italian influence which dominated Spanish music for so long. . . . The best of the work is its picturesqueness. . . . An impression of the land of Spain, a feeling for the countryside, the sky, and the time of day, at every moment surround the characters with a subtle atmosphere; the picturesque is intimately bound up with the development of the drama. And the enchantment of this atmosphere is extraordinarily intense."

Time and passing fashions have not altered these opinions. In the work which he dedicated to his friend Falla, Roland-Manuel praises *La Vida Breve* for the noble style of its declamation, which is devoid of grandiloquence, and the spirit of the ancient *soleares*: "The author subordinates instinct to color and light."

In *La Revue Musicale* J. P. Altermann underlined "the voluptuous, ardent, passionate, yet secret evolution, at once violent and restrained, subtle in its complex simplicity and marked by an authenticity of accent, gripping throughout."[41]

---

[40] J. Pahissa, *op. cit.,* p. 64.
[41] J.-P. Altermann, "Manuel de Falla," in *La Revue Musicale,* June, 1921.

The critic André Coeuroy saw in the opera "a poignant struggle between the conventional forms of the fashionable *verismo* drama and the nascent personality of the musician."[42]

Only V. Jankélévitch contributed a discordant note, in *Europe,* by claiming that Falla in *La Vida Breve* "met his *verismo* puberty crisis with a kind of infallible instinct for ugliness." Fortunately, the rest of the article strikes a different note. Since then, *La Vida Breve* has been performed in the principal opera houses of the world.

Falla's name became well known in artistic circles and with the general public. The nobility glimpsed behind his reserve, his rare distinction, his courtesy, his discreet and winning charm, attracted sympathy and made him sought after as much by his peers as by many interpreters of his works, against whom he did not always succeed in defending himself! He took part in numerous concerts, and in 1911, for the first time, he was engaged to play in London on the initiative of G. J. Aubry. There he played his *Seven Spanish Pieces* and, with the pianist and organist Franz Liebich, Debussy's *Ibéria* in an arrangement for two pianos created by André Caplet. During his stay there Falla deepened his friendship with Aubry, who subsequently dedicated important works to him and always remained a very close ally.

Shortly after his return from London, Falla was afflicted by the periods of bad health which from then on were often to obstruct and complicate his life. One of his most recent biographers, Luis Campodomico, without going into details, mentions an attack of illness in 1912 which required hospitalization. His other friends do not mention it. Although he was received with great cordiality wherever he went, Falla's reserved nature made him uninterested in fashionable society. He was very rarely seen in such circles, and this may explain why the illness went unnoticed by the others.

The spring season of 1914 shone with an exceptional brilliance. Paris opened her doors wider than ever to the world of art and artists as though she wanted a splendid display of fireworks

---

[42] A. Coeuroy, article in *La Revue Musicale,* after a revival of *La Vida Breve* at the Opéra Comique, April, 1928.

to mark the inevitable and already approaching end of an era. Falla's situation now seemed assured, his future full of hope; he decided to settle down in a house on the outskirts of the capital and to invite his parents to come and live with him. He was just about to sign a lease when the war broke out. He stayed for another month and tried to remain in Paris even longer, but all his friends were leaving, including Florent Schmitt and Ravel, who had just managed to sign up for military service. And so he gave up his plan to settle in Paris and resigned himself to returning to Madrid where his parents were overjoyed to see him again.

His single suitcase contained the *Nocturnes* (the first title of *Nights in the Gardens of Spain*), which was then a work in progress, and the *Seven Spanish Songs,* which had been completely finished.

In Madrid Falla found himself in a situation radically different from that of seven years before. After the laurels he had won in Paris, he now found the doors of the Teatro de la Zarzuela opened to him. Moreover, the musical situation had also undergone a profound change. The energetic director of the theater, Arturo Serrano, who was preparing a season of Spanish lyrical art with operas by Turina, Guridi, and Conrado del Campo, immediately put *La Vida Breve* in rehearsal under the direction of Pablo Luna. The latter was the composer of successful *zarzuelas* staged by Paco Meana, an artist of great talent but small reputation. The two principal roles were assigned to the tenor Rafael Lopez and to the soprano Luisa Vela, a famous singer who performed admirably as Salud.

The first Madrid performance, on November 14, 1914, enjoyed a success far beyond all expectations. Falla had to appear on stage several times to accept the stormy applause of an enthusiastic public, some of whom later escorted him home in a triumphant torchlight procession. The critics were as lavish in their praise as those in Paris had been and celebrated the event in glowing, almost flowery terms. First of all, the critic of *Epoca* deplored the fact that Falla had had to score a triumph abroad before his native country became aware that it had fathered a composer of great merit. The *Heraldo de Madrid* gratefully hailed Falla as another valiant champion of the musical renaissance in Spain. "In Granada, in the center of Albaïcin," wrote Eduardo Muñoz in *El Imparcial,* "in the intense and golden evening glow a poet has come to relate the sad story of the tiny bird who dies of love, and a musician of infinite poetic gifts has caught the essence of azure spaces, of languorous nights and blood-stained twilights, and has converted them for our souls into notes which are indolent, resplendent, and eloquent tears!" . . . Martinez Sierra, in *El Imparcial,* found the music "savage, cruel, and sweet, harsh and vibrant, heart-rending, desolate, at once Moorish and mystical!" The critic of the *ABC,* less poetically, merely praised the fluid and diaphanous orchestration and observed that the composer had succeeded in asserting his indisputable personality by means of the modern technique of the French school of D'Indy, Dukas, and Debussy.

The opera enjoyed twenty-six equally successful performances. At the performance of January 23, 1915, Luisa Vela, accompanied by the composer, sang the *Seven Spanish Popular Songs,* which she had publicly performed for the first time nine days before at the Ateneo in homage to Manuel de Falla and Joaquin Torina.

THE SEVEN SPANISH POPULAR SONGS

As we know, Falla finished working on them before he left Paris. He wrote them after harmonizing a Greek folksong according to his own ideas and his system of harmony. The result was so satisfying that he decided to apply the same techniques to the *canciones* of his own country.[1] This system stemmed from his close study of the book by Louis Lucas, *L'Acoustique Nouvelle* (mentioned in the third chapter). It recognized that the sounds produced by natural resonance, whether these are harmonics of a fundamental note or whether they derive from one of these harmonics considered in its turn as a fundamental, are suitable for a polyphonic support. Thus we can glimpse the logical superpositions which can be obtained in this way and which would naturally enter into the plan of the composition. Let us recall that Roland-Manuel emphasized the care that Falla lavished on the "arrangement of the internal rhythm . . . on the judicious placement of related notes." The transformation of tonal functions plays, in fact, an important role in Falla's harmonic system, a third degree, for example, becoming the leading tone, or a dominant forcing a new reaction in the tonal scale. Moreover, when establishing his arrangements, Falla closely observed not only the modal nature of each song, as advocated by his teacher Pedrell,[2]

---

[1] J. Pahissa, *op. cit.,* p. 82.

[2] "The folk song must be established on the basis of the ancient modes sung *at random,* as it is dictated by natural music. I cannot admit artificial music issued from conventional and arbitrary bases; suppression of the ancient modes, subjection of any tonality to the absolute of major and minor. I hope the time comes when we will be able to sing on all the strings of the lyre, as man has sung natural music since the beginning of time." (Pedrell, preface to Vol. III of the *Cancionero Popular Español.*)

but also their place of origin without in any way neglecting the grace, the sensitivity, the delicate style of his pianistic inspiration.

Nearly all folk poems of the *Seven Songs* belong to the style called *arte menor* or *quebrado* (broken), comprising two with eight syllables, the usual meter of *cantaras, canas, redondillas, letrillas, polos*.[3] The first song—*El Paño Moruno* (The Moorish Cloth) comes from the almost Andalusian province of Murcia.

Garcia Matos, who made a detailed study of folklore sources in Falla's work, found mention of this famous song in the collections of José Inzenga (*Ecos de España, Cantos y Bailes Populares de España*), of Isidore Hernández (*Flores de España*), and of José Verdu (*Coleccíon de Cantos Populares de Murcia*), for all of which he gives complete references in *Música*.[4]

The pianistic prelude of *El Paño Moruno* presents the usual motif, which comes from and returns to the dominant; it is sustained by a rhythm accentuating the second beat and repeated a second time on the minor third (measure 9). After a ninth chord richly ornamented with *acciaccaturas*,[5] a device that the composer was to develop subsequently, arpeggiated in the manner of the *rasgueado* (strummed chords) of an invisible guitarist (measure 16 to 23), the song enters on the dominant B minor.

I. EL PAÑO MORUNO

It is composed of a *copla* in stanzas of two periods each, the second widening the rhythm and compass of the first—a seventh instead of a sixth. The second beat is always strongly accentuated.

---

[3] Songs, lullabies, quatrains in octosyllabic verse, satirical compositions, Andalusian songs.

[4] *Música*, Madrid, *op. cit.*

[5] "A discordant note sounded with a principal note or chord and immediately released." (*Webster's Third New International Dictionary*)

At the end of the first period we note the use, so common, of the cadence on the dominant, B, A, G, F sharp, which Trend calls a Phrygian cadence characteristic of the *jondo,* which is very much in place in this song of Moorish origin (measures 28 to 30). The theme is transposed to D at the beginning of the second strophe (measure 46), separated from the first by the reprise of the accompaniment, followed by the *copla* (measure 53) and finale *con sordina* with a very long *"Ay"* on the dominant ornamented with an *acciaccatura* (measure 68).

The ornamented finales of the *copla* are found again in Salud's first aria (p. 22, measure 7). Compare this with a *granadina* cited by Pedrell in his *Cancionero.*[6]

The *Seguidilla Murciana,* as its name indicates, is likewise a dance form of the province of Murcia. Garcia Matos saw its transcription, almost free of any retouching, contained in the collections cited by Inzenga, Hernández, and F. Rodriquez Marin: *Cantos Populares Españoles,* and Julien Tiersot cites it in the *Encyclopédie de la Musique.*[7]

A copla of two strophes on a rapid tempo *allo spiritoso,* a very voluble song of muleteers, made of a repeated note descending twice to the minor third. The range is of a fifth, and of a sixth for the repetition of the first verse. The accompaniment imitates the crackling of a guitar played in the *punteado,* or contrapuntal style, with pianissimo passages that have the heaviness of a *tambora.* The second strophe identically repeats the first. Note the alteration of the third degree at the penultimate bar.

The *Asturiana* takes us to the north of Spain. Tiersot likewise notes its theme in the *Encyclopédie.*[8] According to Garcia Matos, the melody and text were transcribed faithfully in the collections of José Hurtado (*Ciento Cantos Populares Asturianos*) and B. Fernández (*Cuarenta Canciones Asturianos*).

It is a peaceful lamentation. The vocal arrangement pre-

[6] F. Pedrell, *op. cit.,* Vol. II, p. 224, no. 303. This *granadina* has been harmonized by Joaquin Nin.

[7] *Encyclopédie de la Musique et Dictionnaire du Conservatoire,* IIᵉ Partie, art. *"Chanson Populaire,"* p. 2908.

[8] *Encyclopédie, op. cit.,* p. 2907.

sents an antecedent (the first five ascending notes), a consequent (the four descending notes), and a finale (the reversion to the tonic). There is a similar repetition for the second verse.

The accompaniment offers a curious example of displacement of tonal functions, the fourth degree being employed as pedal point, creating a highly enjoyable modal feeling (Hyperdorian mode, key of F).

The *Jota* belongs to the province of Aragon. The folk theme is strongly modified here, although Garcia Matos has found in the *Gran Colección de Jotas* of J. M. Alvira some that were very similar. A similar *jota* is cited by Raoul Laparra in his article *"Folk Music and Dance in Spain."*[9]

Tiersot remarks that the instrument and the voice alternate in the *Jota.* And so a long pianistic motif of thirty-two bars, based on five notes (E, D sharp, E, C sharp, B), bringing in the dominant of E major, repeated three times, and accompanied by a rhythm spread out two against two and breaking off on a chord in widely spread fourths, introduces an atmosphere of bravura up to the first strophe—*poco meno vivo*—which is of a voluptuous languor. The declamation closes on a triplet ornamented in the manner of the *cantaores* and extends to the following bar. The end, diminishing gradually, presents a canon on the five notes of the beginning. There is a distant recall of the last phrase: *"Aunque no quiera. . . ."*

The *Nana* is a cradle song, an Andalusian lullaby. Pedrell mentions in the first volume of his *Cancionero* a *nana* of Malaga which is almost similar.[10] Garcia Matos views it as a very retouched transcription of folk melodies noted in Inzenga and J. Calvo: *Alegrías y Tristezas de Murcia. . . .* Pahissa recalls that Falla heard it as a child from "his mother's lips before he was old enough to think."[11] Different from all other "cradle songs" of Spain, the sources of the Andalusian *nana,* according to the composer,[12] appear to lie in India (as is true of Andalusian vocal music in general), whereas the instrumental music derives its origin from the more or less impro-

[9] *Encyclopédie, op. cit.,* p. 2353.
[10] Pedrell, *op. cit.,* Vol. I, p. 3.
[11] J. Pahissa, *op. cit.,* p. 78.
[12] *Ibid.*

vised music of the Persian or Moorish *kithara, laud, quitar,* and *gaita.*

It is a brief song in A minor. The voice rises, tonal, from the dominant to the tonic, after which it descends, modal, on the usual Phrygian finale of the dominant. There is an ornamented finale and then a similar repetition. The accompaniment offers a syncopated rhythm between the two hands, representing the rocking of a cradle. It likewise passes from the tonal to the modal by imposing the dominant. In his article in the *Encyclopédie* Laparra cites a very ornamented *cantar de labrador* (song of a worker) of Murcia whose melodic root is strikingly similar to this *nana.*[13]

According to Garcia Matos, the sixth song, *Canción,* is the faithful transcription of a popular theme (cf. Inzenga) "with an insignificant retouching in the last cadence." The character, in G major, is tonal. A single musical phrase in two periods, on a daring rhythm in 6/8 time, is contained within the compass of a descending fourth of the dominant in the second degree. The second period (measure 9) goes from the fourth degree to the tonic. Melodic form is that of antecedent, consequent, and finale. The accompaniment is a double pedal point (dominant-tonic) *ostinato* rhythm. A canon intervenes at the end between voice and piano, followed by a curious descent from a pedal note of the sixth degree (measure 24) to the third, the dominant, and embellished tonic.

The *Polo* belongs to the flamenco or Gypsy world. Garcia Matos came upon it in E. Ocón's *Cantos Españoles: Colección de Aires Nacionales y Populares.* He admits it is "retouched and enlarged."

[13] R. Laparra, *op. cit.,* pp. 2353 ff.

In the Hypodorian mode of A, it begins with a brilliant and rapid *punteado* with accents evoking the *palmadas* (hand-clappings) of the spectators, which continue to the end. The *cantaor* begins on an *"Ay,"* the plaintive cry of Andalusian singers, in which Ramon Gomez de la Serna felt he heard the sighs of a "poor little heretic tormented by the Inquisition!"[14]

"The guitar strikes its *falseta* with a sweet and melancholic sound in E minor, the left hand passing alternately from one position to the other, while the right hand strums the strings in the *rasgueado* style, at first softly, then louder and with passion."[15] The pianistic accompaniment faithfully follows this plan. Then the *cantaor* begins his introduction or *pasero* (p. 29, measure 16), on three of the characteristic notes of the guitar style, A, B, D, enriching the last with embellishments. There are numerous repetitions in staccato, a long vocalization, and a termination on the dominant which ends by being brilliantly asserted as the tonic of E major, offering a new example of those felicitous displacements of tonal functions that have already been pointed out.

The *Seven Spanish Popular Songs,* dedicated to Mme. Ida Godebska, were published in 1922 by Eschig in Paris, with a French adaptation by Paul Milliet. The first Paris performance, delayed by the war, was given in May, 1920, in the auditorium of the Conservatory, sponsored by the Société Nationale de Musique.

These songs, which are simultaneously music and dance, have a strange, evocative power. Listening to them, we find ourselves dreaming about the stamping feet, the long voluptuous spasmodic movements, the heel-clickings of the woman dancer who twists her arms as she strikes the castanets. We hear the raucous notes, cleverly broken and lowered, the vocal tremolos, the harsh sobs of the *cantaor* who sings *El Romance de la Pena Negra.*[16]

But Jankélévitch claims that "Ravel haunts *El Paño Moruno.*" Perhaps he furnished the necessary link of stylization that contributed to their immense and universal success? Likewise Goléa

---

[14] Cited by Valentin Parnac, "Notes sur les Danses Espagnoles," *La Revue Musicale* (May, 1931), p. 456.

[15] R. Laparra, *op. cit.,* pp. 2353 ff.

[16] Federico Garcia Lorca, *Romancero Gitan.* Paris, 1954–55.

remarks that Falla "discovered Spanish folklore much more through the subtle detour of the music of Debussy and Ravel than through the study of Pedrell's researches." Thus he belongs to those who "laid out the first guideposts of that musical humanism which was not to come to full flowering until after 1930."[17]

We shall leave the responsibility for their assertions to these two authors. Yet the influence of the French school on Manuel de Falla's development is undeniable. It is not surprising that his success even reached Japan, where in 1934 a young singer, Mlle. Nakamura, scored a triumph with the *Jota*—"the real thing," as Rafael Moragos noted in the Madrid daily *Luz*, not the *"jota* of the zarzuelas!"

Subsequently, Ernesto Halffter, a pupil and great friend of Falla, orchestrated the accompaniment of the *Seven Songs*. Since then, there have been numerous adaptations for different instruments.

On February 8, 1915, the Sociedad Nacional de Música de Madrid inaugurated its concerts with a program of chamber music. It consisted of works by Turina, Granados, and, with the *Seven Songs*, the first presentation of a song by Falla, *Prayer of Mothers Who Hold Their Children in Their Arms*. The composer, at the piano, himself accompanied the singer Josefina Revillo. The text by Gregorio Martinez Sierra begins as follows:

> Sweet Jesus, who art asleep;
> By the holy breast that suckled thee,
> I pray thee that my boy may never be a soldier!

The great musician was expressing the horror, sadness, and compassion which had swept over him when the violence of war was unleashed, feelings which were at the base of his unswerving and deep humanitarianism. Curiously, Debussy, animated by the same feelings only a few months later (December), was to write his *Christmas for Children Who No Longer Have a Home*. According to Sagardia, these two songs, belonging to the same time and to the same poetic and musical vein, are very close to each other. Strongly influenced by the grace of French music, Falla, like Debussy, utilizes

---

[17] A. Goléa, *Esthetique de la Musique Contemporaine*. Paris, 1954.

in this song the supple melodic recitative of which he had given examples in *La Vida Breve*. The *Prayer* remained unpublished. The poet Gregorio Martinez Sierra, an already famous dramatist and journalist—his praise of *La Vida Breve* in *El Imparcial* should be recalled—recognized in Falla a composer capable of endowing his works with the deepest essence of Andalusia; he proposed to Falla that the latter write the music for a *gitaneria* that he, Martinez Sierra, had just begun.

EL AMOR BRUJO

The first idea for the opera goes back to Pastora Imperio, one of the great *bailarinas* of the time, who belonged to a Gypsy family dedicated to Andalusian dance and song. She told Martinez Sierra that she would like to interpret "a song and a dance" written by himself and by Falla. The idea pleased Falla, especially when he made the acquaintance of Pastora and her mother, Rosario la Mejorana, who had also been a great and famous dancer. She sang many *soleares, siguiriyas, polos,* and *martinetes* for Falla. These he carefully noted down, while Martinez Sierra listened attentively to the old Gypsy woman's rich store of legends and fables. He drew from these stories the plot that transformed the song and dance that had been originally requested into a sung ballet. Falla enthusiastically set to work in November, 1914, and although he generally composed very slowly, he finished the music in April, 1915.

With *El Amor Brujo* the composer described a new aspect of his native Andalusia, the life of the Gypsies in the caves of the Sacro Monte of Granada. For Falla, Salud of *La Vida Breve* was not a Gypsy but a simple *muchacha* of the Albaïcin quarter. "Carmen is the Gypsy, not Salud," he said. It must be recognized that in Andalusia the affinities of native soil and origins are mingled in a dim, distant past; the Gypsy and the pure Andalusian are often mistaken for each other. Can we be sure that Albaïcin is the Gypsy quarter, or is it that the Gypsies chose to settle in the congenial quarter of Albaïcin? Be that as it may, the Gypsies, settled down and assimilated for centuries, have preserved the characteristic features of the race. "The Gypsies," wrote Théophile Gautier in that charming account of his travels, *Tras los Montes,* "are generally black-

75

smiths, mule-shearers, tinkers, and, above all, horse-dealers. Their real trade, at bottom, is thievery. The Gypsy women sell amulets, tell fortunes, and practice the suspect industries habitual to the women of their race." This is the country of the "people of the caves," sings Federico Garcia Lorca in his admirable *"Poema del cante jondo."*[18]

> Oh, lost people
> In the Andalusia of tears!

Falla's main emphasis in *El Amor Brujo* lies in human character and in our yearning for mystery and tragedy. It would be a great mistake to see in it, as did the Madrid critics, a mere search for a facile picturesqueness. The magic, a reflection of racial antiquity, the ritual incantation, the "ghost" who possesses a being and breathes into it the obsession of desperation, death, and all that which forms the very base of the *cante jondo* are expressed as much by the somber hue of the harmonies and of the orchestra as by the almost motionless throbs of the rhythm. However, it must be acknowledged that the first version of the libretto is closer to this ideal. At that time it included two scenes.

The first scene took place in the house of Gypsies. The unhappy Candelas is waiting for her *novio,* who is neglecting her. She consults the cards for a sign of her future.

The sound of the nearby sea—which supplies a justification for the *Fisherman's Song*—and the answer of the cards are an evil augury. In despair, she throws incense on the fire and dances the famous *Fire Dance.*

An interlude leads to the second scene, which is set in the cave of a witch. Candelas appears. Terrified by the cries of frightful night birds, by the flicker of the will-o'-the-wisp which follows her, she dances the *Dance of the Tarantula* so as to exorcise the evil spirits, who vanish in a flash of light.

Then Candelas' incantations bring about the return of her lover. Her face veiled, she bewitches him with her dance until, utterly fascinated and believing her to be the witch of the cave, he

---

[18] Federico Garcia Lorca, *op. cit.,* pp. 71–75.

falls into her arms, conquered. Dawn breaks and the ringing of the morning bells provides joyous accompaniment to the reconciliation of the two lovers. In this version the ghost exists only in Candelas' hallucination, and there is no mention of the rather artificial and puerile character called Lucia.

The orchestra of this first and very abridged version included piano, flute, oboe, trumpet, French horn, viola, violincello, and double-bass.

Pastora's whole family took part in the rehearsals: Vito Rojas, her brother, who played Carmelo; a sister-in-law, the beautiful, statuesque Gypsy, Agustina; and her daughter, who was to become famous under the name of Maria del Albaïcin. Moreno Ballesteros, the organist, conducted. The first performance took place on April 15, 1915, at the Teatro Lara in Madrid. Naturally, the theater was packed, and the intellectual community and the theatrical critics of the press were on hand for the occasion. But the outcome was quite different from that which had followed the premiere of *La Vida Breve.* Indeed, it was not at all a success, either with the public or the critics, whose reactions were far from gentle. For one, the assertive orchestra, with inadequate timbres, overwhelmed the purity of the melodies and destroyed the Andalusian color, which comes exclusively from the guitars, castanets, hand-clapping, and tambourines. Another criticized the score as uninspired and facile and dismissed the work as Spanish exoticism. Another critic counseled Falla to give up these "minor essays" and to consecrate himself to "a great work." Only the Gypsy world marveled at the work and applauded it enthusiastically. It had discovered itself in *El Amor Brujo,* and this was a source of comfort to Falla.

Fortunately, everybody did not share the same opinion, as attested to by the singer Paco Meana, who attended the premiere with Amadea Vives and prophesied that "this music will soon become world famous." His opinion was ratified by the immense and universal success that was to follow the premiere of *El Amor Brujo* in Paris, at the Théâtre Bériza[19] where the still largely unknown Argentina[20] and the already famous Escudero danced.

[19] June, 1925, in the auditorium of the Trianon-Lyrique.
[20] Her real name was Antonia Mercé.

But Falla had revised his ballet before that performance. He deleted some songs and recitatives and expanded his orchestra, making it more suitable for a concert suite. He added a second flute, two clarinets, a bassoon, a second French horn, and a second trumpet, kettledrums, bells, and the normal string complement. Madrid heard *El Amor Brujo* again in this new form on March 28, 1916, in a concert organized by the Sociedad Nacional de Música with the participation of the Orquesta Filharmónica. Both organizations were newcomers on the musical scene. Falla had played a role in their establishment alongside Adolfo Salazar and Miguel Salvador, who was appointed president. Two performances were given under the baton of Bartolomé Pérez-Casas, with Turina at the piano. One year later the great orchestra director E. F. Arbós directed it at the same time as the first presentation of *Nights in the Gardens of Spain*. Martinez Sierra, it should be said, set down the definitive version of the scenario as it has been presented ever since.

THE MUSIC

The music, charged with the task of evoking the Gypsy setting, naturally had to borrow the design of its songs and *jondo* or flamenco dances. On the other hand, having placed the greater part of the dance on a binary rhythm, nonexistent in flamenco, which is nearly always ternary, Falla generally had to interpret folk themes and meters, many of which are recognizable. Thus, from the beginning, two themes are heard as a leitmotif, both in 3/4 time, and both belong to the most significant forms of flamenco. The first, issuing from a vibrant orchestral call installed on the dominant of A and entrusted to the flute, oboe, and piano, with its savage accents cut by lengthy pauses, presents the melodic and rhythmic oscillations and poignant character of the *polo*. It symbolizes the fury of the ghost who will not release his victim.

The first-scene curtain rises on the setting of a *cueva* of the Sacro Monte in Granada, hollowed out in the cactus-studded limestone. It is night. A shadowy, mysterious cave, dimly lit by smoldering embers and the lamp swaying in front of the Madonna. The Gypsies are gathered together. In the orchestra the somber strings rumble on an A flat (p. 7, No. 1).[21] The muted call of a French horn resounds in the distance (No. 1, measure 12). Gradually and menacingly the rumbling of the strings swells, like the wind in the sierra. The second theme, a twangy improvisation, rises from the oboe (p. 9, No. 3). It presages the *solea,* the song of sorrow and loneliness.[22]

Falla utilizes these two leitmotifs by varying their form in the course of the score, principally in the pantomimes tying together the threads of the plot. The *Canción del Amor Dolido* (Song of Sorrowful Love, p. 10) immediately follows, in which we hear the contralto voice of the Gypsy girl.

The melodic line of the *solea* is sketched further here and twines around the two strophes of a *copla* describing the jealous passion of the ghost, more terrible than fire:

I feel in my soul an indefinable dull fire;
I fear your flame less than your jealousy.

The melodic range is enclosed within a perfect fourth (F, B flat) that turns upon itself and whose melismas, ornaments of the *tercios,* further accent the pathos.[23] There is a dissonant harmony based on the double pedal point of the dominant. The strings, very divided, execute the *rasgueado* of the guitarists. The *taconeo* rhythm is marked one against one by the woodwinds and the piano, which is employed as percussion. There is the same harmonic arrangement, reinforced further, for the second strophe:

Cuando el rio suenaque, querrá decir?

[21] The numbering corresponds to the pages and to the referential numbers of the minature orchestra score as published by Chester, London, 1921.

[22] Cf. Laparra, *op. cit.,* p. 2353.

[23] The *tercios* are the different sequences of the *cante,* each of which generally contains an introduction, a development, and a conclusion called *macho* or *remate.*

Three measures on an embellished dominant serve as a liaison with the apparition of the ghost, which occurs with strange glissandos of the piano and the strings (p. 20, No. 4). The beginning of the *Dance of Terror* is outlined by a muted trumpet (no. 6). This striking theme is based on a very ancient Gypsy dance, the *baile de la tarantula,* which has the same Italian origin as the tarantella. It is composed of a breathless repetition of semiquavers which afterward move within the frame of a fifth descending to the tonic, and serve to describe the terror of a lost soul that does not know where to find refuge, like a moth fluttering around a flame.

The syncopated rhythm of an even more tightened second theme—an ascending and descending third—accentuates the feeling of terror produced by the ghost pursuing his victim. The orchestration is particularly refined. The first theme is divided (No. 6, measure 6) between the trumpet, which is given repeated notes (arsis), and the oboe and the clarinet (thesis). Gradually, the composer amplifies his orchestra and varies it, thus avoiding the monotony of repetitions of persistent rhythms. There are oppositions of fortissimo and pianissimo shadings. A piano glissando in the Hypodorian mode (No. 21) rather curiously leads to a finale in D, ornamented with double appoggiaturas.

This is followed by the episode of the *Magic Circle* (p. 38) and the calm *Fisherman's Song,* certainly better placed in the initial version—where it was sung by Pastora—than in the present version. But the music has a calming gentleness, a tranquility that is in welcome contrast to the violent action that preceded and will follow. Its modal character and its contrapuntal notation evoke pre-Renaissance music. Pahissa suggests a closeness between this motif and certain extracts of the *Analecta Montserràtensia,* in which Father Sunyol of Montserrat has collected a great number of songs sung by pilgrims who climb the holy mountain.[24] The tale is conveyed by two muted trumpets and picked up by the two flutes (*dolce con un eco,* p. 39, No. 23) against the exquisite effects of distant chimes, obtained through simple broken octaves at the piano supported by the viola. According to Falla, the unexpected conclusion on an E flat of the

[24] J. Pahissa, *op. cit.,* p. 98.

initial period in the mode of D is a new example of his system of utilizing harmonics (p. 38, measure 4).

The clock strikes twelve, but no bells are heard (p. 40). The strings, subdivided, the blend of harmonics, including those of the double bass, of pizzicatti, of arpeggios of the first violin, the tremolos of the piano, the sustained notes of the French horns, the kettledrums—all produce a striking effect of vibrations. It fades away to make way for muted trills, lengthily imposing the dominant of A. This is the signal for the *Danza Ritual del Fuego para Ahuyentar los Malos Espírituse* (p. 41).

This world-famous dance, whose transcriptions for different instruments terminate innumerable concerts and recitals, reproduces the two strophes of a *copla* followed by a coda. It is made up of three motifs. All three, the first two especially, give it the intensity of an obsession, emphasizing its incantational nature. The first (p. 42, No. 24) belongs to the ancient and forgotten form of the *alboreas* or of the *garrotins,* whose ritual genre was celebrated in secret by the Gypsies of the Sacro Monte. Intoned by the woodwinds, its distinct Arab incantational character is sustained by a changeless rhythm based on equivocal modals (C major, C minor) with trills, hammerings, and pianistic touches in which we believe we hear the onlookers accompanying the dance with their tambourines, their *"Olés,"* castanets, and hand-clappings. This is another proof of Falla's orchestral virtuosity, which allows him to suggest sonorous effects without using special instruments. No. 25 of the orchestra score offers a particularly significant example, thanks to a simple but very skillful combination of the piano, clarinet, and oboe. The second and third motifs are, above all, rhythmic, and the second offers the dancer an opportunity to show her knowledge of the *zapateado.* Still in 2/4 time, pianissimo, there follow quavers in syncopation with quarter notes, tirelessly repeating a chord formed by the harmonics over a double pedal point of D (p. 46).

Candelas accompanies the beat with the almost imperceptible stamping of her heels. The second theme, consisting of four notes revolving around the dominant of C (p. 46, measure 9), erupts suddenly with the two French horns doubling the first violins. The *taconeo* is intensified, and there is a repetition of the second theme (*pianissimo subito*) by two flutes in the bass as a distant echo of the French horns (p. 47, measure 5). Several well-chosen modulations precede the beginning of the third theme with the violins (No. 27). Like the two preceding themes—and, for that matter, like most of them—it is made up of a very small number of notes: A, G sharp, F sharp.

Despite the long repetitions required by the ritual nature of this music, monotony is avoided by strongly accented shadings and certain devices of intensification and orchestration.

At this moment the Gypsy girl is in the grip of a frenzy. Her loins arch, she bends from side to side, her waist twists with snakelike suppleness, and she leaps like a young jaguar showing its muscles of steel.

Suddenly she becomes calm as the orchestra makes a very expressive descent, and she resumes her initial dance (No. 30). She continues it exactly as before, and the orchestra, too, except for some light modifications, is the same. At the end (No. 34), really possessed by the "ghost," the dancer enlivens the rhythm of the orchestra by stamping her heels. This she does until she is totally exhausted. After a final undulation of her arms and hips, she falls to the ground while the orchestra throws off a rapid arpeggio in the tonic A.

The two leitmotifs heard at the beginning reappear in the pantomime that follows (p. 68). The oboe improvisation, picked up by the flute in the treble, is ornamented like the vocalizations of the muezzin. It announces the Song of the *Will-o'-the-Wisp,* a brief *copla* in two strophes, cut by the *estribillo* (refrain):

Woe to those black eyes that wanted to see his flame at play.
Love is a will-o'-the-wisp. You flee from it, it pursues you.

Laparra, in the *Encyclopédie,* has noted a cradle song with a similar melodic line.[25] Here the rhythm is that of a rapid *buleria*[26] with its subtle syncopations, its pace at once bedeviled and anguished, so characteristic of the flamenco. The very light orchestra (strings, piano, French horn, clarinet, flute), thanks to the scoring, this time

[25] R. Laparra, *op. cit.,* p. 2353.
[26] Some Spanish critics see in it a *vito* instead. Also see *Encyclopédie,* II, Tiersot, p. 2910.

is able to borrow the *punteado* of the guitar. Again (p. 75) the first motif reappears in a grand instrumental *tutti*. Its nostalgic anxiety is slowly calmed (No. 43), preparing for Carmelo's return and his dance (p. 78, *andantino tranquillo*). It is a tender dance, using the languorous rhythm of the *guarija* in 7/8, borrowing from the second leitmotif, now stripped of its wildness, the form of an amorous *tanguillo,* an echo of Cádiz, which had imported it from the isles.

Falla had originally destined this passage for the *Nights in the Gardens of Spain* as homage to his native city.[27] He preferred to insert it into *El Amor Brujo,* thus creating a climate of voluptuous tenderness appropriate to the victory of love over the curse.

Suggested at first by the cello solo (p. 79, measure 9), the song uses the extreme treble of the violin (No. 45). The muted trumpet (No. 45, measure 10) evokes from far away a final menace of the ghost whose defeat will be completed with the *Dance of the Game of Love.* It is a *malagueña* (p. 85), and it is also constructed around the first four notes of the second leitmotif, which now the somber fury of the desire to vanquish animates with a panting rhythm, 2/8 and 3/8 within a double measure in 3/8 time (p. 85, measure 4).

At No. 48 a voice *in modo popolare* sings, "You were that evil Gypsy" to the trills of the flute and the sounds of the oboe, used like a Moorish *gaita,* and the strings. The almost immobile harmony is merely the vertical reunion of th*e real* notes of the melody, i.e., those that characterize its particular mode. This close kinship between melody and harmony explains the continuity of the chord, which at no time ceases to belong to the vocal line. This device, frequently employed by Falla, is merely the application of the precepts which he had absorbed from the book by Louis Lucas.

Announced by skillful modulations, the morning bells finally ring in the hour of light and happiness for the lovers (*Finale,* p. 101). The effect is at once unexpected and delightful. In A major—A minor (No. 69) contrasting rhythms, semiquavers on the clarinets and the piano, sustained notes on the woodwinds, light pizzicatti, finally the crystalline timbre of the bell, support the delicate

[27] Cf. Pahissa, *op. cit.,* p. 89.

arabesques, the elegiac meanderings of a *granadina,* and prepare for the introduction of the second *leitmotif,* the symbol of love, which the strings express ardently and fortissimo (No. 66).

It seems useless to recall here the triumphant career of this nineteen-minute ballet, which has appeared in the opera houses of the whole world. It was and still is in the repertories of both ballet companies and symphony orchestras. There have been a great number of recordings made, as well as many different instrumental transcriptions. This success is due to the flavor of its Gypsy-Moorish style, "which is rich in wit, color, oriental drama, dissonances, sonority, and pulsating accents."[28] To this we can add its internal rhythm, the richness of its orchestra, and, especially, its mysterious and always profoundly human feeling.

It would take volumes to reprint the different articles and commentaries inspired by *El Amor Brujo.* Therefore, we shall limit ourselves to citing one that particularly drew Falla's attention, as much because of its author, Charles Koechlin, writing in the *Gazette des Beaux-Arts,* as because of its succinct accuracy: "Purity of line in the writing, simplicity amidst richness and unexaggerated originality simply leap forth from this work."

The score of *El Amor Brujo* was published by Chester of London in 1921. The first symphonic performance in Paris was given by the Concerts Colonne on January 28, 1923. The first performance on stage (with La Argentina and Escudero) took place at the Trianon-Lyrique in Paris on May 22, 1927, as part of the series of theatrical spectacles presented by Marguerite Bériza. It was received enthusiastically. The program of that memorable evening also included Goossens' *Le Carrosse du Saint-Sacrament* (based on Mérimée) and Stravinsky's *l'Histoire du Soldat.*

[28] G. Hilaire, *op. cit.*

CHAPTER VI / *Nights in the Gardens of Spain*

After the failure of his ballet in Madrid, Manuel de Falla spent several weeks in Barcelona. He composed some incidental music for the performances of *Othello,* then being staged at the Teatro Novedades. The work includes some trumpet calls, which unfortunately have not yet been published.[1] It was about this time that Pastora Imperio presented *El Amor Brujo* in Barcelona, and with considerable success. Falla was also finishing his concerto, *Nights in the Gardens of Spain,* which he had begun in Paris.

Falla stayed in the coastal village of Sitges, in an old hotel near the shining beach. White fishing boats and a sunlit patio whose walls, covered with mirrors, reflected the sunlight. This, incidentally, inspired *El Pati Bleu* (The Blue Patio) by the Catalan painter Santiago Rusiñol. Falla also worked in Rusiñol's luxurious villa El Cau Ferrat[2] on an old piano but in an ideal setting—in solitude, among paintings by Greco, precious Talavera tiles, medieval ironwork, and, from the wrought iron balcony, a view of the bluest sea imaginable. After finishing his work, he returned to Madrid where Maestro Arbós, who had commissioned *Nights in the Gardens of Spain,* presented its first performance at the Teatro Real, on April 9, 1916, with his Orquesta Sinfónica and featuring a young pianist from Cádiz, José Cubiles. (*El Amor Brujo* was also on the program.)

Three movements make up these symphonic impressions for piano and orchestra: *In the Generalife, A Distant Dance,* and *In the Gardens of the Sierra de Córdoba.* Falla experts do not agree about the source of inspiration. A. Sagardia[3] claims, according to José Pla in *Rusiñol y su Tiempo,* that the musician was inspired by an exhibit in which the celebrated painter had depicted the gardens of Spain in about thirty canvasses. Since Falla was then working in Sitges, in Rusiñol's house, it is possible that these works might

---

[1] All the manuscripts left behind by Falla are in the possession of his niece, Señora M. I. Garcia de Paredes.

[2] It was bequeathed to the city by the great painter and man of letters (1861–1932) and has been transformed into a museum.

[3] A. Sagardia, *op. cit.,* p. 33.

have been somewhat of an inspiration. But work on *Nights* had been started in Paris in 1909. Falla had left Spain two years before that, and even if he had already known Rusiñol's paintings, the fact remains that his admiration for the expressionist symbolism of the French school of that time was at least equally important in the gestation of the work. One should probably give greater credence to Henri Collet, composer and close friend of Falla, who assures us that Falla found the point of departure for his *Nights in the Gardens of Spain* in a poem by Francis Jammes which Collet had brought to his attention. "The lines are great and peaceful. But," says Collet, "such was his genius for transformation that I would have never perceived [the connection], had he not told me. . . ."[4]

French influence, to which Falla succumbed body and soul when he lived in Paris, clearly shines through the three sections of the *Nights,* and Jankélévitch rightly asserts that "they would not have this brightness, this unmatched liquidity, this impressionist freshness of sight, sound, and smell, if Ravel's *Rapsodie Espagnole* and Debussy's *Ibéria* had not existed." Further: "It is the same mystery—the mystery of voluptuousness and a scented darkness—which suffuses the *Gardens of the Generalife,* Debussy's *Parfums de la Nuit,* and Ravel's *Prélude à la Nuit,* just as it is the one and the same vernal intoxication which leaps up from the orchestra of Ravel's *Feria* and the orchestra of *Nights.*"[5]

"After you pass the Gothic arches of the portal and the tower of Cautiva, before you stands the Generalife, a dream garden without parallel. . . . From the gazebo we see the high, dull-red, square towers of the Alhambra and the Sierra Nevada, whose white spine grotesquely knifes the sky."[6] The sounds of a night festival come from the Albaïcin quarter.

Technical Analysis[7]

A *canto* with a very narrow range—a minor third—like the most elementary but most deeply felt songs originating in the

[4] As cited in *La Revue Musicale,* January, 1947.
[5] V. Jankélévitch, *op. cit.,* in *Europe.*
[6] Théophile Gautier, *op. cit.*
[7] As previously, the numbers correspond to the pages and numbers of the miniature orchestral score, Max Eschig, Paris, 1922–23.

folk idiom, is the only basis for the supple variations that are later developed. On the rhythm of a *jaleo* (a piercing undulation, a very ancient dance whose name has given birth to the Arab *ala,* the Egyptian *olouloulou,* and the Spanish *olé*[8]) the violas and the harp seem to rise from a mysterious orchestral mist, like the peaceful stirrings of the breeze in a setting of greenness, a setting redolent of luxury and beauty. "Nowhere," exclaimed Alexandre Dumas, "were so many orange trees, so many roses, so many jasmines gathered in so small a place. . . . Nowhere will you see so many springs, so many leaping waterfalls, so many rushing torrents."[9]

These waterfalls stream into the treble notes of the piano, which resumes the same *canto* (p. 5, No. 3) on a dominant of the first violins, enlarging and embellishing it with sparkling roulades of thirty-second notes. The horns and flutes take up this theme and answer each other (No. 4, measure 3), prefacing a pianistic accompaniment fashioned of rich broken harmonies accompanied by orchestral runs (p. 8, No. 5). There is a ruffling of trills, buzzing of distant guitars being tuned, and the oppositional play between the piano, which takes the principal part, and its associates subsides. The harp then recalls, in a new rhythm, the initial *canto* (p. 12, No. 7), and this is followed by a passage (*poco stringendo,* p. 13, No. 8) which stresses the evocation of an impressionist atmosphere through the punctiliousness of the notation, the scoring of the strings, and the broken and contrasting chords of the woodwinds. Alternations of shadows and pools of moonlight follow, soon blending in a melody set forth by the piano (p. 17, No. 10), which is simultaneously a development of the first motif and a curious, sudden recalling of a song heard before in Madrid when Falla lived in the Calle Serrano, a stone's throw from the house of Amadeo Vivès. An old blind beggar used to play it all day long on a badly tuned violin, and the subconscious of both musicians had duly noted it. Vivès introduced it into a *zarzuela,* Falla into *Nights.* It is really an element of folklore, a *zoronco* theme descended from flamenco. The orchestra takes it over (*con ampiezza,* p. 18, No. 12), but then subsides, after which, on a quite traditional broken cadence (No. 12, measure 13), it

[8] V. Parnac, *op. cit., La Revue Musicale,* May, 1931.
[9] Cited by H. Collet, *Essor de la Musique Espagnole au XXe Siècle.* Paris, 1929.

leaves the work to the horns. A somber flute responds from a distance. This is followed by a very beautiful altered chord, a sort of homage to Albéniz or Debussy. It is boldly spread throughout the strings (p. 19, No. 13), and it supports the theme, which the piano resumes in a variant that sweeps from the top to the bottom of the keyboard. There are sonorous outbursts, glissandos, *punteado* guitars, and a magical cadence of the piano (p. 23, No. 17) in which are distinguished twice, and as if in a dream, the first four notes of the *canto* arising from the three solo strings: viola, cello, and violin.

Now it is the piano's turn to imitate the guitar in what properly could be baptized a re-exposition (p. 27, No. 20), if such pedantry were in keeping with such enchantment. But Falla's mastery enables him to express the charm of his musical thought completely, while keeping it within the limits of an ordered construction. The orchestra in turn resumes the motif in tutti (p. 30, No. 20), rises to a fiery pitch of passion for the last time, and the piano part glistens with tiny cascades of arpeggios (p. 31, No. 24). Night asserts her rights, and everything becomes peaceful. A horn resounds in the distance (p. 34, No. 26), and all is silent.

In what garden is the *Distant Dance* performed? It consists of fragments of dances, shreds of melodies, harmonies, punctuated by guitars and tambourines, that suddenly burst forth and then are gone almost as quickly. It is music carried on the breeze of a balmy night. What are these rhythms that are too vague to be defined exactly (p. 35, No. 1)? The somber flute, first of all, sketches the hesitating rising and falling of a *malagueña* punctuated by the vocalizations of the violas. Doubled and ornamented, it rises, then falls back again on the four fatal notes that could be called the Andalusian cadence, simply because they are characteristic of so many variants of the *cante jondo* or flamenco (p. 36, No. 2).

A modal feeling of D dominates this beginning and confers upon it the unreal atmosphere in which the invisible ballet unfolds. A persistent rhythm of cellos continues up to the entry of the piano, which resumes and elucidates the initial rhythm (p. 37, No. 3). The tattoo of the Basque drums is imitated by the strings, since the kettledrums provide the only percussion. This is a subtle device of the composer to protect him against the facile effect of real castanets, tambourines, guitars, and cries of *"Olé!"*; the whole is fashioned of arpeggios, trills, glissandos, runs on the strings *pianissimo sul ponticello,* sonorous *jetés* from the harp, and piano octaves that repeat and vary the motif. Everything is intensified and clarified on a new theme (p. 42, No. 7), which, according to Falla, is a sequence "of the second phrase of the first canto of *En el Generalife."*[10] In fact the kinship is evident, as we can confirm from the finale. Should we read in this a brief homage to the cyclic form still predominant at this time? Be that as it may, *tempo giusto molto ritmico* (p. 43), there is a dance on this theme assisted by orchestral tutti. But the wind subsides, and the piano is heard only in some chromaticisms in the manner of Borodin (p. 46, No. 10, measure 6). Calm is restored, but not for long. The piano struggles in the higher register, and the entire orchestra, dominated by two blaring trumpets (p. 47, No. 12), flashes a few instants more, then dies out in a vivid descending chromatic. The horns, on a final echo, recall the rising and falling of the *malagueña* (p. 48, No. 13). The bassoon picks it up, and then the English horn—which the oboe doubles in thirds—unfolds the pattern of the *jota,* which the celesta embellishes with its iridescent sound, and the guitar—alias piano!—punctuates the whole with its repeated notes (p. 49, Nos. 14–20).

But suddenly a new liveliness transforms the scene. A high-pitched note crystallizes into a rapid transition that discloses the setting of *In the Gardens of the Sierra de Córdoba:* "a long sweep of vaporous blue underneath a mother-of-pearl sky pierced by a metallic azure."[11]

Both Gilbert Chase and J. B. Trend, in their important works on the great Spanish composer, see in this third section, this brilliant finale, the portrayal of a *zambra gitana.* Trend explains how the *zambras*—a deformation of *samira* or of the Arab *zamara*—which are night festivals with music and dances, accompanied the sacrament during the village *Corpus Christi* procession even at the time of the severe Cardinal Ximenez.[12] After being forbidden by Philip II, they were taken up again by the Gypsies. According to

---

[10] J. Pahissa, *op. cit.,* p. 94.
[11] A. T'Serstevens, *Nouvel Itinéraire Espagnol.* Paris.
[12] J. B. Trend, *op. cit.,* p. 74.

this eminent historian, Falla might have been thinking of a *zambra* in a village near Córdoba. Other writers see in it an homage to the Gypsy *polo*. Jaime Pahissa disputes these two assertions. He states that Falla, as was his custom, was not trying to portray anything, but simply to suggest an ambiance which would give free rein to the listener's imagination. "As for the *polo*," he adds, "it is a song and not a definite type of rhythm."[13] In the *polo* only the longish prelude played on the guitar has a fixed external rhythm which persists while the *cantaor* improvises a particular cadential movement.

In reality the finale of *Nights* is built in the form of a *copla* with an *estribillo,* or refrain, a section similar to the classic rondo. According to the highly interesting study signed T. A. de S. in *Música,*[14] the rhythm of the dance is an ancient motif of the *sevillana* which belongs to the genre of the Andalusian fandango, a kind of flamenco transposition of the peasant sequidillas of La Mancha and Castile. The *sevillana* mimes "the games of coquetry" writes Georges Hilaire, "the quickly kindled and promptly denied temptation." Its melody reflects the essential tradition of the fandango, which culminates in the glissandos of the cadence and recalls the large inflections of the *tercio flamenco.*

The *estribillo,* or refrain (the sevillana motif), is expressed in the mode of D by an orchestral tutti shared between the strings and the woodwinds, stoutly sustained by the brass joined for the first time, in this brilliant finale, by the triangles and cymbals (p. 57). The atmosphere is one of folk gaiety shot through with strident sounds, somewhat discordant, *marcatissimo.* Suddenly there is a feverish swirling of long skirts, which, clinging to the hips, spread out and twirl, balancing the movements of the fluttering fans above the dancers' heads. This is followed by a passionate *taconeo* (the rhythmic heel-stamping) emphasized by the castanets and the *palmadas* (hand-clappings) of the onlookers. It is easy to believe we hear cries of *"Olé, nina!"* and *"Anda!"* coming from the *jaleadoras,* the women who encourage the dancers.

The entry of the piano in the Hypodorian mode continues the motif of the refrain, embroidering it (p. 59, No. 27,

[13] J. Pahissa, *op. cit.,* p. 95.   [14] T. A. de S. *op. cit.*

measure 3). There is a *calmando appena e gradualmente* (p. 61, No. 27) of the whole orchestra on a pedal point of B and Russian-like chromaticisms. Thereupon begins the first strophe of the *copla* (No. 28), preceded by a call of the horns echoed by others in the distances of the Sierra.

Then there is a brilliant cadence on the keyboard (p. 64, measure 5) which leads into an assertion of the dominant aided by an ensemble imitating guitars (strings, horns, and bassoons) *tenuto e pesante*; this is followed by a repetition of the *estribillo,* now blended with the rapid scale runs of the piano, harp, and celesta (p. 64, No. 32). The second strophe, which is merely a new rhythmic transformation, now greatly enlarged, of the *estribillo,* begins at No. 36, p. 70. Its *ben misurato* pace in 2/4 time and its strongly emphasized blend of binary eighth notes and triplets give it the noble gait of the *fandango grande,* a characteristic dance of Córdoba. Harsh, supplicating, tense, the piano imposes its fierce *taconeo* (p. 72, No. 38) on the heel of the violin bows *sempre molto marcato.* Decisive, sonorous, it introduces a new rhythmic design (p. 74, No. 39) of the *petenera* in 6/8—3/4 time, which the cello takes over on a sudden *pianissimo* (p. 74, No. 40). The glowing brilliance subsides into sweetness. The line of the *estribillo,* modified by this last rhythm, slackens until it enlarges the initial semiquavers (p. 76, No. 42) into minims (half notes) leading to a last *copla* by way of a coda (p. 77, No. 43). This beautiful, voluptuous phrase seems to take no account of a distant rhythm of the fandango that the kettledrum beats, but descends slowly all along the bows of the strings like a tender farewell to the moonlit Sierra. The piano tries a last vocalization (p. 78, No. 44), a last vibration of guitars is borne on the breeze, and everything gradually dissolves into languorous dreaminess.

The aforementioned article in *Música* reproduces an interesting discussion among some Spanish critics who felt that *Nights* was of slight interest and novelty in terms of pianistic notation. T. A. de S. rightly replies that *Nights* is not a concerto, that the piano is used in a search for exceptional timbres to enrich the orchestra with characteristic or expressive sonorities. The way in which the piano suddenly stands out in the instrumental ensemble or dissolves into it, according to the necessities of the moment, proves the composer's intention. Roland-Manuel puts it more poetically: "The designs that the piano blends with the orchestra are subtle arabesques corresponding with the subtle arabesques of the Alhambra.[15] The purely technical point of view likewise calls for some discussion. The entry of the piano in *En el Generalife,* with its theme in bold relief on the capricious arpeggios of thirty-second notes apportioned between the two hands, is a heritage from Liszt and Chopin which Debussy and Ravel often utilized. The repeated notes, translating the *punteado* of the guitar, derive from the toccata style, which certainly belongs to the keyboard. We could also cite other examples proving Falla's scrupulousness in his treatment of pianists, even if, according to Jankélévitch, he was not greatly concerned with "making the most of the soloist, his interesting attitudes, his precious technique, his heroic performance."[16]

Shortly after the first Madrid presentation, Falla experienced the joy of listening to his *Nights in the Gardens of Spain* in San Sebastián as part of the concert program presented by the Orquesta Sinfónica directed by Arbós. There it was interpreted by Ricardo Viñes, his dear friend, to whom the composition had been dedicated. The great pianist Artur Rubinstein was present at this concert. He was to play the *Nights* at the Teatro Colón in Buenos Aires during his first musical visit to that city.

Paris had to wait until January, 1920, to hear *Nights* as played by Joaquin Nin under the baton of, once more, Arbós. In London a year later, Falla scored a triumph for his *Nights,* playing it himself at the Queen's Hall on a program of modern music directed by Edward Clark. Max Eschig published the score in 1922, and we can be indebted to Gustave Samazeuilh for a piano arrangement for four hands that is as faithful as it is meticulous.

[15] Roland-Manuel, *op. cit.*
[16] Jankélévitch, *op. cit.,* p. 85.

CHAPTER VII / *The Corregidor and the Miller's Wife, The Three-Cornered Hat*

On Saturday, April 7, 1917, the curtain rose at the Teatro Eslava in Madrid on the premiere of *The Corregidor*[1] *and the Miller's Wife,* a pantomime in two acts by G. Martinez Sierra based on the novel by Pedro Antonio de Alarcón,[2] music by Manuel de Falla. This was the initial version of the ballet *The Three-Cornered Hat.* Alarcón, it is said, heard the story, set in the beginning of the nineteenth century, from an old goatherd who hired himself out as a teller of tales at weddings and feasts. Doubtless it was *The Miller of Arcos,* the well-known *romance,* which, combined with the *saynète* or *zarzuela, The Corregidor and the Miller's Wife,* gave birth to the novel, which was first published in July, 1875. It teems with misunderstanding and adventures that make it very difficult to transfer to the stage, especially as a lyric drama, and, incidentally, difficult for an audience to follow. Nevertheless, the story had already inspired one musician, Hugo Wolf. His opera in four acts, *Der Corregidor,* with a powerful polyphonic structure, barely survived its first production in 1896. The fault, at least in large part, may have been due to the very bad libretto by Rosa Mayreder.

The genesis of the future ballet is rather confused. The plot had interested Falla even before the competition at the Academia de Bellas Artes. According to Pahissa, fate decided—by way of three titles drawn like lots from a hat—for *La Vida Breve* against *El Corregidor* and a treatment of the Paolo and Francesca story. Since then, Falla had always toyed with the idea of drawing a lyric work from Alarcón's novel. Diaghilev had also been studying its possibilities as a ballet for his company. Encouraged by G. Martinez Sierra, his choice finally fell on *Nights in the Gardens of Spain.* Diaghilev would even have journeyed to Granada in order to get a better idea of the setting in which his dancers would have to perform. He was already imagining a night festival at the Alhambra, with amorous

[1] A magistrate.
[2] Spanish poet and novelist (1833–1891).

caballeros and Gypsy girls whose sumptuous shawls fluttered in the enchanted night. It was a fine idea for the music hall but, understandably, it had little appeal for Falla. Instead, the Spaniard suggested to the Russian the project of *The Three-Cornered Hat*. Happily, Diaghilev was as enthusiastic about this possibility as he had been about *Nights*. But World War I prevented its immediate staging. Meanwhile, Falla obtained permission from the impressario to present as a pantomime what was still merely a first version, a sketch of the future ballet. At that time Falla was already at work on the composition of the song of the *Will-o'-the-Wisp* and on the beginning of *Master Peter's Puppet Show*.

The Madrid performance was an immediate hit with the public, which was delighted with the Corregidor's frustrations, but the critics exhibited greater reserve. They had high praise for the quality of the music, but they picked on certain defects in the staging, especially of the pantomime. The profusion of details which the composer was forced to include destroyed the unity of the whole. The critic of the *Heraldo de Madrid* was devasting: "By dint of describing and showing the action in its minutest detail, the author ends up by describing and showing nothing. Moreover, he thwarts an inspiration that on other occasions we have known to be more facile and vigorous!"[3] Diaghilev's reaction while watching a performance must have been similar, because the ballet incorporated important modifications made at his request and agreed upon by the authors.

Diaghilev meanwhile was struggling with the usual difficulties brought about by his own character and especially by his lordly manner. They were now compounded by the war and the Bolshevik Revolution. Financial complications had reached a point where it seemed that the Ballet Russe definitely faced disaster. Leopoldo Matos, an able lawyer recommended by Falla, managed to settle the thorniest questions,[4] and with the war over, Diaghilev prepared to resume his spectacular productions in all their former splendor. One of the first beneficiaries of this change of fortune was *The Three-Cornered Hat*, given in London on July 22, 1919.

---

[3] Cf. Sagardia, *op. cit.*, p. 35.
[4] In appreciation, Falla dedicated the ballet to him.

Although the plot was shorn of many useless details, it is still hard to follow for anyone who is not completely informed beforehand. The plot bears no relation to the somber, disturbing, eerie atmosphere that completely pervades *El Amor Brujo*. We are still in Andalusia, but an Andalusia characterized by that joy of life so vividly evoked by Goya in his tapestry cartoons. We see couples dancing the seguidilla to the strains of a guitar to which the tambourine gives the rhythm. Some boys are amusing themselves flying a kite; later others wave a cape before an imaginary bull. They form a circle and play at blind-man's bluff. Some *manolas* toss a straw effigy of the Corregidor into the air with a blanket. A sunburnt landscape outlines the sharp features (in the original production) of Picasso's very beautiful décor, accentuating it by the background aridity and dazzling whiteness. It is a milk-white night of the Feast of St. John, a night shot through with outbursts of laughter, song, and amorous intrigues. The pretty miller's wife, the very jealous miller, the slightly foolish teacher, the gouty, ridiculous Corregidor in his grotesque hat, which is a sign of his lofty office, the neighbors, a blackbird, a cuckoo, are all having a thoroughly good time, which cannot be darkened by the wicked constables at the Corregidor's beck and call.

For the first time, with this portrayal of a luminous Andalusia, Falla applied his talents to other Spanish provinces. Pahissa[5] relates that in order to steep himself in the character of the final *jota,* Falla accepted an invitation from his friend, the famous painter Zuloaga, to spend several days in Aragon, the central region preeminent for the *jota.* The pretext was the inauguration of a school built at the painter's expense in Goya's native village, Fuendetodos. As was customary on such occasions, festivals were also organized. After the Mass, celebrated in the church where "the frescoes painted by the young Goya still retain their vivid colors,"[6] a banquet took place at the town hall. From the balcony overlooking the great square of the village, the singer Aga Lahowska sang the *Jota* from the *Seven Songs,* naturally without accompaniment. (The

[5] Cf. Pahissa, *op. cit.,* pp. 101, 102, 103.
[6] Pahissa, *op. cit.,* p. 102.

villagers, not recognizing *their jota,* gave it an icy reception.) On the same evening, in all the lanes and illuminated squares, the real *jota Aragonesa* resounded in *rondas* and *serenatas* danced and sung by all the young people of the village. This is how Falla saw and heard it, and not at a table of a café-concert or from the stage of a variety theater.

Contributions were likewise sought from Navarre and Murcia so as to create characters closer to the original types. And Falla broadened his ambitus in time as well as in space. He went back as far as Domenico Scarlatti, whose long stay at the Madrid court had to all intents and purposes made a Spaniard out of him. *The Three-Cornered Hat* randomly strives for the dry-point effects, denuded and allusive, which introduce the harpsichord of *Master Peter's Puppet Show* and of the *Concerto,* and if the orchestral palette is gradually enriched until the final flowering, its delicate hues are more related to the Goya of the tapestries than to the Goya of the violent colors crushed "under a heavy thumb."[7]

Musical Analysis[8]

The composition of the orchestra includes woodwinds with piccolo and English horn, four horns, three trumpets, three trombones and tuba, harp, celesta, piano, kettledrums, percussion (castanets, triangle, bass drum, cymbal, xylophone, drum), and strings. In keeping with the laws of a wise economy, the instruments are gradually integrated into the action so as to display the climactic moments of the composition to good advantage; the third and fourth horns and trombones are not heard until the finale.

The origin of the folk motifs used in the score of *The Three-Cornered Hat* has been minutely studied by Garcia Matos,[9] and the author of the present work has tried to verify this study as far as possible.

Before the curtain rises, we hear a rapid and joyous fanfare

[7] Th. Gautier.

[8] The reference numbers are to the score for piano and voice published by Chester of London, 1921. The numbers referring to the miniature orchestra score are indicated separately.

[9] Garcia Matos, *op. cit.* (Cf. *Música,* Madrid, 1953).

introduced by the kettledrum, to which are successively added two trombones, two horns, castanets, hand-clappings, and cries of *"Olé!"* uttered by invisible dancers. Finally we hear the voice of a woman. (This introduction was written in London shortly before the premiere so that the audience could have a chance to admire Picasso's drop curtain.) The song, for mezzo-soprano without accompaniment, is an old children's roundelay that differs somewhat from region to region. Pedrell[10] is of the opinion that it comes from Malaga, whereas F. Rodriguez Marin[11] claims it for Seville. But Falla was also able to hear country children singing,

> *Casadita, casadita, cierra con tranca la puerta.*
> (Little house, close your door with a crossbar.)

After the song, the orchestra begins with a dance theme presented by the second violins in tremolo, the first clarinet, and the English horn, and sustained by the pizzicati of the first violins and the *picchetati* of the harp. This is a motif coming from Murcia, in homage to the miller, a native of that province (orchestra score, p. 3).

The curtain rises on the tiny esplanade in front of the mill. It is the hour of the blackbird's lesson. The bird's perverseness in whistling the wrong hour of the day is expressed by the piccolo (Nos. 2 and 3). The miller's angry outburst is expressed by runs in the strings and woodwinds. This is followed by the cautious intervention of the miller's wife in a delightful duet of four measures between the flute and the piccolo (orch. score, p. 9, measure 4), portraying her triumph in teaching the bird how to whistle the hour of the day. Then there comes a combination of the two themes, forming a leitmotif of the miller and his wife. The first theme is from Navarre, like the charming miller's wife, and will be the basis of the grand *jota* of the finale.

Doubtless this is the *jota* that Falla heard at the time of the festival in Aragon. According to Garcia Matos, it also appears in different traditional variants, and he cites one of them in *Lírica*

[10] F. Pedrell, *Cancionero Musical,* II, p. 115.
[11] F. Rodriguez Marin, *Cantos Populares Españoles.*

Popular de la Alta Extremadura.[12] The loop of the terminal *tercia* is very characteristic of the *jota* and at the same time well suited to different choreographic episodes.

The other motif is that of *El Paño Moruno,* the first of the *Seven Songs,* and like the miller himself, of Murcian origin. As has been said, this was a real song that enjoyed great popularity. The orchestra at first indulges in allusions (orch. score, p. 11, No. 4). Barely expressed by a crescendo of strings and woodwinds, the theme of the miller's wife gives way so that the bassoon *con grazia*— and the cellos—*pizzicato e marcato*—can introduce the theme of her spouse. They look at each other admiringly and kiss while dancing. There is no suggestion of melancholy in an unexpected minor (No. 13). The miller and his wife are wildly happy together. They set about their chores. Here the music becomes imitative. The pulley of the well grates at the same time as the piccolo (orch. score, p. 13, No. 7) and the harmonics of the strings. The miller's wife throws grain to the chickens on the *picchetati* of strings in solos and *sul ponticello* (same number). The miller whistles snatches of a ridiculous, childish song, which the piccolo expresses and which turns out to be a popular march tune Falla and his friends used to sing in Madrid before he set out for Paris (orch. score, p. 16, No. 9).

The dandy intervenes. This is a scene of coquetry finely expressed by the orchestra. He is very much in the manner of an Andalusian *majo,* a gallant ever ready to toss a compliment to a pretty girl (orch. score, pp. 16 to 18).

But a pompous procession appears on the scene (Syn. No. 20), announced by the kettledrum and somber strings. The Corregidor and his wife the Corregidora, in her sedan chair, advance to the discordant, nasal strains of a solemn march blared in the treble of the strings and piccolo. This also is a well-known children's song, *El Sereni* (The Night Watch). Pahissa cites it,[13] and Garcia Matos, according to Marin,[14] establishes its origin in Seville. Obviously, the intention is to make the Corregidor look ridiculous by

[12] G. Matos, *Lírica Popular de la Alta Extremadura.* Madrid, 1944, p. 78, No. 70.
[13] *Op. cit.,* p. 101.
[14] F. R. Marin, *op. cit.,* p. 53.

using a children's song as his symbol, and this absurdity is stressed even more by the choice of instruments.

The procession passes, the miller and his wife resume their chores, which are again interrupted by the arrival of a young woman, which gives rise to a scene of jealousy, followed by a reconciliation. The orchestra and the choreography follow the action closely. The composer develops it in able counterpoint. But then the wife weeps— a sorrowful motif expressed by the violins and violas. This development, finely presented by a reduced orchestra, ends with the reunion of the two themes of the miller and his wife as a sign of reconciliation.

The Navarese *tercio,* barely terminated on an arpeggio of the harp, announces the Corregidor's reappearance, accompanied by a constable. We again hear the bassoon play the motif of the important personage, still in C major, followed by a march in the same key with light pizzicati accompanied by the ironic comments of the woodwinds, the staccatos of the harp and piano (orch. score, p. 30, No. 15). The miller's wife makes fun of the Corregidor and imitates his limping gait. There is a retard on a dominant of G and then begins the *Fandango of the Miller's Wife* (orch. score, p. 34).

All that this famous passage has of the classic *fandango* is the 3/4, 6/8 rhythm and the imitations of the guitar *rasgueado* by the repeated notes of the doubled strings, the chords of the piano, and the thirds of the clarinets, with constant shadings from forte to piano. Later, to the rhythm of the dance, Falla links a new motif which has an expressive relation to the theme of the miller's wife, as well as to her husband's moods (orch. score, p. 42, No. 20).

The orchestra becomes impassioned and leads to a forte tutti giving the effect of a *taconeo,* clearly indicated by the strokes of the bow (orch. score, p. 55, No. 24). The woodwinds burst with vocalizations, and we are back to the beginning of the fandango with its blends of G major and minor, and its cello pizzicati.

Suddenly there is an interruption, an exclamation point on the dominant of D: the miller's wife claims she sees the Corregidor! He advances, waddling, his face inflamed by the fandango danced by the pretty miller's wife, whom he greets in his most ceremonious manner, to the strains of a very well-known Andalusian dance, the *olé gaditano* (orch. score, p. 62, No. 29). Falla uses these *olé* variations of it up to the finale. Garcia Matos has located it in several publications, including one by F. Garcia Navas.[15] The bassoon introduces the theme solo in a grotesque march tempo in 2/4. The miller's wife mockingly and vigorously responds with ironic curtsies to the accompaniment of a light minuet given to the strings, in which the outlines of a *montanesa* (a mountain melody of a slightly affected delicacy) and the hoarse, ponderous fifths of the bassoon[16] are contrapuntally interlaced.

An outburst of laughter on a rapid scale of the flute introduces one of the most charming parts of the score: *The Grapes.* The mischievous woman offers a bunch of grapes to her grotesque admirer and, miming the feints of a picador exciting the bull with his *banderillos,* she indulges in all kinds of flirtations as she circles the poor man who does his best to grab the grapes. The harp begins with some arpeggios on a clear E major (orch. score, p. 63, No. 32). The motif, chiefly rhythmic in character, unfolds its groups of irregular values in capricious ornamentations. We can recognize in it a utilization—now quite ornate and sublime—of the Andalusian *Canción,* the sixth of the *Seven Songs,* whose shape is apparent beneath the delightful baroque quality of the ornaments. But everything has an end. The Corregidor, out of breath, slips, falls to the ground, waving his arms and legs frantically as he vainly attempts to get up. Groans rise from the horns, accompanied by appropriate glissandos from cellos (orch. score, p. 74, No. 37). The guilty miller and his wife make effusive explanations in a skillful, rhythmic distortion (in rapid sixteenth notes) of the grapes motif (orch. score, p. 37, No. 38). Furious and limping, the Corregidor goes away. The miller and his wife continue to make fun of him. There is an animated reprise of previous motifs (*marcato* and *molto ritmico*), but a menace arises, announced by the horns with the theme of the Corregidor and exactly spelled out in an ironic tone by the constable. His trumpet plays a song which bodes ill (orch. score, p. 83, No. 46):

[15] F. Garcia Navas, *Collección de Bailes Españoles.*
[16] R. Calleja, *Cantos de la Montaña.*

> *Con el capotin, tin, tin, tin,*
> *Que esta noche va allover.*

> (I put on my little cape,
> for tonight it will rain.)

This is a humorous allusion to the arrest of the miller and to the rain of complications that the next night will bring. Pahissa notes that this song "of a common type is quite popular in Spain."[17]

But nothing casts a shadow yet over the joy of the couple, delighted at having hoaxed the old man, and the curtain falls on a final fandango teeming with the themes already heard.

For the second act the curtain rises on a *tertulia* which brings together the neighbors of the miller and his wife. This is in honor of the night of the Feast of St. John.

They dance a seguidilla based on two themes. The first is a ritual *canto* of the Gypsies of the Sacro Monte of Granada, the *alborea,* or *albola,* whose ancient beginnings are now but dimly remembered. It was sung at marriages, after sacramental rites had confirmed the *novia's* virginity.[18] During his sojourn in Granada, Diaghilev had heard and passed on to Falla the second theme, played by an old blind man on a discordant violin. Later, the theme was recognized in a *zarzuela* by Jerónimo Jiménez, *La Boda de Luis Alonso.*[19]

Falla treats and develops these two folk fragments with a delicacy of touch in both the harmonic and orchestral refinements, which not only endows those melodies with a new savor but makes the seguidilla danced by the neighbors one of the high points of the score.

The first violins expound the theme pianissimo in an unadulterated D major. Several vigorous *taconeos*—on the dominant— separate the diverse modulations (orch. score, p. 100, No. 1). Binary rhythms are likewise interpolated into the initial 3/4 time. The mood is generally piano with sudden strong outbursts. It is

[17] Pahissa, *op. cit.,* p. 109.
[18] *Ibid.,* p. 109.
[19] *Ibid.,* p. 107.

night. At times the breeze stirs the leaves, and the whirling of the skirts is accentuated. The celesta now adds its crystalline notes, like the thousands of stars which shine in the velvet Andalusian sky (orch. score, p. 104, measure 3). The second theme—that of the blind man—is introduced by somber strings (orch. score, p. 105, No. 5). A flute and a bassoon solo in double octave (orch. score, p. 107, No. 7)—a Mozartean device. Falla repeats it before it is taken over by the orchestra, and particularly develops its terminal form. There succeed rapid scales, embroideries, trills, harp glissandos, resumption of the initial theme on the flute (orch. score, p. 111, No. 10) with a light accompaniment of the strings. It all gives an impression of nocturnal, languid voluptuousness, a mysterious sweetness that is expressed particularly by the extremely subdivided strings and the skillful responses of the woodwinds.

The miller's wife now invites her husband to dance the *farruca. The Miller's Dance* is the apex of the score, certainly the best known part of it. Its arrangement for piano, like that of the *Ritual Fire Dance,* is on the program of many a recital.

It was composed in twenty-four hours at Diaghilev's request, in order to have a solo for his premier danseur Leonide Massine, after the *fandango* of the danseuse. Upon hearing it for the first time at a rehearsal of the orchestra, Massine and Picasso expressed a boundless admiration for it.

The *farruca* is a flamenco dance. G. Hilaire[20] describes it as a "solemn dance with redoubled and redoubtable syncopations." In keeping with custom, the neighbors gather in a semicircle and begin to *jalear,* or spur on the dancer with their hand-clappings and their *"Olés!"* A horn prelude makes for a poignant, nostalgic, heart-rending touch (orch. score, p. 122). The English horn terminates it in raucous accents. The dance begins in the mode of A on the staccato and heavy rhythms of the strings *sul ponticello.* The dancer, almost motionless, accentuates the music with his heels.

A second theme intervenes on the oboe (orch. score, p. 125). It is still the popular *olé gaditano,* as collected by F. Garcia Navas,[21] of which Falla preserves only the melodic core contained

[20] *Op. cit.*
[21] *Op. cit.*

in a fourth—E-A. Harp arpeggios accompany it. The line of this *olé,* modified and developed, will form, as it were, the strophes of a *copla* which will be separated by the motif of the *farruca.* This dance seems to claw at and beat the ground furiously, passing through the changes of mood natural to the capricious, unpredictable character of the Gypsy. The miller, in the grip of the *duende* (ghost), gradually intensifies his dance to match the fierce rhythm of the orchestra. We hear the furious scraping of the strings of imaginary guitars. The cries of *"Olé!"* burst out. The animation is frenzied, sensual (orch. score, p. 132, No. 9). The dancer seems to disconnect himself from the ground in a stunning gyration and then suddenly he is motionless —at the very moment that the whole orchestra is stilled. The on-lookers approve wildly. Their congratulations are offered accompanied by a motif of a *granaina murciana* whose guitaresque arpeggiated rhythm runs through the whole orchestra and will be utilized later in different modifications (orch. score, p. 135, No. 11).[22]

The miller thanks his audience, thus providing a pretext to reintroduce his theme on the first violins (orch. score, p. 138, measure 2). Suddenly "fate knocks on the door," so to speak, with a well-known Beethoven theme sounded by the horn (orch. score, pp. 139–140), and, with a flourish of the piano, the door opens. The constables appear, black-clad and unnerving, as solemn as inquisitors. They advance in measured steps, with grand gestures underlined by sudden fortissimos. To Falla's great regret, Diaghilev wanted to delete this march at the first performance on the grounds that it slowed down the action. Besides the pain any author feels at the slightest deletion, Falla had a special fondness for this march because his mother had sung it to him when he was a child. Moreover, its introduction into the final *jota,* among the themes reflecting the crucial moments of the plot, would be meaningless. Be that as it may, since the fundamental tones of the march—tonic, dominant— are in minor, whereas those of the Corregidor's motif are in major, the requirements for the relation between flunkeys and their master are fully satisfied.

The miller's astonishment at his arrest is expressed by an

[22] G. Matos cited several variants. Cf. *Música, op. cit.*

interrogative phrase which first is taken up by his wife and then by the onlookers. The constables insist. Here follows a polymodal drama: the miller protests in D major, the constables command in minor (orch. score, p. 144, No. 16). Tension grows—*poco a poco affrettando.* Skillful harmonic arrangements modify the theme without breaking the melodic line. But might makes right. The law's minions lead the prisoner away, and his neighbors, choosing discretion over valor, withdraw. The miller's wife stands alone.

Garcia Matos asks: "What can best express the theatrical instant, if not a *soleare?"* An allusion to this song of separation and loneliness is expressed as an aside by the somber strings and the harp (orch. score, p. 151, No. 18). A voice sings in the distance:

> The cuckoo sings in the night.
> It cautions us to bolt the door,
> For the devil is awake.

And the voice repeats: *"Cucù, Cucù, Cucù!"*

The source of this very beautiful song remains a mystery. On the basis of its sustained notes and its rhythmic and modal imprecision, it could be compared to a *granadina* cited by R. Laparra in his study in the *Encyclopédie.*[23] The *granadina* is one of the most melodious expressions of the *cante grande flamenco,* whose "elegiac arabesques, delicate downstrokes, and voluptuous meanderings seem to be a response to the Alhambra's fragile decorations in stucco and tiles!"[24] Its melismas also recall a *pantoum* of Granada noted by Tiersot.[25]

The theme of the song saddens the miller's wife who sighs and goes back into her house. But the seguidilla continues amid the fragrances of the night. The cuckoo clock strikes the hour. All is silence.

Suddenly, a bassoon twangs the theme of the Corregidor (orch. score, p. 157, No. 23). The old gallant returns, knowing the square to be empty. He moves timorously, simpering, and then

---

[23] R. Laparra, *op. cit.,* IV, p. 2353.
[24] G. Hilaire, *op. cit.*
[25] J. Tiersot, *op. cit.,* p. 2906.

104

dances a minuet in the style of the miming in the first act (orch. score, p. 157, No. 25). It is unfortunate that this pompous, playful minuet is generally shortened or deleted in the theater, for this very eighteenth-century pastiche is both enormously charming and comical. Jankélévitch and other critics see in it "the shade of Scarlatti." We recall that Falla had introduced the first measures of this dance into the best of his zarzuelas, *La Casa de Tócame Roque*, which was never published. Written in a very simple style in A major, the dance is wittily divided between strings and woodwinds up to the moment when, just as the bassoon is about to play the final chord, a false step precipitates the Corregidor into the millrace. Then comes a great orchestral agitation of tremolos, a hubbub of the percussion instruments (orch. score, p. 165, No. 33). The miller's wife reappears and takes part in the general disorder to the motif of the *Dance of the Grapes* (orch. score, p. 168, No. 34). But the Corregidor, undaunted, continues his amourous pursuit as before, and the orchestra reflects the minutest details of the action. The bassoon, which symbolizes the old Don Juan, resumes a variant of the *olé gaditano,* to which attention was called at its first appearance (orch. score, p. 174, No. 29).

To the rapid triplets of her Navarre leitmotif, the miller's wife flees while syncopations accompany the Corregidor's pursuing steps. Here Falla uses violent contrasts of shading and rapid modulations. We hear the explosion of a beautiful romantic declaration from the horn and cellos (orch. score, p. 181) answered by outbursts of laughter from the woodwinds. The miller's wife puts an end to the scene by brandishing her husband's blunderbuss to the strains of a very popular tune:[26]

> *No me mates, dejame viver en paz.*
> (Don't kill me, let me live in peace.)

(orch. score, p. 183, No. 46).

Thereupon, the miller, who has escaped, comes back, whistling his song to himself. He flies into a rage when he finds the Corregidor's three-cornered hat on a chair, and we hear the motif

[26] Pahissa, *op. cit.,* p. 109, and Hernandez, *op. cit.,* cf. p. 46.

of the *granaina murciana,* previously expounded after the *farruca* (orch. score, p. 185, No. 49). The flute twits him with a recall of the Corregidor's little song (orch. score, p. 186, No. 51). The whole scene, through its medley of different themes, is a recapitulation of the thoughts of the unhappy miller as he recalls that day's events. All of them flit through his mind up to the pompous march of the first act, which most opportunely reminds him of the Corregidor's wife (orch. score, p. 192, No. 55). This time his whistling strikes a note of triumph; the flute assumes the task of expressing his malicious joy, and the piano accentuates it (No. 56). He disappears, full of ideas for revenge. Dressed in the miller's clothes, the Corregidor, to the motif of his grotesque walk, now returns (No. 38). A new distortion of the theme of the *olé gaditano* follows, still assigned to the bassoon (orch. score, p. 196, No. 62) and developed in a skillful harmonic progression expressing in turn the Corregidor's hesitation and despair and the ridiculousness of his situation. Now follows an ample orchestral crescendo, leading to a pause after a fortissimo chord which announces the brilliant final dance, the *jota.*

Immediately the confusion seems at its peak. Each character reappears, including the neighbors, and the orchestra undertakes to clarify the situation by presenting the different themes in their proper place. The constables look for their prisoner to the theme of the march of the Corregidor played in a very rapid tempo (orch. score, p. 199). The cries of the miller's wife on the two first notes of her leitmotif (orch. score, p. 200) lead into the *jota* danced on this same element by the crowd of neighbors drawn by the hubbub. This may be viewed as the *estribillo* (refrain) of this immense *copla,* simultaneously summarizing and climaxing the action.

Now we hear the complete orchestra, with the four horns, the three trombones and tuba, and the ensemble of the percussion instruments. The key of C, solely on the tonic and the dominant, struts to an *allegro ritmico, molto moderato e pesante* (orch. score, p. 201, No. 1), as becomes peasants on a festival night, for we must not forget that this is still the night of the Feast of St. John.

The constables do not give up their search for the miller. The phrase of the *olé gaditano* reappears in 6/8, in E, in the strings (orch. score, p. 206, No. 4). At the same time the horns, followed by the trumpets, play a fragment of a well-known song of children playing hide and seek:

> *Que no me coges.*
> (You won't catch me!)

This reflects polytonally, and just at the right moment, the game of cat and mouse between the hero of the festival and his persecutors.[27]

The movement quickens its pace. The *jota* theme, blared out by the woodwinds, becomes increasingly impetuous and alternates with the harp glissandos (orch. score, p. 210, No. 6). An orgiastic excitement comes from the strident notes of the percussion instruments. But new arrivals appear. The procession of St. John passes over the bridge, and the participants mingle with the crowd of neighbors. The orchestra recalls the "grapes" motif, deeply modifying its rhythm, before presenting a new variant of the *olé gaditano* in the manner of a song of the procession (orch. score, p. 219, No. 9).

Repeated and ornamented at length by the strings, these two motifs with a sudden pianissimo and a *doppio meno vivo,* prepare the crescendo entry of the *olé gaditano,* this time in its entirety. It is trumpeted fortissimo by the orchestral tutti (orch. score, p. 228, No. 14). Garcia Matos cites this popular theme, not only in the aforementioned collection of G. Navas and in the *zarzuela* by I. Jiménez, but also in the rare and ancient *cancionero* of Núñez Robres.[28]

The orchestra becomes increasingly intense and highly colored. There is a general brawl. The constables and the Corregidor are made sport of. The *jota* bursts forth joyously with great support from the orchestra (orch. score, p. 234, No. 19). The different themes—the miller, the constables, the song *El Capotin,* the *Dance of the Grapes,* the children's hide and seek song—follow one another in the demoniacal movement of the dance, whose design, *meno vivo e pesante,* undergoes the classical modulation to the subdominant (orch. score, p. 244, No. 27, measure 4) before reappearing in still more rapid rhythms at the moment when the crowd grabs the Cor-

---

[27] G. Matos, *op. cit.*
[28] Lazaro Núñez Robres, *La Música del Pueblo*. Madrid, n.d.

regidor and tosses him in a blanket (orch. score, p. 248, No. 31). The crowd's joy and the clicking of castanets die away only on a final chord of C and the fall of the curtain.

As was mentioned previously, *The Three-Cornered Hat* was presented for the first time at the Alhambra Theatre in London on July 22, 1919, by Serge Diaghilev's Ballet Russe with the following billing:

THE THREE-CORNERED HAT

Ballet by G. Martinez Sierra
After a story by P. A. de Alarcón
Music by Manuel de Falla
Choreography by Leonide Massine—
Direction: Ernest Ansermet

The drop curtain, décor, and costumes by Pablo Picasso created a sensation and marked an important date in the history of stage design. Paris, in turn, applauded the work in 1920.

It would be an endless task to quote the accolades earned by the huge success of Falla's new ballet. Like *El Amor Brujo,* it is in the repertory of all the ballet companies of the world. The two suites for orchestra extracted from the score, the dances of the miller and of his wife, as well as the seguidilla, transcribed for different instruments, appear on the programs of many symphony concerts and recitals. The scores—orchestra and piano and voice—were published in 1921 by Chester in London.

CHAPTER VIII / *Fantasia Baetica*

One year later (1922) Chester in London published the *Fantasia Baetica,* a piece for the piano.

Its origin goes back to a meeting between Falla and the famous pianist Artur Rubinstein, who had made a concert tour of Spain during the war, in 1914. The two musicians had been brought together by a letter asking Falla to solicit Rubinstein's help on behalf of Stravinsky, who was then living in Switzerland in straitened circumstances. Always tactful and generous, Rubinstein responded by commissioning two pieces for piano, one from Stravinsky, one from Falla, and by sending two checks. The commission to Stravinsky brought forth *Piano Rag Music.* Falla responded to his commission with *Fantasia Baetica,* which was completed in 1919.

Baetica was the name of the Roman province which roughly coincides with present-day Andalusia. The term itself comes from Bétis, "the poetic name of the river of Seville, the Guadalquiver."[1] With the *Fantasia Baetica,* Falla was still celebrating his beloved Andalusia, but this time he went back beyond the annals of the caliphs and plunged into the distant and glorious past, the past that had given two emperors to Rome, Trajan and Hadrian, as well as Seneca, the Cordovan philosopher. A few years later Falla was to stress this homage to the Roman origin of his people by founding the Orquesta Bética.

This return to origins was in the air at the time in literary and artistic circles. The Moorish and Gypsy elements had become hackneyed and were gladly rejected in favor of a more remote antiquity. This tendency was to prove lasting.

Falla had been broadening the horizon of his heritage since *The Three-Cornered Hat.* He was to continue doing so up to his last work, *Atlántida,* in which he was not only to actualize the national consciousness but to make "of it a universal European value," as A. Salazar has noted.

[1] *La Revue Musicale,* May 1, 1931.

This work, dedicated to ancient Andalusia and to an already famous pianist, was burdened with the double task of celebrating the region and the artistry of the man. The borrowings from folklore themes, flamenco rhythms, and from one of its most representative modes of expression, the guitar, had to be all transposed into the domain of the keyboard. But this time it was not a question of concrete thematic utilizations neatly outlined through pianistic notation, or contrapuntally set in contrast, as it had been with the *Four Spanish Pieces,* which were dedicated to Albéniz and were similar in style to the latter's *Ibéria.* In honor of the famous virtuoso, the piano dominates by borrowing from the guitar its characteristic effects of arpeggiated chords (whose rapid *rasgueado* furnishes the polyphonic features), of repeated or *punteado* notes, and of the persistence of the dominant in the form of a pedal point.

The first motif outlined on this ornately wrought texture is made up of two very short and simple fragments, born of the rhythm of the *buleria,* which belongs to the *muy flamenco* genre of the *solea.* The interlude features the outline of a tender ballad, stemming from the exotic domain of the *guarija.* The general form is among the most common: A-B-A:

A. Exposition of the two themes.
B. The interlude.
A. Textual return to the exposition, save for some modulations preparing the coda.

The general tonality, notes G. Chase, is on the Phrygian mode with the interlude in the Aeolian mode, frequent in Spanish folk music. Expressed more clearly, its inspiration is based on the chord of the guitar, E-A-D-G-B, with a frequent alteration of the minor third, G-B flat, which gives a particularly tragic and melancholy character to the two A parts.

From the beginning, through thematic repetitions, Falla strives to accentuate the incantational character of the work in conformity with its Gypsy essence. The caprices of the *taconeo,* the sudden turns of *baile jondo,* the long sustained notes followed by the rapid vocalizations of the *polo,* and the Andalusian cadence are the distinguishing features of this work, the last that Falla dedicated to the land of his birth.

Rubinstein wanted to give the work its first presentation during his Spanish tour, and Falla immediately sent him a copy. The time was too short, however, and the pianist postponed the premiere until his return to New York. He played it again on several occasions, but the work is still little known and is seldom performed, a fact which Alfredo Casella deplored in his important work *Il Pianoforte.* Jankélévitch, generally hard to please, ranks it among "the sequence of incomparable masterpieces, *El Amor Brujo, Nights in the Gardens of Spain, The Three-Cornered Hat.*" Henri Prunières, after the first performance at a concert organized by *La Revue Musicale,* with Falla at the piano, hailed it as "direct, profound music, gushing forth from the heart and expressed in a form as beautiful as it is original." Unfortunately time has yet to confirm these enthusiastic appraisals.

Meanwhile deaths in his family had brought grief into Manuel de Falla's life. In May, 1919, his father died. Two months later, on the evening of the London triumph of *The Three-Cornered Hat* at the Alhambra Theatre, he received a telegram from his brother: "Mother very ill, return as soon as possible." Falla set out for home immediately, but in 1919, with the war barely over, international travel was still difficult. The channel could be crossed only between Southampton and Le Havre. Le Havre to Madrid was always a long journey now made even more arduous by the discomforts resulting from the war. En route, he learned of his beloved mother's death from a newspaper, and he arrived only in time for the funeral. Thus the great composer's second journey to London ended sadly despite the sympathy extended to him by the entire Diaghilev company, something he was never to forget. Falla returned to London in 1921 in order to give a public performance of *Nights.* At that time the city was in the grip of a coal strike. Despite the discomforts of the journey and of his stay, Falla loved to recall later how beautiful London seemed, rid of her coal dust and her fogs, resplendent under the pure and luminous sky.

After his mother's death, Manuel de Falla decided to leave Madrid and to live with his sister Maria del Carmen in Granada, a dream which he had been cherishing for a long time. Before leaving the capital, Falla was invited by the Princess de Polignac to write an opera for marionettes to be staged at her home in Paris. As we know, Falla had already started work on *El Retablo de Maese Pedro* (Master Peter's Puppet Show).

But before proceeding to an examination of this major work, several of his projects which remained more or less unfinished and his very brief but very beautiful work dedicated to the memory of Debussy should be mentioned.

Falla had been haunted since sometime before the premiere of *La Vida Breve* by the idea of writing a one-act opera to be called *The Death of Carmen*. He wanted it to adhere more closely to Mérimée's story than Bizet's opera had done. Among the critics who were sounded out, Pierre Lalo was favorable, but other persons prominent in the musical world violently opposed the project as "sacrilege"; it was abandoned. Much later, Ernesto Halffter, pupil and friend of Falla, took up the project, the same one "in conception, in dedication, and even in music."[2]

Falla also planned to write a new *Barber of Seville,* very different from Rossini's work, with scenes that do not figure in the comedy by Beaumarchais. For example, the opera was to begin in Figaro's shop and conclude with his wedding. Debussy liked the idea, but Dukas formally advised him against it, counsel which Falla followed.

What aberration led him to follow the advice of G. Martinez Sierra, who brought him a libretto for a comic opera in three acts in the old style of sung and spoken numbers? The title was *Fuego Fatuo* (Will-o'-the-Wisp), and the music was based on Chopin themes. This was an idea as bizarre as it was fatal! The first performance was to be during the 1919–1920 season at the Teatro Eslava in Madrid, at that time under the direction of a friend of G. Martinez Sierra, the composer Penella. Falla worked furiously during the summer of 1919 in Madrid's scorching heat—"nine months of winter, three months of hell," says the proverb—ten hours a day behind closed shutters. The work was partially ready for copy-

[2] J. Pahissa, *op. cit.,* p. 109.

ing when he learned that the season would go by without the performance of his comic opera. Disappointed, Falla presented it for consideration elsewhere, but without result. His name and his previous successes seemed to make no impression on theater directors. He was to get a clue to the riddle from Albert Carré, manager of the Opéra Comique, to whom he offered his score when he made a trip to Paris. Carré asked: "Why do you use Chopin's music instead of your own?" Thereupon, Falla locked his manuscript in a drawer and decided that "it would remain unpublished forever." Not only did the work remain unused—and there is slight chance that it will ever see the light of day—but it was also the reason why Falla, for lack of time, had to decline Diaghilev's offer to write *Pulcinella,* a ballet on themes of Pergolesi. Diaghilev then, of course, entrusted the project to Stravinsky.

At the beginning of 1931, the musicologist Juan Maria Thomas, an eminent Majorcan musician and a great admirer of Falla (who was his guest in later years on the island of Majorca), asked him for the score of *Fuego Fatuo* for inclusion in the program of one of the festivals being organized at Majorca in honor of Chopin. The composer's sister Maria del Carmen told him that Falla was studying the possibility of giving him a fragment of his work for the celebration. She explained that he had neglected it for ten years, that he wanted to look at it again before deciding, and that he would get to it as soon as time allowed. This "time" never came, and thus an opportunity to know at least a part of *Fuego Fatuo* was lost forever.[3]

Falla's great admiration for Bizet, Mérimée, Beaumarchais, Chopin, when translated into a musical homage in the form of operas, each time led him to an impasse. Only the *Homage to Debussy,* more modest in intent but lofty in conception, turned out to be a complete success. These two pages were the result of a request and an encounter. The request came from the celebrated Catalan guitarist Miguel Llobet, pupil and successor to the great Tarrega, who for a long time had been begging Falla to write a work for his

[3] Falla's unpublished manuscripts are in the possession of his niece, daughter of his brother-german, Señora M. Isabel de Falla de Garcia de Paredes.

instrument. Falla had agreed, but before doing so, he wanted to familiarize himself completely with the technique of the guitar. This was in keeping with the advice he had received from Dukas many years before. The encounter took place in Paris shortly after the war, when one day he met Henri Prunières, editor of the newly founded *Revue Musicale,* who asked him to do an article for a special issue dedicated to the memory of Claude Debussy. Falla said he preferred to write a musical work that would be suffused with the spirit of his deceased friend, one in which here and there he could touch lightly on one or another of those works of Debussy that had been inspired by Spain; for example, *La Soirée dans Grenade* or *La Puerta del Vino,* which owed its inspiration to a postcard Falla had sent to him. Finally, he wrote both the article and the music, the latter in the form of a piece for guitar, which he quickly dispatched to Llobet. This was *Homenaje,*[4] published in the special number of *La Revue Musicale,* December 1, 1920. In an insert entitled *Le Tombeau de Claude Debussy,* Falla's homage lies beside those of Dukas, Roussel, Malipiero, Eugene Goossens, Bartók, Florent Schmitt, Stravinsky, Ravel, and Erik Satie.

Musical Analysis

Falla's piece is a funeral dirge, a symbolic threnody, so frequent in Spanish poetry, influenced by the musical essence and spirit of his departed friend. Its harmony rests essentially on the fundamental fourth of the typical—and so beautiful—chord of the guitar, E-A-D-G-B. Falla places a short rhythmic phrase on this fourth, a kind of muted and bitter lamentation which resounds like a knell throughout the piece. Several echos of *Ibéria*[5] form the beginning of a theme, a brief motif in triplets marked by the characteristic chromaticism and the augmented second (measures 8 to 15). The special resources of the guitar are skillfully exploited through arpeggios, very open chords, glissando scales, *punteado* effects, and octave harmonics.

Toward the end a sudden modulation leading to a *piu*

---

[4] Not *Homenaja,* as was published by mistake.
[5] *Ibéria,* symphonic poem by Claude Debussy, 1909.

calmato section (measure 63) sets in bold relief, like a brief ray of moonlight, the clear appearance of a textual citation of the habanera motif, evoking *La Soirée dans Grenade.* It is followed by a brief pause. The knell sounds for a last time and gradually fades away in the silence.

Written in Granada in August, 1920, the *Homenaje* to Debussy was given its first performance in Paris on January 24, 1921, at one of the concerts of the Société Musicale Indepéndante in the Salle des Agriculteurs. Mme. Marie-Louise Casadesus performed the work at that time on the harp lute. On December 2, 1922, in the auditorium of the Conservatory it was heard played by the eminent guitarist Emilio Pujol.

Soon after its appearance in *La Revue Musicale,* the critic Émile Vuillermoz reviewed it in *Le Temps* as follows: "A burst of music, perfumed like a garland of flowers. Falla sings his melody on the vibrant and vigorous instrument of the improvisers of his race: the guitar. The rhythm of the Spanish dance admirably suits a dreamer who wishes to lull his sorrow. Manuel de Falla's *Homenaje* is a work of penetrating, irresistible emotion."

In 1920 Manuel de Falla finally settled in Granada with his sister Maria del Carmen, who was to take care of him for the rest of his life. They found a tiny house, a *carmen* on Calle Antequeruela Alta on the slopes of the hill crowned by the Alhambra. The house is fondly remembered by all who had the privilege and the good fortune to visit it. Etymologically, the word *carmen* stems from a pair of Arab homonyms, one meaning "vineyard," the other, "terrace." Actually, a *carmen* in Granada signifies an orchard on a height; a closed garden could not be considered a *carmen* unless it was in a high place dominating the countryside. They are small rustic estates built on the slopes around the Alhambra or the Albaïcin, often hugging the ruins of high walls or towers, and their charm springs from the richness of the vegetation, their fountains, as well as from the spirituality emanating from these places laden with artistic and historical lore.

"M. de Falla," writes one of his first biographers, Jean-Pierre Altermann, "lives in Granada, near the Alhambra in an atmosphere that is voluptuousness itself, enveloped in the most beautiful tranquility. He lives in a setting as enticing and fragile as a dream. Though real, it does not seem real unless it is indeed a fable. . . ."[6] Another friend of Falla, the late critic Émile Vuillermoz, recalls: "Beyond the threshold, several steps lead you to a shaded courtyard full of flowers. On one side of it is the house, tiny but perfectly proportioned; on the other, a delightful terrace overlooking a marvelous panorama: the immense Andalusian plain stretches before you all the way to the horizon. . . . A fountain spills into two basins, one above the other. . . . Beautiful trees lend a delicious freshness to the air; the garden walks are hidden under a rich tapestry of ivy. There are masses of foliage, flowers, birds, and all of these compose a setting full of charm. It is a miniature, private paradise fit for a sage, the abode of a sensitive and pure being."

The Carmen de l'Ave Maria, where Falla lived for about fifteen years and which he left, never to return again, in November 1939, is preserved just as he left it thanks to one of his friends and admirers, the Duchess of Lecera. She maintains the house in a spirit of love and piety and is happy to open it to musicians and Falla admirers. I had the privilege of being received there in September, 1960, and spent some unforgettable hours on the enchanting terrace now presided over by a beautiful bronze bust of Falla made by the sculptor Vicente de los Ríos. The fountains sing, cats roam the lanes as before—Falla loved these silent and faithful friends —and the Sierra Nevada crown the countryside with a dazzling diadem, "the Sierra Nevada, which one glimpses at the end of every street, so close, or so the transparency of the air makes us believe, that one might touch it from the top of the balconies and belvederes."[7] At twilight "the mountain tops, struck by the light, become rose-colored but it is a dazzling, perfect, fabulous rose glazed with silver and shot through with the colors of the rainbow and reflections of opal. . . . Where the rays of the setting sun cannot reach, all is of a blue that rivals the azure of the sky and the sea, of lapis lazuli and sapphire. The contrast between light and shadow makes

[6] J.-P. Altermann, *op. cit.*
[7] Théophile Gautier, *op. cit.*, p. 209.

for a fantastic effect." Then night comes. "Little by little the splendid colors dissolve and melt into half tones of violet; shadows invade the lower ridges, the light withdraws toward the high summits, and the whole plain is enveloped in darkness while the silver diadem of the Sierra still glitters in the serenity of the sky under the farewell kiss of the sun."[8]

No one has better described the setting in which Falla had chosen to live. But what impression did the interior of the house make on his visitors?

A staircase with an iron railing leads to "white rooms with black furniture, rooms adorned with choice engravings, and taffeta-cloth banners hanging from ancient ironwork," wrote Roland-Manuel after visiting Falla in 1925.[9] The total effect was "a harmony without ostentation, a simplicity full of freshness, an air of voluptuousness and severity, all of which sums up the proud grace of Andalusia."

The arrangement is no longer the same because Falla, who was only a tenant of the house, had his furniture taken away before his departure. But the Duchess of Lecera refurnished it in the Spanish style, in which baroque is blended with a monastic severity. Felicitously arranged mementos, books, and portraits evoke the memory of the great composer. Another bust, executed by the sculptor Juan Cristóbal in 1927, so strikingly resembles its subject, with its severe lines, that one cannot contemplate it without being deeply stirred.

Nearby, at the campo de los Mártires, St. John of the Cross, the sandaled Carmelite who authored *The Living Flame of Love* and *Spiritual Canticle,* lived for seven years. Inflamed with mysticism, the saint was a firebrand in the place where lived one who already blazed in the symbolic meaning of his name[10] and in his musician's heart. A hundred yards away, in dramatic contrast, are gardens of voluptuousness, the incomparable Generalife, celebrated by the solitary and contemplative musician-poet. Here are numberless arabesques in stucco, glittering glazed tiles, the fragrance of flowers and

[8] *Ibid.,* pp. 216–17.
[9] *Revue Pleyel,* October, 1925.
[10] *Falla* means firebrand. They are burned in Valencia on the night of the Feast of St. Joseph.

fountains, all the arcane poetry of Moslem gardens whose subtle charm has been grasped only in the music of Manuel de Falla.

Nevertheless, in the course of the first and peaceful years of the sojourn in Granada, the modest Carmen de l'Ave Maria was not always wrapped in meditation. Falla divided his daily life—pleasant and full of a peaceful felicity—between work in the morning and, in the afternoon, the visits of different personalities: artists, foreign travelers, or young musicians eager for some advice from the maestro. Friends came in the evening, gathering on the terrace or around the piano where new works would be played, unless they preferred to recall the memory of the "good old *zarzuelas* of Chueca and Gerónimo Jiménez."[11] Young Federico Garcia Lorca, who already held an important place in Falla's life, as the following chapters will show, was one of the intimates at these *tertulias*. At these parties he undoubtedly read some of his poems from the *Cante Jondo,* "a language of sorcery, in a rhythm of brimstone and blood," written at the composer's instigation, or his descriptions of nearby Albaïcin with its "nooks and crannies and innermost hiding places, which must be explored if one really wants to know the town."[12] And when fatigue or his frequent bouts of illness confined Falla to his room, the famous guitarist Angel Barios, a very dear friend, would come and play for him.

It is in this rarified, delicate atmosphere, an atmosphere meant for creativity, that Falla completed *Master Peter's Puppet Show*. It was to bring Falla's already immense reputation to its peak.

[11] Pahissa, *op. cit.*, p. 154.
[12] M. Pomes, *op. cit.*, p. 150.

CHAPTER IX / *El Retablo de Maese Pedro* (Master Peter's Puppet Show)

At the beginning of 1919, while he was living in Madrid, Manuel de Falla received a commission from the Princess Edmond de Polignac to write an opera for marionettes, which she proposed to stage at her residence in Paris. The same offer was made to Stravinsky and Erik Satie, and to it we owe the former's *Renard,* which was staged by Diaghilev's Ballet Russe, and the latter's *Socrates,* which was performed in concert.

Falla showed an immediate interest in this new prospect, more from an artistic than financial standpoint. He was quite aware that the Princess spent her enormous fortune to enhance her private reputation rather than to be the patroness of the arts she claimed to be. Doubtless the memory of the marionette theater which was the delight of his childhood also contributed to Falla's decision to accept the offer.

After searching for a long time for a theme on which to build the work, it suddenly struck him that an ideal subject would be the scene of the *titeres* (marionettes) of Maese Pedro's puppet show in chapters twenty-five and thirty-six of *The Ingenious Knight Don Quixote de la Mancha,* Part II, by Miguel de Cervantes. He decided to write his own libretto, selecting this or that fragment, deleting this or that passage, all from the original text. With a background of such evocative power, the music perforce drew its inspiration from the age of Cervantes, if not borrowing from it completely.

A total change of style was absolutely necessary. The composer of *El Amor Brujo,* who had just settled in Andalusia, a stone's throw from the *cantaores, tocadores,* and *bailadoras* of the Sacro Monte, for whom he was preparing the *Cante Jondo* competition, did not hesitate to pull back, in time and space, the frontiers of his musical kingdom, even farther than he had for *The Three-Cornered Hat.*

First of all, in addition to the *canto llano,* the plain song, ancestral source of Spanish musical tradition and base of its recitative, and to the *pregones* (cries), which will be discussed later, Falla drew on historical folklore for primary sources that were most in keeping with the situation on the stage. The ancient religious themes of the national heritage, as much Moslem and Mosarabic as Gregorian, were a valuable aid to him, quite as much as the folklore still in existence in different parts of Spain—in austere Castile, for example. Naturally, the use of melodic features, rhythms, and modes stemming from the time of Cervantes required a harmonic and instrumental treatment very different from those of the Andalusian *melos* he had employed up to then and which had been destined particularly for the ballet. In this new project Falla was to employ a technical discipline that was the mark of a distinguished and brilliant intelligence.

This unexpected aspect of the art of Manuel de Falla occasioned admiration and surprise at the premiere of *Master Peter's Puppet Show*. It still similarly affects those who listen to or analyze it today. The mystery perhaps may be explained by a fact not generally known, however, which did not escape Garcia Matos. According to the learned critic, the story is as follows:[1]

When Falla was still a student at the Madrid Conservatory, he had the opportunity in 1905 to witness the sumptuous festivals in the capital commemorating the three hundredth anniversary of the publication of *Don Quixote*. He probably attended some of the lectures that were delivered at the Ateneo by many professors, writers, composers, and musicologists. The prestigious music critic of that time, Cecilio de Roda, discussed on two occasions a book entitled *The Musical Instruments, The Dances, and the Songs of Quixote*. Even if Falla could not have heard them all, the book enabled him to become familiar with the subjects, one of which related precisely to the scene of the puppet show. The lectures were accompanied by concerts featuring music of that time, and the examples studied were also found in the book. At first glance it seemed advantageous to the lecturer to choose his musical program from the immense treasure left by the *vihuelistas* of the fifteenth and sixteenth centuries, work of prodigious interest, of universal significance, revealing a culture that has

[1] "Folklore en Falla," II, Música, *op. cit.*

never been surpassed and barely equaled elsewhere. But the pavanes, fantasias, and galliards written for performance at the court reflected the Italian style then in vogue more than the Spanish. Moreover, the events of *Don Quixote* borrowed more from peasant life than from courtly life, particularly in the scene in question. After finding nothing typically national in character among the *vihuelistas,* nothing that reflected the "freshness, the perfume of the people," Roda turned to one of the most ancient masters of the guitar, Gaspar Sanz.[2] His instructions[3] contain not only the advice to study the guitar "according to the customs of one's province," but also works of "the purest national character, richly varied," with their cadences, turns, and designs almost like those of present-day Andalusian music. Moreover, Sanz exhibits a freedom and a boldness both completely new and very close to the folk imagination.[4]

Roda also referred to the numerous court *cancioneros* (*cancionero de palacio, cancionero de la biblioteca colombina y tonos antiguos y castellanos* of the Medinaceli library), asserting that the most authentic documents are contained in the treatise by Salinas, *De Musica libri septem* (Salmantico, 1575), where he treats of musical scansion and of religious and Castilian songs. According to Garcia Matos, "there is no doubt that at the time he was composing *Master Peter's Puppet Show* Falla recalled these judgments and appraisals and they guided him in the choice of themes that would be in keeping with the poetic meaning of his work. In effect, despite what one might expect and contrary to what some had already thought and asserted, the composer did not employ a single note drawn from the admirable canon of the *vihuelistas,* thus disdaining the easy sources available in the many examples collected by Barbieri, Count de Morphi, and Pedrell. Accepting Roda's dictate, he turned to the treatise written by Salinas and to the guitar pieces in Gaspar Sanz's *Instrucción de Música.*

"In his use of liturgical melody, he follows the famous critic when he underlines the close relation existing between religious

[2] b.?—d. Madrid, 1710.
[3] *Instrucción de música sobre la guitarra española y metodo desde sus primeros rudimentos hasta tañerla con destreza.* Zaragoza, 1674.
[4] E. Pujol, *La Guitare, op. cit.* p. 2008.

music and that of the people, forms of music which, because of their particular archaic atmosphere, are to a great extent suitable to the medieval period in the play."[5]

He adds, however, that Falla, as a grateful former pupil, likewise leafed through the famous *Cancionero Musical Popular Español* of his beloved teacher Pedrell, as can be easily seen in the quotations used by Garcia Matos himself.

Among the artists and men of letters who visited the *carmen* on Antequeruela Alta, there was a young man who was already considered a child prodigy of poetry, Federico Garcia Lorca. He was born in 1898 in Fuentevaqueros, near Granada. The musician and the poet quickly became close friends, and the friendship grew ever warmer until the terrible tragedy of 1936.[6] From his childhood, Lorca, like Falla, had been staging puppet shows at his parents' country estate. Once cordial relations had been established between them, Falla collaborated with the poet and arranged musical shows based on scores extracted from Pedrell's *Cancionero, autos sacramentales* (one-act dramatic compositions in honor of the Blessed Sacrament), classics, pieces by Albéniz, and, subsequently, even fragments of Stravinsky's *Histoire du Soldat*. He transcribed them for a small orchestra composed of a violin, a clarinet, a lute, and a piano "converted into a harpsichord by newspapers inserted between the strings."[7] Marionettes and settings were executed by two artist friends, Hermenegildo Lanz and Manuel Angeles Ortiz. On Falla's recommendation, both were later commissioned by Princess de Polignac to do all the designing for the new work.

Falla set to work with great enthusiasm, wholly in the grip of the new idea. In addition to the aforementioned classic sources, he decided to use *pregones,* the street-cries which he had known since childhood, even in Madrid, and which he had already employed in *La Vida Breve.* The declaiming of the professional storyteller, sur-

---

[5] It should also be said here that while recalling Roda's views, Garcia Matos represses his desire "to discuss some of their questionable extremes." (*Op. cit.* p. 5.)

[6] Lorca, a friend of Antonio Machado, brother-in-law of the Socialist mayor of Granada, Montesino, was shot by the Nationalists in 1936, not far from the Alhambra.

[7] Pahissa, *op. cit.,* p. 116.

rounded by a band of *muchachos* as he tells terrifying tales of the bandits of the sierras, was to be that of the *trujamán,* the narrator of *The Puppet Show.*

Garcia Matos states that "with its modal structure [Falla's *pregon*] is based on the first three verses of a very rare kind of Andalusian *saeta.*" He is almost certain that the *pregon* used in *The Puppet Show* comes directly from the people. A great number of *pregones* of Andalusia are only imitations or variants or fragments of folk songs. Doubtless this musical hawking is doomed to disappear. The variations that the *pregonero* (vendor), introduces into the melody differ according to what he has to sell. We can logically conjecture that the *pregon* of *The Puppet Show* similarly varies the original folklore melody, which is itself a variant of the *saeta.*[8]

The Stage Décor

The staging of *Master Peter's Puppet Show* requires two stage levels and two groups of marionettes. The first level contains the spectators, large-sized marionettes watching a performance in a *venta* (an out-of-the-way inn) of *The Rescue of Melisendra.* The second level is the stage for the tiny marionettes to whom the action has been assigned. The spectators include Don Quixote and Sancho Panza, a student, a page, a lancer, a halberdier, and, of course, Peter, the puppet showman, and his assistant, the *trujamán.* Only Don Quixote, Master Peter, and the narrator have singing roles; the others mime the action that Cervantes extracted from the old Castilian ballad *Don Gayferos y Melisendra.*

The tiny marionettes represent Charlemagne, Don Gayferos, Don Roldán, King Marsilio, Melisendra, the enamoured Moor, plus heralds, lords and guards of Charlemagne's court, the chief of the guard, soldiers of King Marsilio, executioners, and Moors.

Following Cervantes, Falla gives minute details concerning the appearance and bearing of the characters, as well as his own notations about vocal execution and the composition of the orchestra. These are found at the beginning of the score.

The idea of using the harpsichord, "whose employ," ac-

---

[8] Garcia Matos: *Folklore en Falla, op. cit.,* pp. 7–9.

cording to Darius Milhaud, "had been lost since the eighteenth century and whose revival constitutes a veritable novelty," came after a trip that Falla took to Toledo for Holy Week. He went to visit Don Angel Vegue y Goldric, a professor at the university who had an important collection of ancient instruments, among them a harpsichord in excellent condition. The particular character of its sound suggested to Falla that he should include it in an orchestra meant to recreate an archaic atmosphere. Milhaud observed: "The harpsichord alternately clinks and warbles and allows for a variety of which M. de Falla has made good use." It should also be added that he had at his disposal the celebrated and extraordinary Wanda Landowska.

The stage action, preceded by *Master Peter's Symphony,* is divided into six scenes, as follows:

> Charlemagne's Court
> Melisendra
> The Punishment of the Moor
> The Pyrenees
> The Flight
> The Pursuit

It ends with Don Quixote's exploit and song of glory.

Musical Analysis[9]

A sourish-sounding fanfare of a rustic character—the Franco-Spanish composer Maurice Ohana claims it is a Galician chant—prefaces the performance on stage; there's a drawn-out call of the oboe on three notes revolving around the dominant of F, borrowing from both the major and minor thirds and sustained by the harmonics of the strings (p. 1), the alternated rhythm of the kettledrum, and a muffled drum. Writes Garcia Matos: "It is difficult to decide whether this sprightly motif is original or stems from the transformation of a theme of traditional root." It might possibly be compared to a *tempo de bolero* mentioned by Isidoro Hernández.[10]

[9] The indications of pages and numbers correspond to those of the miniature orchestral score, published by Chester, London, 1924.

[10] I. Hernández, *Tradiciones Populares Andaluzas.* Madrid, n.d.

At any rate, the desire to imitate the *gaïta,* the old bagpipe of the strolling storytellers, is clearly evident.

The curtain rises; the puppet stage appears, glittering in the candlelight. Master Peter, ringing a bell, is inviting the people to watch the show (p. 3), to a chant in the style of a *pregon* which Garcia Matos compares to two examples of *saetas* mentioned by A. Aguilar y Tejera[11] and by Pedrell in the first volume of his *Cancionero.* This call can be compared to the proclamation which the rural constable beats out on his drum to announce an exceptional event in the village.

The spectators lose no time in coming. Among them are Don Quixote and Sancho Panza. All admire the beauty of the puppet stage, which they examine with great curiosity. Each one makes himself as comfortable as possible, and Don Quixote sits next to the stage, stretching his long legs. Meanwhile we hear *Master Peter's Symphony,* which serves as an introduction. In this piece Falla ingeniously amalgamates different traditional motifs, in which Garcia Matos discerns the exterior lines of a *gallarda* cited in the *Instrucción de Música* by Gaspar Sanz[12] and transcribed by Pedrell in his *Cancionero.*[13] We can also discern in it the pace of a *folia* by Sanz, which was referred to by Cecilio de Roda in one of his lectures.

Independently of the color of the keys of C and of F, which are often employed simultaneously (not for a polymodal purpose but in an application of Falla's favorite procedure—the utilizing of natural harmonics of chords), we observe the extreme freedom of the scoring of the instrumental groups, treated according to the practices of chamber music, in which each one follows its particular line. After the rhythmic figures of the first three bars—strings, harpsichord, kettledrums, horns, bassoon—and the trumpet calls, a very simple theme is heard on the horns. It is commented upon by the harpsichord, which is joined by the oboes (p. 4, No. 4). Here it is of interest to point out the modifications that Falla applies to certain notes assigned tonal functions: he employs the natural leading tone

[11] A. Aguilar y Tejera, *Saetas.* Madrid, n.d.
[12] Sanz, *op. cit.*
[13] Pedrell, *op. cit.* I, p. 122.

or lowers it, thus producing delightful "false relations" of the octave; likewise he raises the subdominant of C, while avoiding the modulation in G.

Suddenly we hear a brief and delightful motif assigned to the flute—*música lejana* (distant music), just as Cervantes calls for in his text. At the same time the harpsichord joyously improvises in very different tonalities, after which we are quite surprised to find ourselves in C major! Thereupon, Master Peter calls for silence (p. 15, No. 9). This new *pregon* is comparable to the call of a hawker of the Caceres region who announced his arrival to his clientele thus:

The rustic fanfare still resounds, but this time each instrument plays on its own in a joyful polytonal fashion, and the narrator, "shouting and reinforcing his voice," announces and comments upon the "true story" of the rescue of Melisendra. It tells how Don Gayferos frees his wife, Melisendra, a captive of the Moors in the city of Sansueña (now Zaragoza) (p. 15, No. 11).

This recital, without accompaniment, remains within the span of a minor third. The boy narrator's subsequent comments will be treated in the same way, and we observe here a relation between this form of recitative and the Gregorian chant below:

We can also consider these recitations as imitations of folklorist *pregones,* in accord with a reference by the composer to the voice of the *muchacho pregonero.* This cry, "rude, twangy, forced, stripped of all lyrical inflection," possesses a distinct folk character. In Spain, as elsewhere, there are many examples of such public announcements, and they offer frequent analogies with the Gregorian chant. Falla was aware of this and knew how to apply the "cries" to the appropriate situations.

The music critic G. J. Aubry in his analytical article on *The Puppet Show*[14] hesitates midway between the attribution of liturgical or folk origin to this section. He notes that the accents fall heavily on the first syllable of the phrase (or part of a phrase) regardless of the regular tonic accent or of the syntax, changes which are one among the most expressive kinds of license in Spanish folk poetry.

After announcing the events to come, the narrator states that Don Gayferos has been living in idleness and frivolity at Charlemagne's court. This the narrator does through the medieval *tonada* "He's playing at the table . . ." (p. 16, No. 13), which he sings in a natural voice and in which we recognize a kinship with a Gregorian formula of the first key. The meter employed is frequently found in folk songs cited in the treatise by Salinas.

The first scene of the play within a play takes place at the court of Charlemagne. The narrator, interrupted by a fanfare, resumes his recitative and describes how Emperor Charlemagne, putative father of Melisendra, scolds his son-in-law for playing backgammon with Don Roldán instead of fighting to reconquer his bride. Stung to the quick, Don Gayferos wants to borrow Don Roldán's good sword Durindana. Don Roldán refuses; however, he offers to accompany his friend, but Don Gayferos, with true Castilian pride, wants to be Melisendra's only savior. To the accompaniment of the motif of the preceding chant (p. 18, No. 17), the narrator describes his departure.

The heralds sound the horn, there is a roll of drums, and then Charlemagne enters (p. 19, No. 19) to the rhythm of a *gallarda—moderato e pomposo*—which is shared by three motifs presented in their original form. Garcia Matos has recognized the first one among the examples found in Gaspar Sanz's *Instrucción* and also cited in one of Roda's lectures. The *gallarda,* like the pavane, suits solemn and measured movements and perfectly fits an imperial en-

---

[14] G. J. Aubry, *"El Retablo," The Chesterian,* October, 1923.

try. A second motif follows; it is expressed in thirds by the two oboes (p. 20, No. 20). This time it involves a canticle in the key of C extracted from the famous book *Cantigas de Santa Maria del Rey Alfonso el Sabio,* which is preserved in the Escorial.

The third theme is a recall of the *gallarda* outlined by the horns in the introductory symphony. Here it is developed and lightly varied by the harpsichord (p. 21, No. 21), followed by a conclusion on the initial fanfare of the trumpet "such as is heard in Cádiz during Holy Week."[15]

In the second scene the narrator tells the spectators that the lady who is about to appear on the balcony of the Tower of Homage in the Alcazar of Zaragoza is the beauteous Melisendra (p. 25, No. 26). Sadly she gazes toward the distant horizon beyond which lies France, and she despairs at her husband's forgetfulness. A Moor who is observing her approaches her stealthily and gives her a kiss full on the lips (p. 26, line 4). The offended beauty is plunged into a state of deeper despair. The Moorish king, Marsilio, himself in love with Melisendra, is furious; he has witnessed the act of sacrilege and he orders the guards to seize the audacious Moor.

To portray the melancholy of the captive, nothing seemed so apt as Salinas' celebrated ballad:

> *Retraide está la Infanta*
> *Bien así como quería.*

It is found in Pedrell's *Cancionero.*[16] According to the latter, it also belongs to several other *cancioneros* and ancient *tonadas* (tunes) of profane ballads.

The brief scene—*molto lento e sostenuto*—subtly and magically evokes an instrumental color contemporaneous with the Knight of the Doleful Countenance. The muted trumpet presents for the first time the delightful song in the form of antecedent, taken up again by the flute. The response belongs to the first violin (p. 28, No. 31). The same section is found later, with trumpet and English horn (p. 29, No. 32), separated from the first statement by a varia-

---

[15] G. J. Aubry, *El Retablo, art. cit.*
[16] F. Pedrell, *Cancionero, op. cit.,* p. 21, No. 25.

tion in the horn (p. 28, measure 5). The accompaniment, rhythmically refined in the extreme underneath the apparent bareness, is shared between divided strings, pizzicatti and *con sordini,* some chords of the harp lute, and a light clarinet counterpoint. This delightful scene has great charm. Listening to it, we see, as Falla was to do one day as he thought of Wanda Landowska, "the face of Isabella of Parma in the Tocador de la Reina of the Arab palace, playing on her spinet the *Variations on the Song of the Knight* by Félix-Antoine de Cabezón."[17]

At the moment when the orchestra seems about to fade into imperceptible sonorities, furious chromatics rise fortissimo from the flute (p. 31, No. 34). The ballad of the Infanta resounds anew, but this time in the horns, violently transformed, in thirty-second and sixty-fourth notes (p. 32, No. 35). The enamoured Moor has stolen a kiss from the princess, and the punishment is not long in coming. At the piercing order of the trumpet (p. 32, No. 36, measure 4), the narrator describes how King Marsilio's sentence is quickly carried out (p. 33, No. 37), "for with Moors no proof is required, as with us." This calls forth Don Quixote's first reprimand (No. 38); he orders the boy to adhere to the truth of the story and not to lose himself in useless reflections. At this point Master Peter pushes his head out from behind the stage: "Stick to your plain-song (*canto llano*), boy! Don't try any counterpoint melodies, for they only create confusion," he counsels ironically, in order to please the knight, who is so prone to emphasis and rhetoric (p. 34, No. 39).

Don Quixote's declamatory tone is solemn. Master Peter's is equally pompous, recalling the style of a seguidilla popular in the Mancha.

The third scene is based on a popular children's song shared by several provinces. Falla surely first heard it from street urchins. A variant exists in a Madrid roundelay, another in a *can-*

---

[17] M. de Falla, *"Wanda Landowska à Grenade,"* La Revue Musicale, February 1, 1923. The Tocador de la Reina, built atop the Torre del Peinador, one of the towers of the Alhambra's ramparts "where the breeze wafted the fragrances of the Generalife to the dreamy sultanas of the Arab palace." (Théophile Gautier).

cionero of Santander.[18] G. J. Aubry places it in Castile but also recognizes "an Arab atmosphere" in it.[19]

On this theme Falla constructed a march for the entrance of the Moor, who has been sentenced to be bastinadoed, of the herald who reads the sentence, and of the fierce executioners and soldiers who accompany him. The tonality is simple, the rhythm heavily accented. An Oriental atmosphere is created by the percussion instruments—rattle, drum, kettledrums—and by the twanging of the English horn. Ingenious superpositions produce a polytonal effect which is merely the consequence of Falla's customary use of harmonics (p. 38, No. 44).

This apparent disorder produces the confused sounds of a crowd drawn by the spectacle. Blows rain upon the back of the wretched Moor. They are punctuated by the chords of the woodwinds, rapid and blunt. At regular intervals a violent sforzando in the treble bursts forth like a cry of pain (p. 38, Nos. 44 to 47). Meanwhile, the song intervenes in the manner of an *estribillo* (a refrain).

The condemned man falls to the ground. The executioner and soldiers drag him away, leaving slowly in a procession on the above-mentioned motif (p. 41, No. 47), stated now in a simple 2/4 rhythm, barely perceptible in the lower strings, harpsichord, and the kettledrum.

A horn sounds (p. 42, No. 48). The boy announces: "You will see Don Gayferos galloping along the road of the city of Sansueña!"

In the fourth scene the rhythm changes to 3/4 and is exactly defined, suggesting a horse's gallop. Don Gayferos appears and disappears on the slope of a mountain, as if he were following a spiral road. He is wearing a Gascon cape and is holding a hunting horn which he blows from time to time. Other horns echo from the distance, indicating responses from the sentries of the castles that he comes upon en route. The harmonic features of the seguidilla murciana[20] are outlined through the orchestral texture with its sup-

[18] S. Cordova y Ona, *Cancionero Popular de la Provincia de Santander.* Santander, 1948.
[19] G. J. Aubry, *El Retablo, art. cit.*
[20] Compare with the second of the *Seven Songs, Seguidilla Murciana.*

ports on the dominant, its chromatic accents, its ternary and binary rhythmic blends, and its marked differences of intensity. The heroic blast of a trumpet is heard at times in the key of B flat, after which it gradually diminishes on a long sustained note. The curtain falls (p. 54, No. 57). Only the beats are persistently marked in the subdued, sustained notes of the violins and violas, while the echo of a resounding call floats in the distance.

The narrator announces before the beginning of the fifth scene (p. 54, No. 57) that "the beauteous Melisendra" is going to lean over the balcony of the tower and tell the knight, whom she does not recognize as her husband (p. 56, No. 59): "If to France you go, Sir Knight, ask for Don Gayferos." The boy sings this brief ballad on Salinas' melodic formula, which had already been pointed up in *Master Peter's Symphony*. Then he continues his *pregon* in the previous rhythmic pattern effect in order to relate (p. 57, No. 60) how Gayferos reveals his identity and how Melisendra hastily descends from the balcony and gets into the saddle behind her husband. They quickly gallop off along the road leading to Paris.

The curtain rises and the scene unfolds. It is illustrated by one of the most subtle and stirring pages of the score (p. 59, No. 62). The harpsichord, lightly colored with several muted strings, ushers in the scene—*andante molto sostenuto*—with rich arpeggios in the Hypodorian mode. Then we hear the violin solo without accompaniment (No. 63); it is a marvelous melody in Gregorian style of the first mode transposed in F. The melody is original, although Garcia Matos points out a kinship with a fragment of the *Tuba mirum.*

Tú..ba mírum..   spar:..gens só num

It is difficult to decide here whether or not this is a fortuitous resemblance or whether Falla aimed to imply a warning of the fate threatening the couple. A rapid passage on the flute simulates their departure (p. 61, No. 66, measure 4), accompanied by the good wishes of the narrator. "Go in peace, O true lovers! May the eyes of your friends and relatives rest upon you and rejoice in your days of peace to come" (p. 62, No. 67). The boy has thus embellished his text, and Master Peter, again putting his head above the stage, reminds him that "all affectation is bad." His ill humor is expressed by some furious trills in the bass of the woodwinds (p. 68, No. 70).

During this explanation the fugitives have rapidly arrived in the Pyrenees (p. 62, No. 67)—*allegretto vivace*. The pace is quickened, as differences of accents and intensity underline the wanderings. The boy resumes his narration while the scolding trills of his master continue to be heard. But he again indulges in a flight of fancy, proclaiming that King Marsilio, apprized of Melisendra's flight, orders "the bells of the towers of all the mosques to sound the alarm" (p. 71, No. 72). This is a serious error in terminology, which makes Don Quixote spring to his feet and assert that the Moors do not use "bells, but kettledrums and flageolets!" (p. 73, Nos. 73 to 74). In fact, the instrumentation ironically accentuates the boy's mistake by the *quasi campana* effects (p. 71, No. 72). Master Peter intervenes again and bids Don Quixote to excuse the youth and inexperience of his fledgling assistant. "You speak truly," Don Quixote admits. "Continue, lad!" orders the master (p. 76, No. 75), and the boy resumes his narration.

"Behold," he recites, introducing the sixth and last scene, "how many splendid knights are leaving the city in pursuit of the Catholic lovers! Listen to the flageolets, the blare of trumpets, and to the roll of drums and tabor!"

The orchestral score, with an extreme artfulness, imitates these martial sonorities and asserts them in *ostinato* rhythms. Nevertheless, the intensity is accomplished not so much by the accumulation of means as by the skill with which they are used. Through this suggestive agitation and the acerbic and agile arabesque of a *raïta*—doubtless a close kin to the *rueda*[21]—modulated by the clarinet and relayed to the oboes, we are surprised to discern in the horn

[21] Arab song.

solo the theme of the song of *El Amor Brujo: Lo mismo que er fuego fatuo.* It is underlined by the dry striking of the xylophone (p. 76, No. 75).

This stroke doubtless is a technical caprice indulged in by the composer: Berber Andalusia appears before us in the swarming of the multitude in arms. Is this a reference to the symbolism linking *The Puppet Show* to *El Amor Brujo,* just as *The Three-Cornered Hat* is linked to *La Vida Breve,* as G. J. Aubry believes, in keeping perhaps with the ideas of the composer himself who was his friend?

"I fear," adds the narrator, "that all those soldiers will overtake the fugitives and bring them back tied to the necks of their horses" (p. 79, No. 76, measure 9).

No sooner has he finished when Don Quixote leaps onto the stage and draws his sword, crying out (p. 81, No. 77): "Halt, base rabble, cease pursuing them or you shall do battle with me!"

The horns blare persistently, the trumpet in the base repeats a motif suggesting imminent menace, and the precipitate chords of the strings serve as prelude (p. 82, No. 78) to the finale (*allegro con brio*).

Here is the apotheosis of Don Quixote, of his greatness, his valor, his exaggerations, which are, in a way, the price that must be paid by a nobility of soul not of this world and far from its incomprehensible, unacceptable baseness. The finale is presented in the form of an immense *copla,* with the different sections separated by a rhythmic motif in 2/4 time inspired by a Catalan folk song *El Desembre Congelat,* which describes the struggle, and resumes as an *estribillo* each time that Don Quixote's attention, which strays easily, focuses again on his enemies. This brief phrase begins with a strongly plunked out G chord (p. 82, No. 78): "Don't run away, villains and vile creatures. One lone knight is going to deal with all of you!" shouts Don Quixote. "Señor Don Quixote," cries Master Peter, "be careful with my property!"

But the knight pays no heed and shouts into the distance: "Here I am, valorous Don Gayferos and highborn Melisendra" (p. 86, No. 81), as we hear the Catalan song entrusted to the woodwinds, a kind of Christmas folksong with a touch of the zarzualesque about it, marked by a bold rhythm and a simple harmonization.

The first section of the *copla* appears in the form of a seguidilla of the Mancha. "The arrogance of your persecutors will not extinguish my flame," shouts the hero. With an even more impassioned fury he rains blows and slashes and falls with all his might on the Moorish marionettes, knocking some to the ground, beheading others, destroying the rest, and endangering even Master Peter who crouches low to save his head. Sancho Panza, appearing on the stage, looks and acts terrified.

While the knight is brandishing his sword, the Catalan motif (in G) is again introduced in the minor tonality of the previous section (p. 91, No. 84). Proudly, he proclaims that he is Don Quixote, captive of the peerless Dulcinea (p. 92, No. 85). An intermediate fragment in portentous and persistent triplets, forte, then fortissimo, suddenly interrupted by a silence pierced by a lamentation from Master Peter ("Sinner that I am!"), prefaces an enthusiastic, ecstatic evocation of Dulcinea. It draws its inspiration from a *canto* of Salinas, discovered by Pedrell in his study of Castilian folklore of the sixteenth century.[22]

Don Quixote sings, his gaze fixed on heaven. The noble cantilena is accompanied by large bold strokes from the strings with some touches from the woodwinds. The contrapuntal notation is delightful and devoid of harshness. But the idea of combat returns to the knight, and the initial motif is heard again. Turning toward the audience, which he confuses with an assembly of "knights and squires, passers-by and travelers, persons on foot and on horse" (p. 97, No. 89), he calls upon them to bear witness to his prowess and sets out to save Don Gayferos and "the beauteous Melisendra." Then he tells about Tirante el Blanco, the invincible Don Beliasis of Greece, and all those whose feats fill the novels of chivalry. This time the recital borrows the profile of a *zarabanda española* in E by Gaspar Sanz, which is found among the examples cited in Cecilio de Roda's first lecture.[23] The rhythm in 6/8 time is accentuated in the manner of numerous Spanish dances. Falla cuts its development

---

[22] Felipe Pedrell, *Etudes sur le Folklore Musical*. Paris, 1909, p. 256.
[23] C. de Roda, *Ilustraciones, op. cit.*

with recapitulations—in the form of the *estribillo*—of the initial march transposed (p. 98, No. 90, measure 3).

From this moment on, Don Quixote's pompous, declamatory style is placed in bold relief by the treatment of the whole orchestra, which is now increased, a method already used in the finale of *The Three-Cornered Hat.* Then, *con grave espressione entusiastica* (p. 102), the knight proclaims, as the orchestra subsides into silence, the good fortune of the century that witnessed the exploits of the valiant Amadis (p. 103, No. 93). The strings accompany—*allegramente*—note against note, in the manner of a chorale.

On a *tempo gagliardo* that is pompous but animated by a paroxysm of martial exaltation (p. 105, No. 95), the orchestra uses some notes from the royal Spanish march (p. 107, No. 96), punctuated by Don Quixote's shouts of "Long live knight-errantry over all living things!" He addresses a final salute to the glories of Spain, while Master Peter, desolate and defeated, contemplates the personification of Charlemagne that he holds in his hand, its head gone one way, its crown another. The key of C still asserts itself in an echo of Sanz's *zarabanda* (p. 108, No. 97), but despite the traditional perfect cadence (p. 109, No. 98), the conclusion returns to the quasi-liturgical symbol which is expressed—*lento ritmico e pesante*—by the appearance of an F sharp and the major chord of D.

Above the last bar of the score we read: "Madrid-Granada, 1919–22." And on the flyleaf of the score the dedication reads as follows:

> This work has been composed as a devout homage to
> the glory of
> Miguel De Cervantes
> and the author dedicates it to
> Madame the Princess Ed. de Polignac

The first performance took place before an invited audience at the residence of the Princess de Polignac on June 25, 1923.[24]

---

[24] The performers were MM. H. Dufranne, Th. Salignac, Manuel Garcia, and Mlle. A. Peris. Orchestra of the Concerts Golschmann under the direction of Vladimir Golschmann. At the harpischord, Mme. Wanda Landowska.

A first playing—a kind of dress rehearsal—had previously been given at the Teatro San Fernando in Seville on March 23, 1923, under the auspices of the Sociedad Sevillana de Conciertos, a branch of the vast cultural organization which put on plays and concerts in the major cities of Spain. This cultural group also presented Manuel de Falla with the opportunity to establish the Orquesta Bética de Cámara (the Betica Chamber Orchestra).

CHAPTER X / La Orquesta Bética de Cámara

When Falla established the Orquesta Bética de Cámara in 1922, his aim was to obtain an orchestral ensemble suitable not only for classic works—from Vivaldi, Bach, Haydn up to Beethoven —but also for contemporary works which, like *Master Peter's Puppet Show,* were written for a reduced orchestra.[1] These works, whose scoring is close to that of chamber music, require first of all, interpreters who are as proficient as soloists. This standard cannot be required when putting together a large orchestra meant for a large auditorium and a large public; the quantity in that case is as necessary as the quality of the musicians. At the time of Vivaldi and Bach, when concerts were heard in salons, it was customary to establish orchestral balance by having an equal number of strings and woodwinds. If one follows that rule in a modern ensemble, the work of the strings must be more intense in order to counterbalance the effect of the others; therefore, individual responsibility will be intensified, each must strive to do his absolute best.

This is how Falla justified his demand that each member of the Orquesta Bética be of soloist quality. It was met; originally all were famous teachers. The first president, chosen by Falla, was the maestro Eduardo Torrès, assisted by Ernesto Halffter. Adolfo Salazar, in an article in *La Revue Musicale,* stresses the singular sonorous effect obtained by this mathematical equality between the strings, woodwinds, and brass.[2] The Orquesta Bética, which ordinarily did not include trombones, was broken down as follows: woodwinds, two horns and two trumpets, four first violins, three seconds, two violas, two cellos, and a double bass, to which were added, when needed, piano, harp, kettledrums, and percussion.

"It is on this orchestral plan, more or less modified in accordance with the requirements of each work," adds Salazar, "that compositions were played, ranging from Monteverdi, Scarlatti, and

[1] A. Sagardia, *op. cit.,* p. 42.
[2] *La Revue Musicale,* Paris, November 1, 1925.

137

Bach, up to Falla, Stravinsky, Malipiero, and the young Spaniards. With its décor and puppets for *Master Peter's Puppet Show,* the Orquesta Bética, under Falla's direction or that of his young pupil Halffter, traveled all over Spain, spreading both classical and modern beauty and awakening in the young musicians of our provinces an idea of orchestral sonorities wholly different from those of the large orchestra."

At the first performance of *Master Peter's Puppet Show* in Seville the singers were Lledó, Segura, and the young Niño R. Redondo, a member of the *Seises* of the Cathedral. Falla directed his work, as he was also to do at the public Paris premiere on November 13, 1923, where it was given as part of one of the Jean Wiener concerts, which featured only modern music. On that occasion, attended by all of the Parisian music world, the roles were interpreted by the same singers who had sung them at the residence of the Princess de Polignac. The performers included members of the Societé Moderne d'Instruments à Vent and soloists from various symphonic groups.

These three performances, Spanish and Parisian, soon followed by many others in Europe, naturally stirred up much interest in the press and the musical world. Many friends of Falla, as well as foreign critics, had come to Seville to attend the *estrena* (premiere), among them J. B. Trend, Schindeler, and G. J. Aubry. Aubry observed that *Master Peter's Puppet Show* was the first attempt "to express in a musical work the spirit, form, lyricism, irony, pathos, and power of this unique story" and that "the enterprise was worthy of Cervantes."[3] Roland-Manuel, in his book on Falla, stresses the perfection and frugality of the style which, in the midst of the influences from the liturgy, from the *romanesca* music of the Middle Ages, and from the court music of the sixteenth and seventeenth centuries, can blend the recital of the story of Melisendra and Don Quixote into an evocation of austere Castile.[4] Henri Collet, a student of Spanish music, writes that the grandeur, the brilliance of Don Quixote's final song recalls Boris Godunov.[5] And B. de

[3] G. J. Aubry, *The Chesterian, op. cit.*
[4] Roland-Manuel, *op. cit.*
[5] H. Collet, *op. cit.*

138

Schloezer proclaims: *"Master Peter's Puppet Show . . .* is not a pastiche but a creation, an innovation in the ancient style, and like a bold master artist of old [Falla] develops it by introducing new harmonic and melodic elements that do not distort it."[6]

From Paris, the Spanish correspondent of *El Sol,* the famous Madrid daily, described the Polignac soirée in a witty report; he noted the distinguished guests who crowded into the salon: Paul Valery, "the poet of the day," clearing a way for himself "with the gestures of a castaway foundering among the waves of feminine shoulders"; Henri de Régnier, "the poet of yesterday, with a drooping moustache and a haughty monocle"; Stravinsky, "a mouse among she-cats"; Picasso, surrounded on all sides; José Maria Sert, the fashionable painter, and others. But among the famous poets, musicians, and painters—the usual court of Princess Edmond de Polignac—the hero of the evening was Manuel de Falla.

Following the first public performance by the Wiener orchestra, the press continued to shower praise on Falla and his work. One could fill a book with the names of people who were content to utter extravagant praise rather than study the work to find the real reasons for its greatness.

Falla also scored a great success in October, 1923, at the Victoria Theatre in Bristol, England, which was holding a week-long festival of one-act operas. Purcell's *Dido and Aeneas* and works of the English composers Napier Miles and Vaughan Williams were also performed. The exacting critic of the *Times* of London wrote that during this whole week "the special note of distinction had come from Spain with *Master Peter's Puppet Show."*

The first Madrid performance of *The Puppet Show* took place on March 28, 1924, at the Philharmonic Society. Pérez Casas conducted the Orquesta Filarmonica with Falla at the harpsichord. Barcelona heard it in 1926, this time under the baton of the composer. In the same year, the International Society of Contemporary Music (S.I.M.C.) included it in the program of its meeting in Zurich and invited Falla to direct it. Salvador de Madariaga came especially from Geneva, where the League of Nations was in session, to attend

[6] *La Revue Musicale,* December 1, 1923.

the performance, at the end of which he presented Falla with a copy of his *Guid al Lector del Quijote* (Reader's Guide to Quixote) with this flattering dedication: "To Manuel de Falla whose *Master Peter's Puppet Show* brings a second immortality to the immortal Don Quixote." Francisco Rodriguez Marin, one of the greatest Quixote scholars, in similarly enthusiastic terms dedicated to Falla a copy of his annotated edition of the novel.

Berlin commissioned the decorator Buffano to make enormous puppets for the performance of the work in that city. Finally, in Paris, in the spring of 1926, the Opéra Comique celebrated Manuel de Falla's fiftieth birthday with a program consisting of *La Vida Breve, El Amor Brujo,* and *Master Peter's Puppet Show.* Zuloaga, the famous painter and a close friend of Falla, was commissioned to design the décor and costumes for these exceptional performances; his brother-in-law Maxime Dethomas made the marionettes, in carved wood. The decision that singers and dummies would replace the large-sized marionettes witnessing the rescue of "the beauteous Melisendra" gave Zuloaga and Falla the amusing idea of joining that audience, the painter appearing garbed as Sancho Panza, the composer as the innkeeper. At the end, P. B. Gheusi, director of the Opéra Comique, gave each one a five-franc note with his compliments and encouraged them to persevere along the path of their new careers!

On March 12 and 15, 1928, to mark Falla's acceptance of the Cross of the Legion of Honor, the Opéra Comique gave the same production with a brilliant cast: Ninon Vallin sang the role of Salud in *La Vida Breve* and the solos in *El Amor Brujo.* Carmen Granados danced in *La Vida Breve,* while the celebrated La Argentina performed in *El Amor Brujo,* for which she devised the choreography. La Argentina was the very personification of Candelas. The stunning impact she made on the audience in the *Ritual Fire Dance* and the numerous triumphs she scored in the role thereafter are still remembered. This performance was under the direction of maestro Albert Wolff.

Among the most notable performances of *Master Peter's Puppet Show*—the order is chronological—must be cited that given in San Sebastian for the inauguration of the Museo de San Telmo.

L'Orféon Donostiarra, which participated in the concert with Juan Gorostidi, first performed several folk songs. Then Falla took the baton and, under his direction, L'Orféon interpreted the *Ave Maria* and *Sanctus* from a mass by Victoria with such flawlessness and such religious fervor that many in the audience were moved to tears. The painter José Maria Sert told Falla: "Today, thanks to you, God has again come down to this earth."

In September of the same year, Venice placed *Master Peter's Puppet Show* on the program of her International Festival of Contemporary Music and invited Falla to direct his work. The guitarist Andrès Segovia, who at that time lived in Geneva, suggested to Falla that they meet in that city and leisurely travel together to Venice by car. Falla was delighted, and along with Dr. José Segura, a professor at the University of Granada, Falla and Segovia now became tourists, stopping in Verona, Vicenza, and Padua before arriving in Venice.

The program of the Festival programmed *Master Peter's Puppet Show* on the same bill as Respighi's *Mary the Egyptian*. This was a source of conflict for the scrupulous and deeply religious Falla. Could a work of the mystic quality of *The Puppet Show* be placed alongside another which dramatized the very sinful early life of the future saint? Only the international acclaim the performance earned could have made his objections disappear. Venice had wisely chosen to use the marionettes that had proved so successful at the Zurich performance and to engage the orchestra of La Scala of Milan. As it was known that Falla already was working on his great poem *Atlántida*, the management of the Maggio Musicale Fiorentino asked him if they might have it for the following year. At that time no one suspected that so many years would pass before the world would hear what was to be Manuel de Falla's last work.

On the return trip the maestro's fragile health—he had been feeling unwell for a long time as a result of the fatigue of the journey, the rehearsals, and various strong emotions—caused a very serious and very painful boil to develop. He had to stop in San Remo to consult a doctor; then he was able to continue the journey. He visited the town of les Baux, whose Dantesque landscape impressed him, and also Arles, where the Rhone reminded him of

Mireille and the poem of his childhood. At Arles the travelers separated, Segovia returning to Switzerland, Falla and Dr. Segura taking the train for Granada. Worn out by the journey and the debilitating effect of the boil, Falla's appearance, not helped by several days' growth of beard, so frightened his companion that the professor wondered if they should stop the journey. But in Barcelona, after both the bandage and his beard were off, wearing a fresh suit of clothes, and back on his native soil, Falla felt much better. When they arrived in Granada, he looked like a different man from the one who had entrained in Arles.

This section on *Master Peter's Puppet Show,* ought to end with the words of the critic Federico Sopeña, who saw a performance sponsored by the Teatro Maria Guerrero in Madrid on October 15, 1941:

"This return to antique forms, which all too often has been only a recourse to obsolete and arbitrary formulas, here produces a marvelous ambiance of poetic abandon. Immense technical knowledge, which often offers only an artificial paradise, here becomes a meaningful method of creating a delicate illusion. The deliberate reduction to a small orchestra . . . gains for *Master Peter's Puppet Show* a thousand new timbres and unique methods of evocation. And, above all else, the work raises the folksong—from the Castilian *romance* to the Valencian song—to a clearly universal form. Never up to now has the secret of its lyric power been discovered. The continual chanting of the narrator, enameled with the sweet cadences of the *romance,* is the most difficult and the most beautiful form that one can imagine for our language. There is only one thing that can explain this success: the unmatched beauty of the soul of Manuel de Falla, who wished to restore to music its melodic integrity, its purity of illusion."[7]

[7] Cited by A. Sagardia in *Manuel de Falla,* pp. 51–52.

When Falla settled in Granada, he became a close friend of young Federico Garcia Lorca. The two men were brought together by, among other things, a common love of music and of marionettes. Lorca, son of a rich landowner, had had the leisure to pursue his studies and, at the same time, to indulge his passion for poetry and music. As a child he was already acquainted with a vast amount of folklore. Later he harmonized some folk songs such as *Le Café de Chinitas* and *Los Cuatro Muleros*. A competent pianist, he worked "with an old romantic teacher who filled him with enthusiasm."[1] In the evening he and the other young artists would meet in a café on the Alameda, at that time a fashionable promenade, where they endlessly discussed music, flamenco, poetry, and, no doubt, politics. One evening they decided to pay a surprise visit to Falla. Don Manuel received them amiably, expressed an interest in their works, especially in their project of a traveling theater, and willingly played some of his compositions for them. This was the beginning of the intimate friendship between the young poet and the famous musician.

Enveloped in that atmosphere of "divine Andalusian grace . . . drawn by instinct toward beauty, rhythm, song, dance, music, toward all that was life, with profound understanding of the life of trees and plants, people and beasts," young Lorca possessed a charm so extraordinary "that all those who had the privilege of being near to him . . . remember it."[2] Falla was certainly not immune to such charms. A profound knowledge and love for the *cante jondo* must have been one of the strongest bonds between them. According to Mathilde Pomès, Lorca composed his *Poema del Cante Jondo* (1921–22) at the suggestion of Manuel de Falla who was organizing a folklore festival with a *cante jondo* competition to be held in Granada in 1922.

The aim of the competition was to restore original purity

---

[1] Claude Couffon, *"A Fuentevaqueros, sur les Pas de Garcia Lorca,"* in *Figaro Littéraire,* December 26, 1953.

[2] Mathilde Pomès, *"Lorca, Poète de la Tradition Profonde,"* in *Federico Garcia Lorca,* p. 148.

to an ancestral patrimony, then threatened with ruin, if not complete extinction. Falla had made an intensive study of the *cante jondo*—which he chose to publish anonymously, apparently in order to avoid becoming the center of attention at the competition. In a note accompanying his study, Falla explains that with the exception of rare *cantaores,* what one now heard of Andalusian song was nothing more than a pathetic shadow of what it had been and of what it ought to be. The solemn, traditional song of the past had degenerated into a ridiculous *flamenquismo* which had adulterated and modernized those essential elements that once constituted its glory, its patent of nobility. "What a horror!" commented Falla. "The sober vocal modulation—the natural inflections of the song produced by the subdivision of the sounds of the scale—has been transformed into ornamental artifice closer to Italian decadence than to the primitive songs of the Orient. The narrow limits of the melodic range in which these songs unfolded have been clumsily amplified. The modal richness of the ancient scales has been replaced by tonal poverty through the preponderant use of only the two modern scales. Metric heaviness deprives the phrase of rhythmic flexibility, which constituted one of its greatest beauties."

To buttress his assertions Falla had studied the *cante jondo* from its beginnings. We recall that the composer and his teacher Pedrell agreed on the historical factors: the Byzantine liturgy, the primitive systems of the Andalusian *cantaores* based on vocal enharmony, the richness of inflections, the absence of metric rhythm—properties which also distinguish the Andalusian Moorish chant. These features are found primarily in the *siguiriya gitana,* in which we discern characteristics stemming from the settling of Gypsy tribes around Granada in the fifteenth century. All these different aspects culminate in the genuine *cante jondo,* whose essential elements Falla elaborates as:

1. Enharmony as a device of modulation.[3]

[3] It is perhaps unnecessary to point out that this is not the passage from one tonality to another in the manner of the system called "classic," but the sliding of the quarter tones, as required on Oriental scales, in a kind of fluctuation that is almost oral.

2. The use of a melodic range not going beyond the limits of the sixth, which includes, of course, the chromatic subdivisions of the nine half tones.

3. The repeated and almost obsessional usage of the same note, frequently accompanied by a higher or lower appoggiatura, a device belonging to formulas of sorcery and enchantment, some of them antedating the formation of spoken language—a distant "sound of the ages that secretly sighs in these raucous, strangled, and plaintive voices!"[4]

4. Although the Gypsy melody is rich in ornaments similar to those of primitive Oriental songs, these ornaments should be employed only in the moments of passion suggested by the text.

5. The calls or cries with which the public animates and excites the *cantaores* and the *tocaores* spring from something similar to the practices of Oriental peoples.

Thus, *polos, martinets,* and *soleares* are all derived from the *siguiriya gitana,* the only authentic flamenco, and are distinct from the group vulgarly called "flamenco": *malagueñas, granadinas, rondeñas, sevillanas,* and *peteneras.*

This division of the *cante* into two groups seems very simplistic and somewhat authoritarian to contemporary exponents of flamenco. For example, the learned Georges Hilaire recognizes the merit of convenience in the designation "flamenco song" for all *cante grande.*[5] (The *cante chico* designates the lower, bastardized forms against which Falla inveighs, although we can appreciate the value of the *pasos dobles, romances,* and the like in some *"zarzuelas* of quality.")

Hilaire also points out the non-Oriental, modern contribution of some *cantaores,* knowledgeable and respected flamenquists who use not only the rigid framework of verse and prosody but also carefully thought out modulating inflections. Even in its highest form, the purest *siguiriya gitana,* we find alterations dating back to the fourteenth century used by singers who modified or reinforced its "original" accents. But is not Falla attacking "creations by default"

[4] J. Mercanton, Preface to *Andalusie* (F. Roiter). Lausanne, 1957.
[5] G. Hilaire, *op. cit.*

rather than these imperceptible and inevitable transformations due to the passage of time?

Numerous studies have appeared since the competition of 1922 and Falla's article. But in a pamphlet, accompanying a series of records, called *Una Historia del Cante Flamenco* Garcia Matos puts everything in question again and in a few paragraphs bluntly dismisses the assertions of his predecessors, including Falla.[6] He first takes issue with the term "flamenco." According to him, it is a slang expression which cropped up "at the time the Gypsies established their closest contacts with the aristocracy of thieves," namely, at the time of Charles III (1759–1788), whose laws influenced the Gypsies to give up their nomadic life and to settle down in the cities. Then, in contrast to Hilaire, when he discusses the origin of the flamenco song (or *jondo*), he claims there is no difference whatsoever between them.

According to him, when the Gypsies arrived in Spain in the middle of the fifteenth century, they sang and danced only *villancicos, romances, seguiriyas, chaconas,* and *zarabandas*. He also states that the term *seguiriya* (or *siguiriya*), like the other above-mentioned Gypsy songs and dances "assuredly would have nothing in common with what we call *cante* and *baile flamenco*." With that statement, he not only contradicts Falla, but himself, because a little later he cites the *siguiriya* in the repertory of his favorite *cantaor,* Manolo Caracol. Reading further, we learn that he "has not succeeded in proving the existence of the *cante* before the eighteenth century." He goes on to say that the first evidence of the flowering of flamenco was gathered by Don Antonio Machado Alvarez in his *Colección de Cantes Flamencos* (Seville, 1881) and that Don Antonio owed his information to the old *cantaores* who were his friends. From them, he learned about a certain Tio Luis el de la Juliana who was the "king of the *cantaores* around the last third of the eighteenth century and who sang *polos* and *canas* as well as *seguiriyas gitanas,* and indeed *livianas* and *tonás*" . . . all of which tells us nothing about the origin of *cantes*.

In the eighteenth century, in order to earn a livelihood with-

[6] Voga, HH. 1023–24, Hispavox.

out having to do the manual work they detested, the Gypsies sang and danced for money. The cafés *cantantes* where they performed flourished throughout the nineteenth century. To please their audiences, "the Gypsies used all their powers of improvisation and originality in performing the songs they had heard in the cities and earlier, when they were vagabonds, in the country: *tonadas* (*tonás*), *seguiriyas, polos,* and *romances* (ballads) which they called *corridas* or *corridos.* The songs gradually acquired subtle shadings; the special genius and temperament of the Gypsies did indeed add something new to the melodic elements and characteristics derived from the songs' traditional Hispanic origin. Doubtless there were more and more embellishments as the number of *cantaores* increased and their ambition to surpass each other drove them to do whatever would attract the most notice—a phenomenon also frequently observed in our day."

Since the origin of the *cante* goes much farther back than the *cantaores,* the learned investigations of Garcia Matos in no way destroy the validity of these conducted by Falla, Pedrell, and others —including Garcia Matos himself—when they traced this more remote origin. Thus, the *jondo* competition of 1922 simply aimed to restore the variant and modifications inevitable with the passage of time to their true and proper place as innovations.

After studying the roots of the authentic national song, Falla studied its influence on European music. We have seen that it affected Russian music. The Russians, it is true, like the Spaniards, have a few drops of Gypsy blood in their veins. "What was Mikhail Ivanovich Glinka looking for," exclaimed Pedrell "when he roamed all by himself through the quarter of Avapiès or along the Calle de las Sierpes?[7] That very same thing which he sought in the Albaïcin of Granada, where he sat enraptured for hours listening to the guitar of the famous Francisco Rodgriguez Murciano, stubbornly and unsuccessfully trying to translate the essence of a fiery musical imagination, the flow of a torrent of rhythms, forms, and inventions which defy any graphic notation." The Spanish influence was to persist in Russia; Falla recalls that Igor Stravinsky, when he visited

[7] A street in Seville.

Andalusia, was "deeply impressed by the beauty of our songs and our rhythms, and made known his intention of using them as an inspiration for one of his compositions." This intention seems to have been carried out only in the *Espagnola* of the *Five Easy Pieces for Piano* in 1917, written a year after the Russian journeyed to Madrid to meet Diaghilev.

As for France, Falla notes musical affinities, a return to the modes of the past, as we have already remarked in connection with Debussy, or the ties of race as in the case of Ravel. (Falla published his studies of these two French masters in two important articles that appeared in *La Revue Musicale*.[8] He concludes with some reflections on the very important role played by the guitar in the influence or inspiration that foreigners receive from two well-defined effects: (1) the exterior or immediately perceptible rhythm and (2) the purely harmonic-tonal value. By virtue of its easily assimilated cadential formulas, for a long time the first was often utilized whereas, until fairly recently, the value of the latter was barely recognized by composers, except for Domenico Scarlatti. The Russians were the first to grasp its value, albeit on a wholly superficial, ornamental level. On the other hand, Debussy's "sonorous fabric" greatly resembles the *"jondo* touch" and found immediate and brilliant application in Albéniz's *Ibéria*.[9] But here we must observe that chronology is in disagreement with Falla. The first selections from Albéniz' masterpiece appeared in 1906. In fact Debussy was familiar with it when he was working on his *Ibéria for* orchestra; and he celebrated the work of his Spanish colleague in his articles. Moreover, Debussy's composition had not yet been played or published when, in 1909, the fourth part of *Ibéria* by Albéniz appeared. Actually, Debussy's influence in Spain began with Falla himself.

For Falla, the guitaresque polyphony unconsciously produced by performers represents one of the marvels of "natural art." He asserts that "our instrumentalists of the fifteenth century probably were the first who harmonically accompanied the vocal or instrumental melody," especially in Castile.

---

[8] *La Revue Musicale,* December, 1920, and March, 1939.
[9] Leon Vallas, *Debussy et Son Temps.* Paris, 1958, p. 339.

Here we must explain the distinction between the Moorish guitar and the Latin guitar. Pedrell, in his *Organografía Musical Antigua Española,* states that the Moorish guitar, which took root in Algeria and Morocco under the name of *kitra* (*khitara* = *guitarra*), requires the player to pinch the string. On the other hand, the original style of the Castilian guitar is the *rasgueado* (strumming).

This explains why the Moorish instrument was employed melodically and its Latin-Spanish counterpart harmonically. Some call these harmonizations barbaric chords, but Falla, concluding his article, hails them as "a marvelous revelation of sound possibilities that no one ever thought of before."

The competition was open to *cantaores* of both sexes, but paid professionals who appeared in public or private recitals were excluded. The word *cantaor* has no exact English equivalent, but Hilaire's definition explains[10] that the "*cantaor* is not at all a 'singer' in the vocal sense, that is to say, as it is understood in Castilian, a *cantarin* or a *cantante* (a male or female singer). Nor is he a *cantador,* a traditional Andalusian folksinger. It would be more accurate to call him a *chantre* (church singer) because of both the ritual and the esoteric nature of his art. . . . The *cantaor famoso* is one whose reputation for virtuosity and authenticity has been duly established by devotees who themselves are eminent specialists: the *aficionados.* The objective does not mean merely famous."

The note at the end of the contest's list of rules confirms this distinction between the *cantante* and the *cantaor:* "the first is a singer in a theater or concert hall and cannot bestow on himself the title of the second."

After rigorous preliminary elimination the jury selected the *cantaores* and *tocaores* (the guitarists) entitled to take part in the final contest, which took place amid great pomp and ceremony on the night of June 13, 1922—the feast of Corpus Christi—in the Plaza San Nicolás (Albaïcin), which had been splendidly decorated by Angeles Ortiz, Lorca's friend, and one of the painters of the décor of *Master Peter's Puppet Show.* The plaza itself affords an ineffably beautiful view of the Alhambra.

[10] G. Hilaire, *op. cit.*

149

The years that followed Falla's settling in Granada were years of happiness and fulfillment. Shortly after the competition, he spent some time in Seville with Garcia Lorca. Here he became a friend of the cellist Segismundo Romero. It was then that the idea of founding the Orquesta Bética de Cámara took shape, as well as the decision to entrust to it the first concert performance of *Master Peter's Puppet Show*. Pahissa also mentions another journey to Italy, in May, 1923, in response to an invitation from the well-known American patroness of the arts, Mrs. Coolidge, but it seems improbable that Falla would have left Paris when *Master Peter's Puppet Show* was in intensive rehearsal for its premiere in the salon of Princess de Polignac just to establish relations, however useful, with the rich American lady and to attend a concert of the American Academy of Rome. There may be some confusion about the dates. Whenever it was, Pahissa relates how the composer, overwhelmed by his first visit to the Vatican and, of course, to the Sistine Chapel, forgot that he had been invited to lunch with Mrs. Coolidge and then to visit Ostia with her. He arrived in time for dessert, and the lady, accustomed to Northern punctuality and above all to instant satisfaction of her slightest whim, did not conceal her keen displeasure. No commission was offered to Falla, at least at that time.

During his stay in Rome, Falla met Malipiero, Casella, and Rieti, among other Italian composers. He explored the surrounding districts: Tivoli's waterfalls and the Villa d'Este, at that time almost in ruins, seemed melancholy places to him. But Frascati delighted him, and he took up lodging there in a *pensione* near his friend Santiago Rusiñol, the painter of abandoned gardens. Here he began the arrangement for piano and voice of the score of *Master Peter's Puppet Show*. His habits of keeping to himself and of working far into the night aroused the suspicions of the Fascist authorities, who asked him to furnish explanations for his peculiar way of life at the police station. He was received "with great amiability," and when he identified himself, the apologies were profound. Falla then returned to Paris, "slightly ill," according to Pahissa.

Falla's poor health was certainly one of his great concerns throughout his adult life. That he was hospitalized in Paris in 1912 has already been noted. His health worsened again in 1915–16, and he spent several months in a sanitarium in Córdoba. He was suffering from a nervous depression, which may have been caused by the headaches that constantly afflicted him. According to Campodonico, certain Gypsy beliefs "regarding the evil powers of light" made a deep impression on Falla. On the other hand, he sought help and consolation in a strict practice of his religion, which is hardly in agreement with Gypsy sorceries! According to the same biographer, the years between 1926 and 1928 were punctuated by periods of illness "more or less of a nervous character."[11] This has also been confirmed by several old friends of Falla. But these years were nonetheless full of successful performances in many cities, as has already been outlined.

[11] *Manuel de Falla.* Paris, 1959.

CHAPTER XII / *Psyché*

By the middle 1920's Falla was a composer of international reputation, conducting or playing his own works in Spain and abroad. The *carmen* on Calle Antequeruela Alta, presided over by his devoted sister Maria, was his refuge between concert tours or bouts of illness. Even this peaceful retreat was often invaded by friends, musicians interested in performing his works, relatives, curiosity seekers, and journalists, the most persistent of all. To one of them Falla declared: "Granada is the city where I work, but I travel a great deal, unfortunately, and then I don't have time to work. Once a year I go off to a tiny village in Andalusia, and for ten or twelve days I don't talk to anybody. In this solitude I can prepare myself for work. I am absolutely dedicated to music, and music must be lived, must be inside you; it must be formed naturally. Music is a thing of mystery! Life in our society is becoming more and more complicated. This is why the artist must isolate himself. . . . I believe that society needs the beautiful utility of music. It must not be created selfishly, only for oneself, but for others. The artist's problem is that he ought to work for the public and at the same time retain his artistic imagination. This is a constant preoccupation with me. One must be worthy of his own ideal and communicate it in his work. It is an essence to be extracted, sometimes only by enormous and painful effort. . . . Then you must conceal the effort—as if the result were an improvisation achieved by a simple guaranteed means."[1]

These retreats into solitude were also retreats into mysticism, the source of his strength. "Without the powerful aid of my religious convictions I would never have had the courage to pursue a path that lies almost wholly in darkness,"[2] he said. But with it sustaining him, nothing could interrupt his creation of music. These were the years of the harpsichord concerto and, before that, of *Psyché*.

[1] *Excelsior,* May 31, 1925.
[2] Roland-Manuel, *op. cit.*

The poem *Psyché* had been written by Falla's very dear friend, the distinguished writer and music critic G. Jean Aubry. An enthusiastic promoter of Spanish music (with which he dealt at length in his important work *La Musique et les Nations*[3]), the "discoverer" of Albéniz, it was Aubry who sponsored the first concert in France to be wholly dedicated to Spanish music, and Falla was at the piano.[4] At Aubry's request Falla, in 1924, in Granada, set *Psyché* to music. It is a short composition (running seven and a half minutes) for voice (mezzo-soprano) and five instruments (flute, harp, violin, viola, and cello).

Four tercets[5] make up the text of this prettily styled, rather precious poem much like the work of Góngora, whose tercentenary was then approaching.

Although Falla's deep-rooted asceticism, and perhaps also an atavistic remnant in him of Arab disdain, kept him so far away from an interest in women that no feminine name was ever coupled with his, he could create sensitive and sensuous female characters: Salud the Andalusian, Candelas the Gypsy girl, the Biscayan miller's wife, Melisendra the Castilian, and, in *Psyché,* the lady of the court of Isabella Farnese. To create her in the spirit of the poem, Falla first imagined a suitable setting; he describes it in his dedication to Mme. Alvar: ". . . Recalling that Philip V and his consort Isabella Farnese lived in the Alhambra about 1730, I imagined a small court concert held in the boudoir of the Queen, which we call the Tocador de la Reina. It is in a high tower and commands a perfectly magnificent view. The interior of this apartment is decorated in the style that made this period illustrious. I have tried to write in the same style; it is quite natural that the ladies-in-waiting to the Queen play and sing music about a mythological subject very much in vogue at that time. . . ."

It was in the Tocador in 1923 that Falla imagined Wanda Landowska at the harpsichord; this was after a visit the celebrated harpsichordist made to Granada.

[3] Chester, London, 1922.

[4] In Le Havre, November 10, 1910.

[5] *Terceto* in Spanish; a stanza composed of three verses of eleven syllables called *redondilla mayor,* a kind of metric combination used especially in the theater.

153

A brief instrumental prelude (seventeen measures), *andante molto tranquillo e sostenuto,* creates the atmosphere of an epoch earlier than that designated by Falla, when tonality was already firmly established. This beginning is distinctly modal. It betrays something of the influence of Debussy through its melodic lines enclosed in an augmented fourth, its rhythmic imprecision, its harmonic refinements—ninths and elevenths curiously alternated—its light instrumental touches, the flute employed in the low, solemn register, the muted strings, the voice *quasi mormorato.* We find ourselves thinking of the *Ballades de Villon,* of the *Premenoir des Deux Amants,* but at times also of Ravel, inasmuch as several melodic inclinations are like the first and the third *Chanson Madécasse,* as is the section without accompaniment (measures 18 to 28) or the flute passage two measures before No. 8.

At the beginning a free melody is played by the flute in the middle register, accompanied by wide chords from the harp and a counterpoint with a deliberately imprecise line from the first violin. Psyché, having disobeyed, is alone, deserted by her divine lover. The music reflects the distress of the guilty girl and her dark thoughts. On page four the voice enters alone, followed by an expressive recitative in the key of F sharp: "Psyché! Thy lamp is dead." A brief passage for the viola (No. 3) precedes a tutti of four measures; then the flute joins its trills to those of the violin. The voice resumes: "The mirror, the confidant of thy face . . . ," accompanied this time by a viola and cello duet in the form of a contrapuntal interlude. This passage is closer to the Renaissance than to the Italian baroque with which *Psyché* has been compared. It ends in an unexpected way— and here again is the baroque spirit, but in a modern version—on an augmented fifth furnished by the harp (No. 5). Then the color changes: "Noon draws near and dances. . . ." The poet counsels Psyché to yield to nature. The strings sketch more animated rhythms; trills and rapid arpeggios suggest the songs of birds. This passage is dominated by a more marked sonority: accents, an *intenso* crescendo; it softens the remembrance of the abandoned couch (4 measures after No. 7), only to be reintensified (No. 8) at the sight of "the bird singing in the treetop." There are arpeggios and double stops for the first violin. The voice fades away in a prolonged vocalization (2 measures before No. 10), while from the flute ascends a broad, clear note—*largamente ma non troppo*—suffused with sunlight and hope. Then there is silence (No. 10). But once more, from far away, the flute plays the sad cantilena of the beginning and then falls silent.

Psyché inspired Rodolfo Halffter's admiration: "In Europe today (1932) I don't think there exists another composer, with the exception of Maurice Ravel, who writes so perfectly as Manuel de Falla. Everything is calculated and nothing is left to chance. The reading of a score by the maestro from Cádiz gives the impression that nothing is excessive and that nothing is lacking. Each of his works is a lesson in Latin clarity, in precision, discipline, and, also, sensitivity."[6]

The first performance of *Psyché* was in Barcelona in 1924, and was sung by Concepción Badia. In Madrid the same artist performed it over Union Radio on November 14, 1930. Between the two Spanish performances, *Psyché* was played in Paris at the Salle Erard at a concert sponsored by the Société Musicale Indépendante (1925) with Mme. Alvar performing. The famous harpist Lily Laskino and the flutist Louis Fleury also took part.

Reporting on this concert in *La Revue Musicale*,[7] the critic Raymond Petit noted Falla's progression from the large orchestra of *El Amor Brujo* and *The Three-Cornered Hat* to the reduced one of *Master Peter's Puppet Show* and finally this quintet. "The five instruments are delightful, whether the harp is harmoniously sustaining the ensemble or each instrument is playing by itself in a delicately wrought counterpoint. The language often has a rather archaic flavor, although different from that of *Master Peter's Puppet Show*. Here we hardly find that sort of harshness or severity which is part of so many of Falla's compositions. . . . Here we breathe the subtle fragrance of the Italian Renaissance more than that of fiery Andalusia. . . . A few tender sighs of the flute make one think of the charming and rather precious literary lyricism of the early Góngora

---

[6] Sagardia, *op. cit.*
[7] *La Revue Musicale,* January 1, 1926.

of the *Villanceros,* an attractive genre and one that is distinctly Spanish."

The score for *Psyché* was published in 1927 by Chester in London in an elegant little format like that of certain precious eighteenth-century works.

In order to write *Psyché,* Falla had interrupted a work quite different in atmosphere—the harpsichord concerto. Questions about this piece of music are still being raised by the critics.

First of all, why did he write it? According to Pahissa,[1] Falla wrote the harpsichord concerto for two reasons: as an expression of thanks to Wanda Landowska for having taken part in the premiere of *Master Peter's Puppet Show* and as a gratification of her often expressed wish that he compose a work for the harpsichord. He began it in October, 1923.

But what idea inspired the content of the work, the choice of instruments, the structure, and the particular character of its notation? A note Falla wrote at the end of the second movement sheds some light on his state of mind: *"A. Dom. MCMXXVI. In Festo Corporis Christi."* Falla had had a very serious bout of illness at the beginning of 1926. Had it been followed by an access of mysticism? That would explain somewhat the inspiration of this, the most surprising part of the concerto.

We can discern a double reason for the structure. First of all there is the evolution evident in his previous principal works. From 1900 to 1910 he was under the influence of romantic *verismo* lyricism in the Italian manner, but it was already tinged with his interest in folklore, both national and regional. The interest in folklore increases in *La Vida Breve,* and most particularly, in the *Seven Songs, El Amor Brujo,* and *Nights in the Gardens of Spain.* These last three works are permeated with rhythms, themes, a harmonic and orchestral atmosphere symbolizing Andalusia. At first glance, *The Three-Cornered Hat* seems to follow the same pattern. However, the motifs here signify his intention to enlarge his concern, not only in space but also in time; the themes and scenes of the Corregidor denoting a return at least to the time of Domenico Scarlatti. The evolution is completed in *Master Peter's Puppet Show.* Along with the *pregones* of an Andalusian type, the author borrows

[1] J. Pahissa, *op. cit.,* p. 131.

from the dances of the *Instrucción* by Gaspar Sanz, the canticles of Alfonso the Wise, from Salinas, as well as from the Gregorian liturgy, for his musical evocation of the time of Don Quixote. Simply by going backward in time, Falla widens his horizon, because from the sixteenth to the eighteenth centuries, the spirit of the court prevailed, and it was not a distinct national one but almost universal.

As Falla broadened his themes, he wanted to lessen the number of instruments, for example, in *Master Peter's Puppet Show* and in the conception of the Orquesta Bética de Cámara. Falla was following the spirit of the time, "the esthetic which is ascetic."[2] Other examples are Stravinsky's *Histoire du Soldat* and *Rag Time,* with their reduced number of instruments, and later works by Bartók, Milhaud, and Honegger. It was this concern Falla indicated when he confided to his friend Collet about *Master Peter's Puppet Show:* "You will see that with twenty instruments I will make as much noise as with one hundred."[3]

Adolfo Salazar discerns a kinship, not in the styles but in the personal musical atmosphere of Stravinsky, Bartók, Schönberg, and Falla. He establishes a parallel among some of their works conceived during 1923 and 1924: the *Concerto pour Piano et Orchestre d'Harmonie* by Stravinsky, the Second Sonata for violin and piano by Bartók, belonging to his atonal period, Schönberg's compositions in his newly developed twelve-tone technique, and Falla's harpsichord concerto. In these four composers, according to Salazar, there is rooted a deep Oriental principle underlying their European culture. It marks the difference between them and Greco-Roman classicism or the Germano-Roman romanticism of Central Europe. A Slavic strain runs in Stravinsky's blood; there is Bartók, a Hungarian who doubtless is heir to a Mongol strain; Schönberg, a Semite, and Falla, who, like many Andalusians, perhaps had a touch of Gypsy, Berber, or Arab blood. Thus we can understand the difference in these musicians' consciousness of sonority, compared to that of Franck and Debussy, Verdi and Puccini, Strauss, Bruckner, and Sibelius.[4]

However this "Oriental root" is deeply buried in the harp-

[2] Roland-Manuel, *Manuel de Falla, op. cit.*
[3] *La Revue Musicale,* January 1, 1947, *op. cit.*
[4] *La Musica Actual en Europe y sus Problemas.* Madrid, 1935.

sichord concerto, so deeply that we are barely able to discern it. All that remains are the frugality of thought and form, the rigor and austerity of the instrumental notation, which, in fact does bring Falla closer to the aforementioned musicians than to the impressionist symbolism of his French friends, whose spell, so to speak, no longer holds him in thrall.

Pahissa gives an explanation for the choice of instruments, which may or may not be the true one: "The character of the work was influenced by the profound impression made upon him by a tune played on oboes and bassoons in an early morning procession during Holy Week, which he spent in Seville with Garcia Lorca shortly after completing *Master Peter's Puppet Show*. The cellist Segismundo Romero obtained the score of this music for Falla. Perhaps it is possible to trace in the difficult lines of the harpsichord concerto something of the effect which the music had made upon Falla's ever keen sensibilities, sharpened on this occasion by the stirring atmosphere of Holy Week."[5]

Technical Analysis of the Concerto

Falla exactly defines his intentions on the first page of the score. He writes:

"The harpsichord must be as sonorous as possible. It is to be placed on the first level, the groups of winds and strings occupying the second or even third levels. The six soloists, however, must be seen by the audience. . . .

"The strings are always to be soloists. In no case is their number to be increased."

In Falla's own words, this harpsichord concerto is a concerto for solo instruments, among which the harpsichord is simply the principal one. Sagardia cites the note Falla wrote for the program of the first performance: "In this work, the composer felt no constraint to conform to the classic form of the concerto for a single instrument with the accompaniment of the orchestra. . . . And the music's style and character both derive from ancient Spanish melodies,

[5] J. Pahissa, *op. cit.,* p. 131.

religious, court, and folk tunes."[6] Thus Falla remained loyal to the principle of a national base for his music, but he continued to push back its frontiers in time and space, in short, to universalize it.

Several points should be made regarding the treatment of the instruments. In the first two movements the composer rejects the usual ornaments of the harpsichord of the classic period: trills, mordants, *grupettos,* and employs them sparingly in the third. Falla's aim is to obtain the maximum sonority through large extensions of arpeggiated major chords. As for the woodwinds, he gladly avoids the best registers; for example, the flute is almost constantly employed in the extreme treble, doubled frequently on the octave, if not tripled, by the oboe and the clarinet. Thus it creates an impression of taut, primitive music. The notation for the strings is incisive; a sustained style is avoided. Certain strokes of the bows—accents, down-strokes, strokes with the base of the bow—are constant. Forceful pizzicati emphasize the harshness of some of the harmonies, wrested from the very body of the instruments. Alternations of shadings are frequent: forte, piano, *pianissimo subito.* Finally, he rejects the viola, deliberately depriving himself of the softening which fills the void between the lower and higher registers. Consequently, plenitude of polyphonic and harmonic sensuality is rejected.

The first movement is marked *allegro,* and its form is classic: prelude, exposition, development, recapitulation, and final plagal cadence. Falla translates his musical asceticism into the thematic as well as the instrumental domain. Like Debussy going back to Couperin's monothematic pieces, he was inspired by the single theme form of Scarlatti's sonatas. The basic motif of each part of the harpsichord concerto is related to the theme of the initial Allegro; the relation is very distinct in the second movement although just

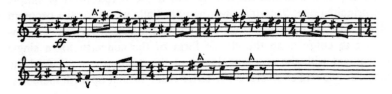

6 *Op. cit.,* p. 54.

perceptible in the third. This generative theme is a Castilian folk song of the fifteenth century, *De los Alamos, Vengo, Madre,* which is found in a sixteenth-century *villancico* by Juan Vasquez.

Introduced by the flute and the oboe an octave lower, it appears only in the twentieth bar of the Allegro, that is, in No. 3 of the score. Before that, a fragment from the last measure of this same theme serves as an introduction. It is confined within an interval of a major third. Falla always found this span, a natural base for numerous folklore themes, very attractive and used it frequently.

This brief fragment stands out on the harpsichord in quarter and eighth notes amid a persistent accompaniment of sixteenth notes and triplets, going from the tonic of D to that of B. The rhythm is punctuated in syncopation by the chords of the violin and cello, based on the same two harmonies and heard simultaneously. Thus Falla, from the first measure, establishes a polytonal intention which he later denied. According to Falla, his harpsichord concerto contained no polytonal affectation but only effects derived from those famous laws of resonance he had discovered in the book by Louis Lucas.

Be that as it may, this beginning creates the general atmosphere of the work: harsh, perhaps even bitter, the sounds of an orchestra in which *gaïtas* and *dulzainas* might be side by side with *vihuellas, tamborillas,* and *citaras.* We hear the *de madrugada* (early morning) procession passing by in Seville.

The falsely polytonal effect is complicated further at the entry of the Castilian song (No. 3 of the score). The motif is in B Major; the harpsichord, doubled in the strings, combines the keys of B flat minor (left hand) and A minor (right hand), while the clarinet runs through an incomplete scale of B flat major. Observes Salazar:[7] "If we replace the flats by their enharmonics, the reader will note that this triple tonality is reduced in reality to a chord of the ninth of the dominant of B major, which, at the sixth measure, is resolved on a ninth of E to return by way of a melodic glissando to the initial key." This judgment is shared by Roland-Manuel.[8]

[7] A. Salazar, *op. cit.,* p. 155.
[8] Roland-Manuel, *Musique, op. cit.*

Salazar compares this effect with the painting technique called *velatura,* which produces a kind of prismatic refraction. Salazar could also have noted the altered fifth and the appoggiatura of the leading tone, heard at the same time.[9] That would complete an analysis conforming with Falla's wish to deny any suspicion of polytonality.

Nos. 4 to 6 (pages 4 and 5) conclude this exposition. A passage on the harpsichord, almost exclusively percussive, a few quickly rapped out notes on the woodwinds and some harmonics in the strings lead to a return of the initial idea (No. 6) in D followed by B major.

Thereupon an extremely refined play begins among the six instruments. At No. 7 the Castilian theme is taken up, this time by the clarinet in an octave doubling of the flute. Chords are heard in syncopation in various tempi: 3/4, 2/4, 4/4, 7/8. Although they are very dissonant, they can be analyzed according to traditional standards, but to label each chord would be an exercise in pedantry. The only way to give even a remote idea of this delightful passage is to assure the reader that it is handled with a delicacy that could come only from the greatest deftness in the art of structuring sounds and that the result is that the ear is amazed and enchanted.

Beginning with No. 8, the harpsichord improvises on the Castilian motif *alla breve* (diminution through sixteenth notes). The cello responds to it with little jumps, strong but *senza stridenza* (1 measure after 9). At Nos. 10 and 11 the violin and woodwind enter, and at No. 12 there is the sound of a rustic fiddler: the violin solo boldly plucks the tune of *De los Álamos* like a Gypsy sorcerer improvising on his guitar. We find ourselves thinking of the satanic violin in Stravinsky's *Histoire du Soldat.* Then we hear the harpsichord play for the first time (4 measures before 13) those large parallel chords—a last legacy from Debussy—in which it will delight in the second movement, perfect chords arpeggiated by a contrary movement between the two hands, a sonorous depth expressing an almost liturgical feeling. This is followed by a canon on the Castilian theme, expounded this time in augumented form, between the strings

[9] A device used by harpsichordists and known as *acciaccatura.*

162

in octave (3 measures after 13) and those two chords of the harpsichord (4 measures after 13) which majestically underline its splendor, while flute and clarinet give this same theme a presto diminution *alla breve*. After many changes the harpsichord, along with the other instruments, resumes the brief and tightened contrapuntal play created by the use of different snatches of the Castilian melody. The melody expands broadly in D major (No. 19), tripled by the flute, the oboe, and the cello in a passage marked *intenso,* accompanied *quasi percussione* by the accents of the clarinet, violin, and the arpeggios of the harpsichord. The harpsichord alone (No. 20) plays a new and noble succession of chords until, after a pedal point and a brief recall of the beginning, the movement ends in a kind of strange and unforeseen plagal cadence made by sliding the chord of D over that of B. Its unexpected savor is emphasized by a long drawn-out *rallentando*.

The second movement is marked *giubiloso ed energico*. To understand this extraordinary second movement, we must recall the inscription with which Falla terminates it: *"A Dom. MCMXXVI. In Festo Corporis Christi."* Corpus Christi Day is marked by religious ceremonies and grandiose processions in all of Spain. Falla's profound religious feelings alone explain the feeling that he wanted to give to this music. Pahissa adds some information with which Roland-Manuel agrees: Falla could not decide what compositional character to give this movement. At a meeting of the Madrid Academia de la Historia, he heard Sánchez Albornoz deliver a lecture about the Middle Ages. In the hall were illustrations of ancient instruments, among which were enormous *chitarrones*. There then flashed through Falla's mind the idea for this central movement: a procession moving slowly around the arches of a Gothic cathedral, to be suggested by the amplitude of the melodic lines and by the clashing resonance of large arpeggios written for the harpsichord. And so, these few pages portray the magnificence of a torchlight procession in medieval Castile, all purple and gold in the smoke of incense, with penitents carrying the sparkling *pasos* and the pious sound of *saetas* and liturgical songs, punctuated by the harsh accents of the *banda*."[10]

[10] Pahissa, *op. cit.,* p. 147.

The form is as follows: modal theme (fragment) arising from the theme of the first movement.

No. 1 (from the score, p. 17), *molto energico* (*non pesante*): Triple canon on the initial theme.

No. 3: Canon, mode of F, still on the initial theme.

No. 4: Theme in C on a chord of E (harpsichord).

No. 6: Augmented recapitulation.

No. 8: Theme in F (woodwind) on an accompaniment in A (harpsichord).

No. 11: Complete recapitulation (first canon).

Conclusion in F sharp major.

The choice and the treatment of the principal motif are significant. The first three notes spring from the beginning of the initial theme (No. 3 of the first movement, p. 2) whose original function was explained above. An *estribillo religioso,* cited by Pedrell in his *Cancionero,*[11] resembles the harmonic support Falla uses. Some commentators also see here the influence of the famous sixteenth-century guitarist Milan.

It is very difficult to explain the distinct superposition here of the keys of C and E major except as a polytonal effect which has nothing to do with the principles expounded by Lucas. Nor, for that matter, does the harmonic glissando (No. 5, p. 20) through which the two instrumental groups join together in E (No. 6) on a long scale running the length of the keyboard. This is followed by a brief effect of discordant bells and of a canonic fragment of No. 1, a blunt stop on a sforzando, a long rest (measure 4, p. 21), and then one of the most characteristic passages of this singular and splendid movement. Several chords begin it pianissimo in the bass (No. 7), after which (No. 8) it is the turn of the woodwind-string group to express the liturgical theme, this time in F major. The harpsichord at the same time repeats fifteen times in A major the chords that we have heard in E at No. 4, that is to say, seventeen measures before. This creates the striking effect of a procession, which we come upon at different points of its journey, always singing the same canticle but at different elevations. The sonorities vary according to the echoes produced in each place. We imagine our-

[11] Pedrell, *op. cit.,* I, p. 35, No. 41.

selves back in the time of Victoria's Gregorian Masses and dramatic Passions.

The finale is *vivace* (*flessibile, scherzando*) and is in D major, the initial key of the concerto; it contains but a single theme, again in the manner of Scarlatti or Pergolesi. And that theme, as explained in the discussion of the first movement, is related to the prelude, itself derived from *De los Alamos*.

There are canons and other bold contrapuntal devices; they give an impression of airiness, but are, nonetheless, absolutely solid. The key of D is established from the beginning by a sonorous chord of the harpsichord, the fifth in the bass, the tonic doubled. This boldly asserted tonality Falla enriches constantly with his free counterpoint.

This same frankness appears in many classic, perfect cadences.

The construction is very simple:

A and A': Exposition and counter-exposition (at No. 6, p. 29) separated by a brief episode (from No. 2 to No. 6).

B: Development (No. 11, p. 32).

C and C': Recapitulation (Nos. 22, 38) followed by the counter-exposition a key above that of the beginning (measure 4 of No. 24, p. 39).

Perfect final cadence—preceded by a brief and traditional modulation to the subdominant—in the form of a coda.

The structure of the theme assigned to the harpsichord is curious. The antecedent presents a sequence of descending intervals —fourth, fifth, sixth—while a diatonic scale, embroidered by a seventh, rises from the dominant of D up to the tonic. A first reproduction in the low register of the flute (third measure), doubled in octaves by the violin and the harpsichord, is accompanied by an arpeggio in E flat, furnished by the clarinet and the bass of the harpsichord. The consequent then intervenes through the oboe (No. 1) and leads to a conclusion (No. 1, measure 4, dominant, inverted tonic) repeated four times, which the harpsichord doubles repeatedly and then amplifies with a joyous cadence *alla Pergolesi* (No. 2). One would almost believe one were listening to a fragment of *La Serva Padrona*.

The music is delightful—spontaneous, witty, and elaborate.

It is baroque art in all its preciosity. At times the play of the canons (for example, beginning with No. 13, a portion in the style of Pergolesi) draws out intervals in the manner of the serial system, which was just beginning to be known in the West; Falla may very well have been aware of it. The differences in intensity also tend to connect Falla with the school of Schönberg. By way of canons, contrary movements, and boldly superposed imitations, this development arrives at a traditional chord of the fourth and sixth (No. 16, p. 35), prepared in the most orthodox fashion. On this solid tonal support, altered and chromaticized scales and arpeggios follow one another and prepare the recapitulation. In conformity with the beginning up to the fourth measure of No. 24, the intensity is generally maintained at the level of an extremely loud fortissimo; indications such as *marcatissimo* and *staccatissimo* precede a brief pause which announces the coda. After repeats of the canonic elements, we hear the last perfect cadence. The finale of the concerto, in conciseness of thought and form, one of the purest ever written, concludes in the most accentuated tonal direction, exactly as it had begun.

The first performance of the *Concerto per Clavicembalo (Pianoforte), Flauto, Oboe, Clarinetto, Violino e Violoncello* took place on November 5, 1926. It was entrusted to the Asociación de Música de Cámara of Barcelona, which was giving a Falla festival, with the cooperation of the Orquesta Pau Casals, conducted by the great cellist himself. The *Jota* from *The Three-Cornered Hat* and *Nights in the Gardens of Spain* were on the same program, with Falla at the piano. Then Falla conducted *Master Peter's Puppet Show* and the harpsichord concerto. Wanda Landowska was the keyboard soloist.

The first reception was mild. Pahissa himself wrote in a review, which appeared four days later in the Barcelona newspaper *Las Noticias,*[12] that he could hardly judge the new work because of the imprecision of the performance. The concerto had not yet been published. The music had been transcribed hastily and contained many mistakes. Rehearsal time had been insufficient. Under such conditions the composer and the principal performer were quite

[12] November 9, 1926.

nervous—Falla, not only because of the insufficient preparation but because of his own lack of podium experience, Wanda Landowska, because of the difficulties of a wholly unusual score. Is this perhaps why she later refused to play this work that had been dedicated to her? When invited to play it in Paris, she declined on the grounds of prior commitments. Falla then decided to play the work himself.

This Paris premiere also took place at a Falla Festival, on May 14, 1927, in the time-honored Salle Pleyel. On the advice of Gustave Lyon, the director of the concert hall, Falla played his concerto twice at the same concert, first at the harpsichord and then at the piano.[13] The program also included his *Fantasia Baetica,* the *Seven Spanish Songs, Psyché,* and the world premiere of the *Soneto a Córdoba,* sung by the eminent singer Madeleine Gresle. Falla had spent many hours at his harpsichord in order to familiarize himself with the play of its pedals. This time the performance went smoothly, and for Falla the evening was always a precious memory. All his friends were there, among them Debussy's widow.

In an article in *La Revue Musicale,*[14] Henry Prunières, observed that many people had not understood the harpsichord concerto. "Yet," he continued, "never before has Falla's art achieved such frugality. . . . If the first movement evokes the period of Velázquez, with its majestic rhythms, its themes embellished as if with plumes, if the third, constructed on a Scarlatian motif, has us mingling with the elegant crowd of Goya's *majos* and *majas,* the second movement carries us back farther into the past, to the age of chivalry: a prayer marked by large chords brandished like swords, a religious hymn sung by warrior monks. The technique, with its persistent repetition and monothematism, is extremely curious. We cannot speak of a return to past techniques; although Manuel de Falla makes use of a contrapuntal style akin to that of the great predecessors of J. S. Bach, it is in the service of a personal science of construction and of the most modern harmonic sensibility. Manuel de Falla has willingly abandoned the elements furnished by folk music, but he has used the rhythm of the guitar, the modes of

[13] The other artists were Moyse, Bonneau, Godeau (woodwinds), Cruque, Pasquier (strings).
[14] July 1, 1927.

the liturgy, all the musical elements that his remembrance of the aristocratic and religious life of ancient Spain offered."

Later, Roland-Manuel in *Musique*[15] wrote: ". . . [Here is] an art which is purified slowly by a series of stubborn sacrifices and rises finally from the rational to the spiritual. M. de Falla has raised himself to mastery by a path which approaches even nearer the "Path of Perfection" of the Castilian mystics. Each work bears witness to a new sacrifice. . . ."

Another writer, Émile Vuillermoz, cited by H. Collet,[16] declared: "Falla has scored the victories of an ascetic and an anchorite over aural voluptuousness."

On the other hand, Joaquin Nin, a deeply learned Spanish pianist, composer, and musicologist, wrote later in the *Guide du Concert*:[17] "Manuel de Falla's masterpieces are neither *La Vida Breve* nor the harpsichord concerto (lyricism and frugality are not his forte) but those in the romantic-realist tradition of his race: *Master Peter's Puppet Show, El Amor Brujo,* the *Seven Songs*. And I told him this many times, with the frankness authorized by an old friendship, when he was my guest in my little house in Saint Cloud." Obviously, this is an opinion shared by too many symphonic societies, to judge by the limited number of performances of the harpsichord concerto!

A month after this memorable premiere, on June 17, 1927, an audience at the Théâtre des Champs-Élysées heard the first performance of Falla's orchestration of Rossini's Overture to *The Barber of Seville*. Was it a reorchestration or a fragment of his old attempt at writing a new *Barber*? The press barely mentioned it, and it fell into a merciful oblivion! But the harpsichord concerto scored more triumphs. The Madrid premiere was held on November 5, 1927, at the Palacio de la Música, once again as part of a festival honoring Falla, and with the composer at the harpsichord. The Madrid press was lavish with praise, and a reception was organized in the Ayuntamiento in honor of the maestro of Andalusia.

In June of the same year it was London's turn to applaud

---

[15] September 15, 1929.
[16] *Op. cit.*
[17] November 11, 1932.

the work, again played by the composer, first at the piano and then at the harpsichord. The singer Vera Janacopoulos sang the role of the narrator in *Master Peter's Puppet Show* at this concert, which was attended by Stravinsky. In 1928, the harpsichord concerto was played at the Festival of the International Society of Contemporary Music, held in Siena, where it created a sensation. The work was published that year by Max Eschig in Paris.

In Granada, once again, Falla prepared the first local performance of the harpsichord concerto and also participated in the festivities marking the three hundredth anniversary of the death of Góngora. It was at this time that he wrote the *Soneto a Córdoba* (Sonnet to Córdoba).

CHAPTER XIV / The *Sonnet to Córdoba* and the Origin of *Atlántida*

The great poet Don Luis de Góngora was born in Córdoba in 1561 and died there in 1627. His fervent admirers wished to commemorate the tercentenary of his death. Why was he so admired by Gerardo Diego, a close friend of Falla, Federico Garcia Lorca and his companions at the Residencia de Estudiantes, Castilians like Salinas, Guillen, and Damaso Alonso, and by famous older writers of the "generation of '98," Miguel de Unamuno, Antonio Machado, exponents of the national tradition in literature? Góngora's *Romances, Canciónes Galantes,* and other works are distinguished by his restraint, his artisan-like craftsmanship, which was precisely what the whole group of these learned young poets was striving for. Lorca demanded an "implacable lucidity," he counseled poets "to observe calmly and dispassionately . . . the quality and sonority of words before elaborating the image," a counsel quite in keeping with Falla's severity with himself. Falla was deeply committed to this brilliant "generation of '27,"[1] and he participated in the tercentenary celebration by setting to music Góngora's famous poem *El Soneto a Córdoba.*

The poem had been suggested to Falla by Gerardo Diego and some of Lorca's friends. Falla was instantly charmed by the poem's evocative descriptions, its nobility of thought, its elegance of technique, and perhaps also by the fact that the poet had actually written the sonnet in Granada in 1585. (Falla's postlude fixes the dates of composition thus: Granada, 1585—Granada, 1927.)

The musical atmosphere is characterized by this quotation from Lorca's 1927 study of Góngora: "The poet doubles and triples the image in order to lead us to different levels of understanding, so that he may communicate the feeling in all its aspects."[2]

The feeling the poet wants to evoke in us is evoked in him by his memory of his native city with its "walls of jasper, towers

[1] M. Pomès, preface cited in *Federico Garcia Lorca.*
[2] *Ibid.*

of gold, high, flaunting."[3] The fertile plains, the mountains "airy crested, that morn delights to gild and noon to favor," the "fair, glorious land, mine forever, mighty with pens and swords" of its sons are present in his memory although he lives far away "in your ruined dome of pleasure."[4] Should he ever forget them, the poet declared, may his eyes never again behold ". . . thy ramparts, thy towers or thy mountains, thy peaks and plains—my country, Hispania fairest!"

Analysis of the Music

This intense, almost religious lyricism corresponded to Falla's state of mind at the time—he had just finished writing the *Lento* of the harpsichord concerto (this second movement was composed last). He chose once more to utilize the long arpeggios of that liturgical movement. Now assigned to the harp or to the piano, these arpeggios set out in bold relief a melodic line which contains elements of an ornate recitative and of a psalmody, marked *lento assai (con lirica esaltazione)*; it is completed by nuances marked *vibrante, marcato e sostenuto, sempre largamente, arpeggiato e con forza*. The allusion to the "mountains airy crested" (p. 2, measure 6) is underlined by arpeggios alternating in opposite movements; their different tonalities open and expand on an A flat *vibrante* (p. 2, line 4), which celebrates the eternal glory of Spain. But the climax is attained on p. 3, line 2. In a return to the tonality of D major, a solemn procession joined by chords to the rich sonority accentuates in a long crescendo the poet's vow to preserve forever the memory of his beloved native city. Here the poet and the musician meet. Falla superbly supports the poet; he, too, doubles and triples the images whose feeling he wants to communicate. The harmonies are intensified *meno lento (poco stringendo,* p. 4). There is a new sequence of five chords thundered *marcatissimo*, which this time heightens a final invocato "Hispania fairest." The melody ends on an immense arpeggio in D; it is repeated three times from bass to treble, and its final point seems to be furnished by a last thunderous effect.

---

[3] English translation by J. B. Trend. See Pahissa, *op. cit.,* p. 143.
[4] An allusion to the Alhambra of Granada.

Some critics see in the accompaniment to this melody a similarity to the methods of the famous *vihuelisto* Luis Milan, which were set down in his book *El Maestro* (1535). According to Pedrell, Milan is one of that group of *vihuelistos* in whose music one finds "the native and original forms of accompanied melody."[5] Lopez Chavarri, in his *Histoire de la Musique,* asserts: "The *vihuelistos* abridge the polyphony by restoring it to simple chords both in notation and in practice."[6] Falla might very well have imposed a smiliar discipline on himself.

The *Sonnet to Córdoba* was published in 1932 by the Oxford University Press in collaboration with Max Eschig in Paris. Falla dedicated it to Mme. Eugenia de Errazuriz, a Chilean.

On the copy of the *Sonnet* which Falla gave to Gerardo Diego, the composer wrote, "In homage to Spanish poetry."[7]

The Paris premiere of the harpsichord concerto and the world premiere of this work were the same occasion: a Falla Festival at the Salle Pleyel on May 14, 1927. Later, the eminent artist Maria Barrientos made the first recording of the *Sonnet to Córdoba,* as well as that of the *Seven Songs,* with Falla as accompanist.

This period—the late 1920's and early 1930's—crowded with work, concert tours, nervous and religious crises, was also marked by intervals of rest and renewal and perhaps of private happiness.

After the English premiere of the harpsichord concerto, Falla stayed for several days in Amboise. He enjoyed the Loire Valley and memories of his youthful arrival in France twenty years or so before. Then came more concerts and festivals in his honor. The concert given by La Argentina at the Théâtre des Champs-Élysées on June 17, 1927, in which the great dancer interpreted her own choreography for *El Amor Brujo,* against a backdrop designed by G. Baccarisas, was followed by performances at the Opéra Comique of *La Vida Breve, El Amor Brujo,* and *Master Peter's Puppet Show,* on March 12 and 15, 1928, in which Ninon Vallin, Carmen Granados and La Argentina appeared. Four days later, on March

---

[5] Cited by E. Pujol in the *Encyclopédie de la Musique,* op. cit., p. 2004.
[6] *Ibid.,* p. 2003–4.
[7] A. Sagardia, *op. cit.,* p. 58.

19, Falla conducted the Straram Orchestra at a concert in his honor at the Salle Pleyel. The program included the premiere of a new suite from *The Three-Cornered Hat, Psyché,* the *Sonnet to Córdoba,* the *Seven Songs,* sung by Ninon Vallin, the harpsichord concerto, with the composer at the piano, and as a finale, *Nights in the Gardens of Spain,* interpreted by Ricardo Viñes.

Shortly after, the harpsichord concerto was recorded for the first time, with Falla at the harpsichord.

In 1934 Falla succeeded Sir Edward Elgar as Foreign Academician of the Académie des Beaux-Arts, the highest honor that France can bestow on an artist. He had already returned to Granada, where the *Homenajes* and *Atlántida* were to take shape.

Even while working on the harpsichord concerto, Falla had been thinking of his next project. He conceived the idea of writing an *auto sacramental* (one-act religious drama) inspired by two works of Calderón, *Los Encantos de la Culpa* (The Enchantments of Sin) and *Circé.* Just at this time the painter José Maria Sert, passing through Granada on his way home from the Salzburg Festival, told Falla that Max Reinhardt, the famous German stage director, wanted to stage his next lyric work. What Reinhardt had in mind was precisely an *auto sacramental* in the manner of Calderón! Sert was to design the décor.

But another coincidence suggested a project Falla found more alluring. The Iberian-American exposition was about to open in Seville. It was 1926, and the fiftieth anniversary of the poem *La Atlántida* by the Catalan writer Jacinto Verdaguer; Falla would also be fifty that year. He had read extracts of Verdaguer's poem in a Castilian translation published by the Madrid daily *El Sol.* Now he read the whole poem and realized that here was a subject that would satisfy him completely. Everything about the poem filled him with enthusiasm, according to Pahissa: its atmosphere of the Hellenic and Roman worlds; its mythological lore drawn from the mysteries of primitive Iberia; its scope—the whole peninsula from the Pyrenees to the Straits of Gibraltar; Cádiz, the Gades of the Romans, before that Gadir of the Phoenicians; the legendary Tartesians; perhaps the fabulous people of Atlantis; and Hercules, whose image adorns the Gaditanian *escudo,* along with the proud motto, "Hercules Fundator."[8] Once again there came to Falla the obscure ancestral memories that had enchanted his childhood, that had inspired the fantastic city of Colón.

He strongly desired to see his native city and the whole Gaditanian region again. He wanted it to be at least the point of departure of the new work. And so, once more, Falla walked through the streets of Cádiz that he had known as a child. He saw, from the harbor, the island of Las Palomas, legendary home of the nymph Calypso. And the Municipal Council of Cádiz declared him officially "an honored guest."

With some friends, Falla proceeded to Jérez de la Fróntera, to Sanlucar de Barrameda, where Christopher Columbus had been. They saw great cattle grazing peacefully, and between their horns were perched ibises, the sacred birds of the Nile, like images of the distant East. Among the ruins of the temple of Hercules they gathered bits of marble and fragments of vases, an activity still permitted at that time. Falla stood for a long time before a bust of Hercules in nearby Medina Sidonia. Finally, he came to Tarifa, and from the top of the tower of the hero Guzman el Bueno, he looked out at the mountains; indeed, they seemed like two pillars supporting the two continents. "Falla was now able to begin his work," adds Pahissa. "During the years to come these intensely felt impressions remained the abiding source of his inspiration."

Another great friend of Falla, the eminent Spanish writer José Maria Pemán, has corroborated this episode in Falla's life:[9]

"One day Falla came unexpectedly to spend a few weeks in his native city. 'Why have you come here?' someone asked him. His reply was almost sibylline. 'I've come to hear the sea!' Toward evening, with a small group of friends, he went to the beach, which is absolutely deserted in winter. For hours he listened to the sound of the waves and wrote down in a notebook the chords that he thought he heard. Back in the house, he explained his project. One of us objected that there seemed to be a disparity between his music, so intellectual and Pythagorean (sic!), and the vast cosmic and pantheistic resonances of Verdaguer's poem; Falla replied that La

[8] Pahissa, *op. cit.,* p. 148.
[9] José Maria Pemán, *Cien Articulos.* Madrid, 1957, p. 165.

Atlántida represented for him, as for the mystic, the search for the First Cause. In reality, it was born of the religious obsession which dominated him all his life. His greatest ambition was to write a Mass, and *Atlántida* was a *rezo de prima,* a matin prayer, a preparation for this ultimate Mass that he never wrote."

Once the two friends visited the tiny island of Sancti Petri, facing Cádiz, where in ancient times there was a temple of Hercules. Today there is only a lighthouse on the island. Seated at the water's edge, Falla contemplated the setting sun, musing perhaps about that ancient Greek who had been told by Poseidon that at the edge of the world one could hear the cry of the blazing sun as it sank into the sea. Pemán writes that he asked Falla whether he had heard the sun cry out. "No," Falla answered, "but I heard many other things." And then he wrote his melodies of the Atlantic.

The mystic has said, "I shall go through mountains and rivers to seek my loves." Falla was to search for his among the immensities of the Atlantic.

In the beginning he had in mind a short work. But as he pursued it more deeply, it began to assume vast dimensions which doubtless met his ideal of a complete synthesis of the Spanish genius, as it had been realized by a Cervantes or a Columbus. To a reporter for the Catalan newspaper *Ahora,* who interviewed him in 1927 about his *Atlántida,* he declared: "It is the work about which I have felt the most enthusiasm. May Heaven grant me enough days and the good health to finish it! It will be a very important work which will fill a whole concert program. It will include soloists interpreting the dramatic text of the poem, choruses, and the orchestra. Verdaguer's poem will be absolutely respected, not only because of the profound admiration the Catalan poet merits, but also because *La Atlántida* has existed in my being since childhood. Cádiz, where I was born, offered me its Atlantic through the Pillars of Hercules and opened my imagination to the most beautiful garden of the Hesperides."

The times, in Spain at least, were hardly propitious for a work requiring concentration, meditation, and tranquility. Besides, Falla fell ill again and for days was unable to work, or even to move about. The social unrest, which had been seething for some time and which was to rock the country, had begun to erupt; its effect was strong in Andalusia. The monarchy was replaced by the republic in 1931. Falla, of course, disapproved of the religious persecution it triggered. He sought a refuge. In 1933, for various reasons, he decided to spend several weeks in Majorca.

Some years before, the Catalan writer Juan Maria Thomas had been a founder of the Associació Bach per la Música Antiga i Contemporània in Palma de Majorca, where he lived. The honorary committee consisted of Falla, Ravel, Bartók, Honegger, and Gustave Bret, among others. The manifesto issued by the group hailed Bach as the most important figure in the evolution of music because in his time he had "shaken the routine minds of those old in spirit and the aggressive non-thinking of pedants," and declared that their aim was always to be inspired by his example; and so they invited "people of good will" to the banquet of beauty.

This association, which grew very quickly, sometimes sponsored concerts. Publishers sent their new works for trial performances; one of the scores Thomas thus received was that of *Master Peter's Puppet Show*.

The first reading among the members of the association elicited such admiration and enthusiasm that it was decided to include excerpts from this work on one of the next programs. Before that, at the premiere of the harpsichord concerto in Barcelona, Falla and Thomas had become close friends. Falla promised to visit Palma, but obstacles to the trip kept cropping up. It was six years after the memorable premiere of the harpsichord concerto when Thomas received the following letter from Maria del Carmen:[10]

"My brother Manuel has recently suffered a very serious attack of nervous illness and now has been ordered to follow a regimen of rigorous isolation, working exclusively on *Atlántida*. The doctors allow him this extraordinary concession only on the condition that he is not to occupy himself with anything else. This is the reason why I am writing to you in his name. . . . After we considered several plans, and remembering the invitations that you have so amiably extended, it seemed to us that nothing could be

[10] January 18, 1933.

better for him than to go to Palma, where he could work in a tranquil atmosphere, which unfortunately is lacking here. . . . Since the visit would be for some time, he would like to find a clean *pension,* comfortable but not luxurious, sunny, with discreet conveniences (sic!), without meals, but, above all, in a peaceful spot, without the noise of gramophones or similar things. . . ."

After some inquiries, "Mossén Tomás" thought he had found just the right *pension* and informed his friends. Meanwhile, Falla's health worsened due to an attack of rheumatism. In addition, during the Corpus Christi festival, public fair stalls had been set up at the very foot of his peaceful haven. His courteous complaints to the Municipal Council about the noise elicited this rude response: "If he doesn't like it, let him leave!"

He did so. On February 28, 1933, Falla and his sister disembarked from the Barcelona mail-boat; Juan Maria Thomas was waiting for them. But the right *pension* had not, after all, been located, and it was only after a series of adventures, wittily recounted by Don Juan Maria,[11] that they found a suitable retreat in a village named, oddly enough, Genoa, which was linked to Palma by a tramway. It was a delightful house, set among pines with a terrace and a tiny garden from which one could see the white sails of boats in the bay. Looking up, one saw, at the top of the hill, an "enchanted castle," which the setting sun transformed into "millions of roses dancing on the green of the pines."

Falla was delighted with his new home, "like a baby with a new toy or a *mozo* wearing a new suit." A former pupil of Tragó lent him a piano, as well as the indispensible *camilla,* a heating apparatus; and so Falla could resume composing *con alegre optimismo* on a minutely detailed schedule. A part of the morning was assigned to the study of Latin and Catalan, the languages used in *Atlántida.* After breakfast Falla would take a short walk, sharing Beethoven's belief that physical exercise stimulates the activity of the mind. After a frugal luncheon and the siesta, the afternoon and evening were consecrated to work. At times he would interrupt his work to contemplate from his terrace the splendor of the setting sun over the bay.

[11] Juan Maria Thomas, *Manuel De Falla en la Isla.* Mallorca, n.d.

At times work other than his major concern would demand his attention. He transcribed an *Ave Maria* by Victoria for the Capella Classica of Palma, another musical organization in whose founding Juan Maria Thomas played a large part, and of which he was director. According to Thomas, Falla's contribution consisted principally in doubling the values of the ternary period of the *Sancta Maria*. He wanted the voice to rest insistently on each of these notes, "large, round, and open, like huge roses of flame, . . . this lamentation being naught else but . . . the sweet echo of the supplications of thousands of lips. A sound full of fervor and hope."[12] Again, according to Thomas, when Falla directed the rehearsal of the new work, everything about him, "his hand, eyes, face implied that he was not conducting but praying, holding between his fingers an invisible rosary of fire." All eyes were moist, all hearts beat faster after the *suavísimo amen*.

On the next day, the Wednesday of Holy Week, April 12, 1933, came the concert, the first public performance of the transcription of *Ave Maria*. At the last moment Falla accepted the invitation to direct it. The audience, mainly foreigners resident on the island, gave the master a standing ovation, in which the members of the Capella joined.

Soon Falla set to work on another new project. A Pro-Chopin Committee had been established in Palma in 1930 to celebrate the centenary of romanticism with a festival to be held annually in the Carthusian monastery of Valldemosa. Artists and conductors such as Pablo Casals, Halffter, Arbós, Tansman, and Rubinstein were to take part in these festivals, and the most celebrated names in the world of music were included on the original honorary committee. Falla's presence had been solicited from the start, and the Pro-Chopin Committee even hoped to give the premiere of *Atlántida* at the monastery. The matter was discussed in an exchange of letters with Falla's sister, Doña Maria del Carmen, but the possibility of a performance was still far in the future. Shortly after, the Committee (again including Thomas) asked Falla for permission to stage *Fuego Fatuo*. Nothing came of their request.

[12] *Ibid.,* p. 97.

However, it was announced that the concert to be held at the Carthusian monastery for the festival of 1933 would feature the first performance of the *Balada de Mallorca,* for a capella chorus, by Manuel de Falla. This was not a completely new work, but an almost literal adaptation of Verdaguer's poem of this title, to the initial *andantino* of the second *Ballade in F major* by Chopin, which he had composed in Valldemosa. Did Falla discern a relationship between the poem by Mickiewicz, which is supposed to have inspired Chopin, and that of Verdaguer? Did the mysterious water sprite of Switez who was changed into an aquatic flower to escape her Russian pursuers seem to him the sister of the young girl who weeps at the edge of a flower-strewn stream? Did he find in the gentle barcarole movement an apt basis for a work blending the poetry and the music of the ocean? Whatever his reasons were, he strictly preserved not only the structure but also the harmony of Chopin's piece, save for several measures, which we will cite here, using Thomas' account since the original manuscript is not available.

In the beginning the contraltos evoke "the sweet sounds of bells" with a prolonged sounding of the dominant, made more explicit by the repeated *la, la* of the tenors. The adaptation is literal up to measure 10, but from the second beat of this measure the tenors present a design, which, combined with light modifications of the basses and altos, produces "sevenths and ninths of a delightful and singular sweetness, denoting the presence of a modern adapter, but one wise enough not to take advantage of the absence of the brilliant romantic composer."[13]

From measure 26, the adaptation jumps to measure 83 and follows the original without any changes up to measure 108. Here Chopin has a long chromatic progression leading to a fortissimo. Falla sums it up in two measures *con gioia.*

The development returns to the original between measures 26 and 44. The adapter then uses a deft artifice "of authentic brilliance" in order to prepare on the deep and prolonged note of the basses (F major), "in which caressing sevenths float like clouds over an abyss," the chord of the fourth and sixth leading to the terminal

---

[13] *Ibid.,* pp. 116–121.

cadence in A minor. This is the cadence which astounded Robert Schumann, to whom the work had been dedicated; he would not admit that a passage in F major could legitimately end in A minor. "Who knows," adds Thomas, "whether Falla's modification, with delicate irony, might not have been aimed at reconciling the feelings of the two great romantic musicians . . . ?"

Thomas also observes the curious effects of onomatopoeia where the basses underline—measures 96, 97, 98—the song of the sopranos:

> *i a trossos lo cánter s'enfonsa rodant*
> (little by little the song is drowned)

and the expressive dialogue between tenors and sopranos:

> *Aii del plor que ella feia*
> (Alas, what lamentations came from her lips!)

The sponsors of the Chopin festival hoped that Falla would conduct the premiere of his *Balada*. But Falla deeply feared the drafts in the old monastery, and the weather threatened to be rainy. He preferred to remain in one of the monastic cells, from which he emerged only to acknowledge the acclaim of the audience. The local press echoed the audience's praises.

Some listeners were astonished by Falla's making an *andante sostenuto* of the original *andantino*. They forgot the requirements of the voices, which would have lost their ease of expression and their flexibility and become unwieldy in a more rapid movement.

Among the other works that interrupted the composition of *Atlántida,* Pahissa cites the revision of the overture to *The Barber of Seville* by Rossini, which involved the suppression of the trombone parts added after the opera had been written. Falla is supposed to have directed this new version for the first time in Barcelona. But, we know that the same arrangement had been announced as a premiere at a concert given by La Argentina on June 17, 1927, at the Théâtre des Champs-Élysées in Paris. It would appear that Pahissa is in error. Nor does Juan Maria Thomas, who saw Falla almost every day during his sojourn in Majorca and recorded his every utterance and deed in his book, mention such a concert.[14]

During this, Falla's first stay on the island, two other notable events occurred. One was a concert performance of the finale of the first act of *La Vida Breve*—the scene at twilight in Granada—all the more striking because, rather surprisingly, it had been preceded on the program by Strauss' *Don Quixote*. The other was on an entirely different level: the death of Enriqueta Albéniz, daughter of the great composer and friend of Falla. This woman, who had inherited "the vivacity and elegant grace" of her father, died at the age of forty-two, two months after Falla's arrival in Majorca. He was, of course, deeply grieved, but besides that, he was filled with remorse. He saw a coincidence in the fact that Albéniz himself had died two years after his—Falla's—arrival in Paris; his superstitious nature made him feel a kind of personal responsibility for these two deaths. (Enriqueta's husband was Don Vicente Alzamora, an excellent musician and the indefatigable secretary of the Sociedad Filarmónica on the island of Majorca.)

Shortly after the festival at the Carthusian monastery, Falla returned to Granada for the summer; he thought that there his precarious physical and mental health would be safer than on Majorca, where the one remedy for the summer's heat was "to close the shutters against the sun's rays and to open all the doors to the breezes!"[15] Obviously, this was unsuitable for one who tried to avoid drafts at all times.

Meanwhile, Spain's internal situation worsened daily, especially in Andalusia. After giving thought to other possibilities, like Provence and Switzerland, Falla decided to spend a second winter on "the island of calm" in the same tiny house as before. He and his sister arrived in time for the festivals of the Nativity that were celebrated in Palma according to an ancient Mozarab rite, which had been prohibited more than once since the Council of Trent. The diocese of Palma was the only one in the world that preserved this forbidden custom. It was called the *Canto de la Sibila,* and it dated from the tenth century. After its restoration by Bishop Vich y

[14] *Ibid.,* p. 154.   [15] *Ibid.,* p. 161.

Manrique in 1575, it was sung, or more precisely, played on December 24, Christmas Eve. The children of the Capella Classica were the dedicated actors. Juan Maria Thomas describes the unusual and charming ceremony "in which the Sibylline child, with flaming sword, emerges from a cloud of incense, while the chorus begins the hymn *Entre Ave et Eva* by Alfonso the Wise, followed by the *Canto de la Sibila,* which, evoking the oracle of Eritrea, announces the Second Coming of the Redeemer and the Last Judgment."[16] Falla listened intently to the songs carefully chosen by Thomas. "Attentive and motionless," Thomas writes, "his face stood out before an eighteenth-century reredos and among the images of three saints, where he seemed to take refuge; he seemed holy, so wise and ascetic in his anxious and pure search for perfection."

Falla's constant search for perfection was at this time concentrating on a short work in homage and gratitude to a friend, the great orchestra conductor, head of the Orquesta Sinfónica of Madrid, Enrique Fernández Arbós, whose seventieth birthday fell on December 24, 1933. A committee organized to render homage to Arbós had asked fourteen Spanish composers each to supply a work for orchestra not exceeding three minutes in length. Falla's contribution was a fanfare for wind and percussion instruments, conceived, as were the thirteen other pieces, on a theme formed by the letters in Arbós' name, to which he added the initials of the conductor's first and second names. The Orquesta Sinfónica performed the premiere of the fourteen homages on March 28, 1934, at the Teatro Calderón, in Madrid, under the direction of Arbós himself. The fanfare was to become the first movement of a suite of four homages dedicated to four very dear friends—Arbós, Debussy, Dukas, and Pedrell.

The intense work of composition—*Homenajes, Atlántida*—plus a copious business correspondence, was interrupted only on Sunday evenings when a *tertulia* brought to Falla's house the many friends, musicians, artists, and foreign travelers, "whom he received in the setting of cordiality, simplicity, and courtesy that he knew how to create around himself."[17] The winter passed peacefully.

[16] *Ibid.,* p. 188.   [17] *Ibid.,* p. 215.

That spring (1934) Alfred Cortot was among the participating artists at the Chopin Festival. The Carthusian monastery was filled. The Capella Classica opened the program with some folk songs harmonized by Pedrell, after which, "like a romantic echo of old monastic psalmodies," it sang a *Magnificat* by Villalonga, a sixteenth-century Majorcan polyphonist; this first part of the concert was brought to a close by Polish works in tribute to Chopin. Then Cortot appeared on the platform and played the *Ballade in F major,* as only he could. When the last chord was played, there was a moment of silence "vast and profound, like the slumbering soul of the old Carthusian monastery itself." Immediately the Capella began, pianissimo, the first notes of the *Balada,* while the great pianist still held his hands above the keyboard. The enthusiasm of the audience exceeded all bounds. Falla had to appear on stage; Cortot had to continue playing, and his interpretation of the *Twenty-four Preludes* seemed to be one of those miracles that happen only once in a lifetime. Cortot himself confided to Juan Maria Thomas that he did not recall ever having played while under the spell of such intense emotion.

On the day after this unforgettable concert, Cortot and Falla went to visit the old *finca* So'n Vent where Chopin had spent a painful month before moving to the Carthusian monastery. In spite of having been abandoned—or thanks to it!—it still seemed to be almost as it was when Chopin lived there, and the pleasantness, the peace of the surrounding countryside, added to the charm of this remembrance from the past.

Shortly after the excursion, Falla, who never lost his keen interest in the activities of the Capella Classica, dedicated to it his transcription of one of the choruses of *L'Amfiparnaso,* a *comedia armonica* by Orazio Vecchi. Falla considered Vecchi to be one of the masters of the best tradition of humor in Italian opera, three centuries before the Verdi of *Falstaff.*

Juan Maria Thomas saw Falla almost daily. By relating their conversations he sketches a moral portrait of the composer that agrees with the memories of Falla's friends. Just as internal rhythm and tonality were the pillars of his musical faith, so did charity and humility support the practice of his religious faith. In church he would become as absorbed in prayer "as a mystic in deep contemplation." He considered those petty verbal attacks that mark the gatherings of professional colleagues to be inspired by the devil; in his view "spitefulness toward our brothers is a most serious offense."[18] His affability with simple people was proverbial, from the *madona* who was the housekeeper in the *casita* to the most humble of his country neighbors.

Already at this time his religious feelings occasioned his concern about the possibility that a bad moral example could be drawn from his works, a scruple expressed later in his will. He hoped that his *Atlántida*—written in homage to the glory and omnipotence of God—would be reparation for what he called his "sins." For a long time he toyed with the project of fusing his religious ideas into a musical work. Thomas cites a letter written from Granada, September 26, 1926, in which Falla mentions his "keen desire to compose a Mass and [his] prayer to God that the time will come when he will be able to realize his project worthily, and with the necessary serenity of spirit."[19] This intention has been reported by many of his close friends, including Henri Collet[20] and J. P. Altermann.[21]

In a way, *Atlántida* fulfilled this keen desire. In Falla's view some elements of prayer may have corresponded to the *Kyrie,* the praises of the Divinity to the *Gloria,* while the affirmation of a robust faith might evoke the *Credo;* the angelic adoration of the *Sanctus* and the sweetness and mildness of the *Agnus Dei* might also be identified there. At least so Falla affirmed to Thomas, who cites F. Garcia Sanchez on this point: " 'Manuel de Falla was not Manuel de Falla. He was the reincarnation of St. John of the Cross. . . . Both followed the purifying, illuminated way that is united with God. . . . And Falla is the saint and scholar of Music, as Fray Juan is the saint and scholar of the Church' "[22]

Second only to Falla's religious feeling was his deep love

---

[18] *Ibid.,* p. 262.

[19] *Ibid.,* p. 270.

[20] *La Revue Musicale,* January, 1947.

[21] *Ibid.,* June 1, 1921.

[22] Letter to Señorita Joaquin Juncá, Director of Ediciones Capella Classica, Madrid, December 22, 1946, as quoted by Juan Maria Thomas, *op. cit.,* n.p.

for his country. "His ideal was that the spiritual unity of the nation be realized beyond its material unity, but not to the exclusion of the immense and diverse richness of each separate province."[23] His work, which began with concern for Andalusia alone, with *Atlántida* came to encompass all of Spain; this was the dream of his whole life.

To penetrate the core and to understand fully Verdaguer's poem, Falla had to subject himself to considerable labor. First, he had to learn the Catalan language, especially the style of Catalan in use in the poet's time. After a scrupulous study of ten cantos of the text, he undertook to form them into a libretto, religiously adhering to the original text, as he had done when transforming part of *Don Quixote* into *Master Peter's Puppet Show*. Thomas relates how Falla compiled a list of terms and fragments from Verdaguer, which he consulted each time he had to connect lines of verse or sentences to others far removed from them in the original. And thus did he also construct the *Balada de Mallorca*. Often, in the interest of greater accuracy he sought the advice or approval of Thomas and other Catalans among his friends. No effort was spared if it contributed to the patriotic spirit symbolized by his new work. He thought it might help to diminish the old rivalry between Castile and Catalonia, which at that time was increasing. In fact, Falla had been thinking about a closer connection between the two provinces when he was working on *Master Peter's Puppet Show*. He introduced into the finale the rhythmic and melodic essence of the Catalan folk song *El Desembre Congelat*. According to Thomas, that was a deliberate attempt to symbolize the closeness possible between the two provinces.[24]

An event of this period, reports Thomas, indicates yet again what greatness of character Manuel de Falla possessed.[25] His friend José Maria Sert brought him a very tempting offer from the United States. In exchange for permission to produce the world premiere of *Atlántida*, Falla was offered, literally a blank check! He would also be able to choose the performers and the orchestra for this performance. And Sert would have complete freedom in his staging of it. The painter, of course, was quite excited over such a

[23] Thomas, *op. cit.*, p. 277.
[24] *Ibid.*, p. 282.
[25] *Ibid.*, pp. 282–3.

project. But Falla flatly turned it down: "I am bound to Catalonia by a moral contract. I promised the first production of my work to the Orfeo Catalá, which will give it at the monastery of Ripoll. I cannot break my word." How rare it is, alas—such integrity and moral strength!

On June 18, 1934, Falla and his sister left Majorca to return to Granada. They stopped in Barcelona, where a special tribute was awaiting the great composer: a concert of his works, which he had agreed to conduct; it was the first performance at the Teatro del Liceo of *La Vida Breve,* and *El Amor Brujo* was to be on the same program. No one suspected then that this would be Falla's last public appearance in his own country before he left it forever.

Now, because of the internal strife in the country, the *carmen* in Antequeruela Alta could no longer offer the peace and quiet that he desired. Falla looked in vain for a more quiet place in a nearby village, then in the Sierra de Córdoba. Finally he returned to Granada, where he celebrated his name day on January 1, 1936, saying then that he had a feeling of well-being such as he had not experienced for a long time. He did not know that he was on the eve of a new, serious, and, unfortunately, permanent state of ill-health. Apparently due to the carelessness of a dentist, the hook of a bridge became loose and it appears that Falla swallowed it. It penetrated his intestines, where it produced the disorders from which he was to suffer until the end of his life. The beginning of the Civil War on July 18, 1936, found him confined to an armchair and incapable of sustained work. But he did not forget *Atlántida* and devoted himself to it any time that his strength permitted, interrupting it only to finish the *Homenajes* (Homages).

CHAPTER XV / *Homenajes*

As we know, Falla composed a fanfare as a tribute to the orchestra conductor E. F. Arbós. And it had been preceded by another tribute, the one which he wrote for a *Tombeau de Debussy* at the request of *La Revue Musicale* and of his friend the guitarist Miguel Llobet. The same magazine asked him for a similar work when they were planning an issue to be dedicated to the memory of Paul Dukas. This issue (May–June, 1936) was to be accompanied by nine unpublished pieces for the piano especially written for this *Tombeau*. We know about the deep bond of affection that existed between the two musicians for a long time before Dukas' death in May, 1935. Falla also felt he owed a great debt of gratitude to Dukas. Thus, Falla's work was to take its place alongside those of Florent Schmitt, Gabriel Pierné, Guy Ropartz, Joaquin Rodgrigo, Julien Krein, Olivier Messiaen, Tony Aubin, and Elsa Barraine, all friends or pupils of the master.

The general style of this brief fragment—forty-two measures, dated Granada, XII, 1935—curiously recalls that of the *Lento* of the harpsichord concerto and is even more similar to that of the *Sonnet to Córdoba*. It, too, is made up of a succession of large and austere chords, characteristics of a long-lasting feeling within Falla. This time he did not extract the thematic material from the name of his friend, as with Arbós, but from the essence of one of his works, the *Sonate pour piano,* published in 1906 by Durand. We can presume that this was one of the first pieces Falla got to know after his arrival in Paris.

A motif of four notes seems to wander amid the solemnity of this brief dirge. It is closely linked both to the second theme of the first movement—*modérément vite*[1]—and to that of the second—*calme, un peu lent*[2]—barely modifying its contours, in accordance with the laws of continuous variation to which Dukas adheres throughout the *Sonate*. Toward the end, there is a textual citation

---

[1] Cf. Paul Dukas, *Sonate pour piano*. Durand et Fils, Paris, p. 3, measure 8.
[2] *Ibid.,* p. 15, measure 4.

of the theme in fugal style which replaces the trio in the third movement—*vivement*[3]—of the *Sonate;* enhanced by two rests, it solves the
enigma posed by the structure of the initial theme:

Theme of the fugue: D-C-A flat-C (transposed).
Initial theme: D flat-C-C-A.[4]

The brief and beautiful fragment displays the richness of
his altered chords and appogiaturas, very much in the manner of his
departed friend, on a binary rhythm which does not depart from its
andante molto sostenuto (*in tempo severo*).

Pedrelliana, the fourth piece of the *Homenajes,* dedicated
to Pedrell, terminates this quartet celebrating the memory of the
four musicians for all of whom Falla felt affectionate admiration.
Like the two just described, this piece was inspired by themes from
the work of a revered teacher, in this case from *La Celestina,* the
opera that was never staged. Conceived directly for orchestra, it is
both the conclusion and the triumph of this suite.

Technical Study

Written for wind and percussion instruments, *Fanfare sobre
el nombre de E. F. Arbós* (Fanfare on the Name of E. F. Arbós)
opens the suite with four horns, three trumpets, two kettledrums, military drum, and muffled drum. The notes given by the seven letters
of the composer's name are:

E F A R B O S
E F A D(*ré*) B flat C(*do*) G(*sol*)

which are introduced by and shared among the trumpets.

The general tonality is a modal D minor in the Hypodorian
mode. After the trumpets, *molto fortissimo,* blare the name of the
great conductor, the horns come in at the third measure on the
dominant, while the drums rumble and the kettledrums, *con bacchette
di legno,*[5] vigorously proclaim the tonic and dominant. The role of
the horns is at first exclusively to provide a rhythmic support. At No.

3 *Ibid.,* p. 22.
4 Supplement to *La Revue Musicale,* May–June, 1936, p. 9, measures 36–38.
5 Wooden drumsticks.

1 of the miniature score for orchestra,[6] they respond to the theme, and their close union, their overlapping with the trumpets, beginning with No. 2 (p. 2), creates delightful chords in superposed thirds. Here we again find Falla's well-known concern regarding the utilization of harmonics. The very brief fragment (only 38 measures) ends on a triumphant chord of D major, affirmed by the violence of the drumsticks.

The second fragment, *À Claude Debussy* (*Elegia de la guitarra*), presents in its new orchestral dress the *Homenaje* to Debussy published by *La Revue Musicale* in 1920. The instrumentation includes woodwinds (with bass clarinet), two horns, two kettledrums, strings, harp, and celesta. The fundamental modality is Dorian E, which, as we know, is the point of departure of the guitar chord. Because this piece was discussed in detail in Chapter VIII, here we shall merely underline some orchestral effects which respect, if they do not affirm, the evocation of the deceased friend in the course of a meditation on the rhythm of a distant funeral march. The brief initial motif is darkened by the pianissimo sonority of the violas, the clarinet, and the flute. Several pizzicati portray the guitarist tuning up, and the harp undertakes, by means of its arpeggios, the task of reproducing the slashing strokes of his *rasgueado*. At the thirteenth bar, page 6, the characteristic theme from *Ibéria* breaks forth clearly in tutti, but Falla, an orchestrator of lofty taste, does not forget to suggest, by way of violent contrasts of shadings, the fluctuations employed by the Andalusian guitarist, a born improviser. The sadness of the first rhythm reappears like a funeral leitmotif (measure 16–19) between the different returns of the supple, voluptuous Iberian melody, in which the woodwinds and strings participate. Falla here and there marks some brief alterations of movement which the conductor is to indicate by lightly holding back the beat. At No. 6, p. 11, the subtle division of the strings, the blending of their pizzicati with sudden accents of the woodwinds, the light arpeggios of the harp, the celesta—all evoke on orchestra of guitars in which each performer might devote himself to achieving unexpected effects. At No. 8, p. 13, the leitmotif this time is expressed by two horns in

[6] G. Ricordi, Milan, p. 1.

octave, and the woodwinds share in the *rasgueado*. The descent of the melody to the augmented seconds leads to chords of the dominant in F sharp and in B; they surround with a halo of soft light the allusion to the *Soirée dans Grenade,* which unfortunately Debussy was never able to savor. Nevertheless, impalpable pizzicati of the violas and subdivided cellos suffice to produce a striking evocation of an invisible guitar in the gardens of the Generalife (p. 15, No. 10, measure 3). After a pedal point, the echo of the primitive rhythm is lost in the distance.

A brief recall of the fanfare leads into the third fragment, *À P. Dukas (Spes Vitae).* (To P. Dukas [Hope of Life]) It is a living remembrance of another great friend. Here again we shall single out just a few instrumental particularities. It is conceived for a large orchestra: woodwinds (with English horn, bass clarinet and contra-bassoon), four horns, three trumpets, three trombones, strings, harp, kettledrums, and percussion. This conception (actually that of Dukas, an added tribute!) enhances the richness of the harmonies and is in keeping with the solemnity of this succession of chords in the changeless rhythm of a procession. At the indication for the movement, *andante molto sostenuto,* Falla adds, in parentheses, *in tempo severo,* and for the strings, *intenso ma dolce.* The strings are in fact assigned the task of expressing the sadness contained in the rise in octaves of a short phrase of four notes, an evocation of the *Sonate pour piano,* which characterizes the atmosphere of the piece from the beginning. Outside of the textual citation (transposed) of the theme of the fugue (No. 6, measure 2, p. 23) and the more or less veiled allusions to the moving melodic lines dear to Dukas, we can discern an orchestral architecture akin to that of the composer of *La Péri* and *Ariane et Barbe-Bleue:* it is a concise, massive notation, with harmonic superpositions that leave no lacuna in the structure of the chords, but nevertheless do not prevent us from perceiving clearly the original musical idea. As usual, Falla lavishes minute care on the shading; the deep meaning of the musical text is set in bold relief by the accents and contrasts. The five notes of the theme of the fugue, well framed in rests, the diminuendo of the last four measures, precede the conclusion on a chord whose deliberate imprecision suggests a sad interrogation.

The last piece, *Pedrelliana,* celebrates the memory of his beloved teacher, Felipe Pedrell. Would not the best homage to him be to cite some extracts from one of his works, disdained by his contemporaries as well as posterity, for example, *La Celestina,* which was never performed on stage? Would not the listener sense an unspoken reproach for the indifference and ingratitude that was shown to this apostle of the renaissance in Spanish music? Falla did not fail to perceive this. The piece is based principally on the hunting theme with which Pedrell's opera begins. Writes Pahissa: "In order to justify his use of these themes and in order that his work would not be taken to be a 'Fantasy on ———' in the old manner, Falla portrays a scene resembling those painted by Orcagna in the famous frescoes of the Campo Santo in Pisa: 'The Joy of Life and the Sadness of Death.' It is the first of these two ideas which Falla wishes to evoke: a scene set against a pleasant and animated background, one in which, while the men are hunting, the ladies are gracefully singing and playing instruments as they sit under the trees on the flower-strewn turf."[7] It is a scene from the time of Fernando de Rojas, a fifteenth-century composer of another *La Celestina.*

Here the instrumental nomenclature includes the quartet of woodwinds, four horns, two trumpets, strings, harp, kettledrums, and percussion. Naturally the theme of the hunt, which is immediately (measure 6) resumed in tutti, is assigned to the horns from the beginning. At No. 2, p. 25, of the miniature score for orchestra, the first violins expound a tender cantilena punctuated by light arpeggios from the harp. According to Pahissa, this is one of the old court songs Pedrell collected and then used in *La Celestina.* Its rhythm— short-long, long-short—evokes that of a *zarabanda,* a dance particularly appropriate to a Spanish opera, although it was hardly widespread at the time Rojas wrote his *Celestina.*[8] The hunt draws nearer (p. 26, No. 4) and the horns are intensified, joined by the woodwinds, while the strings again play their *zarabanda.* This is followed by a grand development (p. 27, 2 measures before No. 6), *un poco*

[7] Pahissa, *op. cit.,* p. 146.
[8] The appearance of the saraband (from *zarabanda,* a dance of oriental origin performed by Jewish or Moorish *troteras*) dates from the sixteenth century.

animato, of the hunt theme, *sempre crescendo,* on a 3/4 rhythm in which triplets abound. Other themes follow one upon the other. In so short a piece the use of so many citations brings a degree of incongruity, despite Falla's delicate and skillful touch; he ran this risk, apparently, because he wished it to be a more complete tribute. Thus at No. 13, p. 35, we have an imitation of guitarists improvising a new dance in 5/4, in which the finales recall somewhat the Corregidor's obsolete minuet in *The Three-Cornered Hat.* Naturally, the theme of the hunt reappears from time to time, enunciated by the horns. Suddenly—*andante,* p. 43, 9 measures before No. 19—a bold modulation leads to a new idea. Is it the *vasco,* a song in the Cantabrian language, which Pahissa cites among the folk motifs borrowed by Falla? Its melodic character and its straightforward rhythm link it more to the northern part of the peninsula than to the province of Andalusia. The development of the theme of the hunt is heard for a last time, not without numerous interruptions in the form of echoes of the previous designs, up to the final *deciso quasi vivo.*

The *Homenajes* suite was to be the last work that Falla performed in public. He finished it in 1938, and directed the premiere himself on November 18, 1939, at the Teatro Colón in Buenos Aires. The work was performed again by the famous Argentine conductor Juan José Castro and by Jaime Pahissa, but not until 1953 was the score published by G. Ricordi of Milan, who are the owners of the work.

CHAPTER XVI / In Argentina

During the thirty months of the Spanish Civil War very little news trickled across the border about de Falla. His friends in Paris were disturbed. How was he getting along in view of the fragility of his constitution and the fact that there was no way for him to receive royalties, his only source of income? Camille Mauclair in an article in *La Page Musicale*[1] vigorously demanded news concerning the fate of Manuel de Falla, whom he hailed as a "brilliant artist and a great soul." Granada at that time was under siege; there was fighting in the street, and the Nationalists were garrisoned in the Alhambra, over which roared the planes of both belligerents.

Later, it became possible roughly to reconstruct the life of the great musician during this sad period. Ill, he hardly left his armchair; he could get up only with great effort, and had to be supported on his sister's arm whenever the sirens shrieked the alarm that meant they had to get to the nearest air-raid shelter. More than ever before he lived like a monk, making the catechism his daily reading —"in French," as his sister later assured the writer André Gauthier, who came to visit her in her retreat at Jerez de la Frontera. Falla wrote notes in the margins of the pages and at the end drew up a list of a number of questions that particularly troubled him. Perhaps he then dicussed them with his close friend Valentin Ruiz-Azna, choirmaster of the cathedral, or with his other friend, R. P. Otaño, who, according to Luis Campodonico,[2] gave him a thousand pesetas a month to help in his support. One day some government officials came to see him and asked him to compose an anthem. All that he could offer them was an arrangement of the *Song of the Almogávares* from Pedrell's *Los Pireneos* for a capella choir in unison. Apparently, this choral work did not suit the wishes of the "patriots," and they could not use it. However, the Estado Mayor school is supposed to have sung it in Burgos. The Republican government offered him the presidency of the newly founded Institute of Spain. He could not

[1] October 16, 1936.
[2] L. Campodonico, *op. cit.,* n.p.

—or would not—accept it because it would have required him to go to Burgos, a move which his health did not permit. Doubtless, his religious and political views did not permit it either.

Juan Maria Thomas reproduces a letter that has often been cited by commentators on Falla, in which he exclaims:[3] "What is to become of us? I assure you, *querido* Don Juan, that this is not living, and the worst thing is that I cannot manage to cure my illness, nor to terminate this poor *Atlántida,* which always loudly summons me and which I can barely attend to. In the end, since this is the way things are, there is nothing else to do except to submit to the guidance of the Supreme Will when our paltry human means turn out to be useless, or nearly so."

Several days earlier the Majorca radio had broadcast the news, attributed to the military command of Seville, of the death of "the great Spanish composer and musician, the great patriot Falla, better known in Seville under the name Maestro Falla." There was a feeling of great loss among his many friends on the island. Fortunately, three hours later, it was learned that there had been an error in transmission and that Falla's name had been confused with the name of the civil governor of Seville, a man named Farias. For Mossén Tomás here was the opportunity for a humorous note to which Falla replied ". . . this has allowed me to know what your feelings and those of our friends will be at the time of my future departure from this poor planet. May God reward you for this anticipated *Requiem aeternam.*"[4]

The Civil War ended in April, 1939, with the country in ruins. Many intellectuals went into exile. Federico Garcia Lorca had met a violent death at the beginning of the upheaval. And the clouds of war hung menacingly over the whole world.

An opportunity arose for Falla to find elsewhere the peaceful refuge which Europe could no longer assure. The Institución Cultural Española de Buenos Aires was preparing to celebrate its twenty-fifth anniversary, at the end of 1939, with a series of events, four of which were to be concerts devoted to Spanish music. Falla

[3] Letter dated February 15, 1938. Quoted by Thomas, *op. cit.,* p. 310.
[4] *Ibid.,* p. 312.

was asked to direct them, with the understanding that one of these concerts would be exclusively devoted to his works. After long consultations with his doctor, Falla accepted. According to a letter of Valentin Ruiz-Azna, he is even supposed to have envisaged giving up his *carmen* in Granada and, after his return, living in the Sierra de Córdoba where he had been offered a *finca*.[5] Be that as it may, he embarked from Barcelona, October 2, 1939, on the steamer *Neptunia,* with his sister Maria del Carmen, accompanied by several faithful friends, among them the pianist Frank Marshall, his former fellow student at the Madrid Conservatory. When the steamer docked in Tangier, he managed to avoid an interview with a correspondent of the Radio Nacional de Madrid on the grounds that he had not been making public declarations for twenty-five years and had no desire to alter this practice. He also refused to be photographed because he felt too sick and did not know how he could even have undertaken this journey. But he did promise that on his return he would accept the invitation and disembark in Tangier, since he regretted that he had no acquaintance with Africa.[6]

Upon his arrival in Buenos Aires, on October 18, he was welcomed by the members of the committee of the Institución and many admirers.

Rehearsals began shortly thereafter. This process was even more than usually exhausting because of the precarious state of his health. But fortunately Falla received inestimable support and cooperation from the eminent composer and conductor Juan José Castro. The concerts took place at the Teatro Colón and included works by Moralès, Victoria, Guerrero, Juan del Encina, Escobar, Albéniz, Granados, Turina, Halffter, Esplá, Pahissa, and Rodrigo; the last—November 18—was entirely devoted to Falla, as prearranged. As we know, the program included the first performance of *Homenajes.*

The physical and moral strain which the direction of an orchestra requires, the state of nervousness into which he was plunged by every public appearance, the various obligations, and the excitement of the great city had such an effect on Falla's fragile state of

---

[5] Cited by L. Compodonico, *op. cit.,* p. 151.
[6] A. Sagardia, *op. cit.,* p. 67.

health that a long rest and a change of air and altitude became absolutely necessary. The doctors advised him to settle in the mountains. He first chose Villa del Lago y Carlos Pax, near Lake San Roque in the Argentine province of Córdoba. His letters to his friend, the cellist Segismundo Romero, a founder of the Orquesta Bética, mention a new operation, attacks of fever followed by a slow convalescence, but also periods of well-being which he took advantage of to direct some concerts in Buenos Aires in order to improve his increasingly distressing financial situation.

In 1941 he moved to Alta Garcia, a charming little village in the same province, and settled down with his sister in a chalet called Los Espinillos (Mimosas). Pahissa gives a beautiful description of it:[7] "Los Espinillos . . . stands in the oldest and highest part of the town, at the end of a wide street. . . . It is surrounded by a garden with very stony soil, cypress trees by the gate, and pines at the back. Many orange, pomegranate, mimosa and other trees stand amidst aromatic shrubs, and large-leafed cacti grow against the walls of the house. The veranda, which catches the sun, looks out onto a nearby sierra, with its dense vegetation of evergreens interspersed with trees which the autumn turns to yellow or red and dotted here and there with black cypresses."

Falla loved "this delightful countryside, half-Spanish, half-Italian, with mountains, a verdant and flower-strewn prairie, and a climate which would be magnificent if it were not for this interminable summer and the wind frequently so torrid. . . . As for the rest, one might imagine himself in Spain."[8] From the Andalusia of his childhood and his maturity, his path ended in "New Andalusia," as it had been christened by Gerónimo de Cabrera, founder of the city of Córdoba.

Nothing was lacking in the interior of the residence, but Falla's room was as bare as a monk's cell: whitewashed walls, a simple iron bed, a chair, and a table covered with books. In his well-lit workroom a large table supported a pile of papers and many books arranged with care. A wide bay window looked out on the

[7] Pahissa, *op. cit.*, p. 163.
[8] Cited by Campodonico, *op. cit.*, p. 163.

sierra. If it became necessary to open the windows or the doors of the veranda overlooking the dining room to let in some of the pure air, Falla would have them closed when he went from one room to another, so absolutely terrified was he of drafts. His good friend Jaime Pahissa, likewise in exile, frequently visited him at this time. Pahissa relates that when Falla was in Buenos Aires, in the winter of 1942, to direct two radio concerts, he asked that the slightest cracks in the window frame of his hotel room, which was suffocatingly hot, be stopped up with towels to prevent any air from getting in.

The hours of his day flowed in a very normal rhythm at the time of his peaceful sojourn in Alta Gracia, although his timetable was minutely regulated. Falla rose late and devoted long hours—more than five, according to a letter that he wrote to Romero, and Pahissa corroborated it—to the care of his person and of his health. After that, he would attend to his correspondence—no letter addressed to him went unanswered. About three-thirty or four o'clock in the afternoon, he had lunch. After the siesta he took tea and began to compose, working at it until midnight, when he had supper. No servant could adjust to a schedule of this kind and, therefore, none endured it for more than a week! Pahissa dwells at length, and not without a touch of impatience, on the extremely meticulous habits of his friend, even in connection with trifling, everyday acts. In addition to his correspondence, the many visits that he received took up precious time, as formerly in Granada. But friendly, or simply human, relations were necessary to him: in private he was still "a great talker," to the point where he forgot his illnesses and the doctor's advice to avoid any needless effort. He would "raise his voice and become extremely voluble, until all at once he remembered and would drop his voice again and suddenly end the conversation."[9]

The conversation of such an artistic and subtle mind captivated his listeners in Alta Gracia, as it had those in Palma or Granada. Far from his native country, he was fond of evoking the years of his young manhood in Madrid, with his comrades of that time, Amadeo Vivès, Chueca, and others. "His observations were

9 J. Pahissa, op. cit., p. 168.

always acute and penetrating," whether he was talking about painting or music, about the early Byzantine influences on El Greco or the relations between certain Wagnerian literary themes and Catalan-Provençal literature: Montsalvat, Parsifal, and Tristan (whose Catalan equivalents, *Montesalvo, val per se,* and *Tan trist* mean "safe mountain," "value for itself," and "so sad.")[10] As for Debussy, commenting on his style as a pianist, Falla recalled how his friend always wanted "only the hammers to strike and that the fingers not be transformed into hammers." In Falla's view the value of Debussy's work lay first of all in the music itself, in the purely musical ideas, more than in its novelties. Therein resides the true beauty of a work of art, the divine spark which human labor causes to fructify until, purified, simplified, freed from all inessentials, the new work is finally ready for presentation to the public, like a house ready for habitation after it is cleared of all the materials that were necessary for its construction. Was he thinking of his harpsichord concerto when he made this assertion, which is so perfectly applicable to this work?

Thus passed Falla's days in this peaceful and charming retreat, interrupted only by some rare concerts, those for radio or the recitals organized in October, 1945, by the Music Circle of Córdoba. Falla had promised to attend, but at the last moment he had to give up the idea for reasons of health. He hardly left the house any more. Despite his piety, he even stopped going to Mass, unless the weather was exceptionally fine. At such times a car would take him to the Chapel of Lourdes, about a quarter of an hour from his house. On other Sundays he obtained permission to have the Mass read at home at the hour it was announced by the bell. His letters mention emotional crises, bouts of fever, and hemorrhages, which he attributed to the malign influence of the moon. We know that this heavenly body was one object about which he was superstitious. He was especially afraid of the equinoxes and the periods of the full moon, as at the time of *El Amor Brujo* and his Gypsy friendships.

But his financial situation was becoming a matter for concern, although he never complained. Royalties were no longer being

[10] J. Pahissa, *op. cit.,* p. 169.

paid to him because of the war, and one day he told Pahissa: "We have only enough left in the bank to last us a month, but God will provide."[11] His friends immediately set to work on his behalf. Articles were sent to Spain, where they caused a great sensation. The representative of the Sociedad General de Autores de España received instructions to pay the composer one thousand pesos a month as an advance on his accumulated royalties. Shortly thereafter he received a payment in dollars in exchange for the authorization to use the *Ritual Fire Dance* in a film in which Artur Rubinstein appeared. But he chose to decline his royalties until his colleagues, exiled Spanish musicians, could also receive theirs.

Another superstition of Falla's was the belief that his life was divided into seven-year periods. He thought that the tenth one would be his last; his presentiment was almost exactly accurate. The first two seven-year periods—childhood and adolescence—were spent in Cádiz, the third between Cádiz and Madrid. He definitely settled in Madrid in the seven years following, and then left for Paris, where his sojourn likewise lasted for seven years. The other periods were more or less clearly defined and were spent between Granada and his many journeys. The ninth seven-year period comprehended the beginning of the 1930's and the internal and external torments of war. Then the tenth seven-year period began in 1939 with his departure for Argentina.

Struck by this pattern, Falla wondered what fate the end of the year 1946 reserved for him. On the morning of November 14, 1946, several days before his seventieth birthday, the maid bringing his lunch knocked on the door. Hearing no response, she entered the room. Falla was dead.

Doctors diagnosed the cause as a cardiac attack. His body was taken to Córdoba for embalming. On November 19 an impressive funeral service was celebrated in the Cathedral in the presence of the civil authorities and the Ambassador of Spain. The coffin was then left in the sepulchral vault of the Carmelites in the cemetery of San Jerónimo until it could be placed on the steamer *Cabo de Buena Esperanza* on November 22. It was accompanied by the

[11] Pahissa, *op. cit.*, p. 179.

faithful Maria del Carmen, Falla's inseparable companion. On arriving at the Canary Islands, it was transferred to a Spanish warship and finally brought to Cádiz.

In his book Juan Maria Thomas tells how the Comisaria General de Música requested the Capella Classica to sing at the funeral service of the composer who had listened to it so often in life and so greatly esteemed it. On the morning of January 9, 1947, the cortege left the town hall under a leaden sky. During the procession the Capella intoned a Bach chorale which Falla had heard it sing many times. "Our eyes were like the sky, covered with clouds laden with sadness," writes Mossén Tomás. In the choir "near the magnificent stalls from the Sevillian Abbey of Santa Maria de las Cuevas," the *cantaores* sang a Requiem by Tomás Luis de Victoria, whose ardent and harmonious fabric, as Joaquin Rodrigo wrote, was "the only drapery worthy of covering the coffin of the foremost Spanish musician of our times." The coffin was placed in the crypt to the sounds of *In Paradisum*. Here Falla reposes under an inscription that he himself had requested: *"El honor y la gloria solo son de Dios."* (Honor and glory belong only to God.)

On September 8, 1960, a monument executed by the architect José Menéndez Pidal was unveiled in homage to Manuel de Falla. Very simple, it is in the form of an altar and rises above the tomb. But Falla's real memorial is in the hearts of the innumerable people who have been stirred by the music of this immortal composer.

Moreover, his memory lives wherever Manuel de Falla lived. In Córdoba, in Argentina, which welcomed him and softened his bitter years of exile, a committee was formed in 1946 for the purpose of erecting a monument to the glorious memory of its distinguished guest. His friends in Córdoba, who had often visited him at the Villa del Lago and in Alta Gracia, with a zeal of love, collected funds for the monument by means of recitals and concerts featuring Falla's works. A stamp was issued, reproducing the charming rustic retreat of Los Espinillos. Finally, a competition for a monument was held, and the commission was assigned to the sculptor Vicente Torró Simo, who is of Spanish descent. Since 1956 this monument has stood amidst the luxuriant shade trees of the Parque Sarmiento.

Many years had passed since 1926, the year Manuel de Falla decided to devote all his energies to what he considered the chief labor of his life. So many circumstances were to impede the completion of this work, begun with such enthusiasm. And death did not allow Falla to write *finis* in his own hand on the last page. More years were to pass before this posthumous work was presented to the world. It may be helpful to recapitulate the circumstances that so markedly slowed the actual composition.

First of all there was the minute timetable which inflexibly ruled Falla's days. Falla followed his daily ritual even before his exile. There were the hours devoted to the meticulous care of his person, even in normal times when his health did not call for such extreme measures. There were the numerous visits of friends, journalists, curious strangers (and Falla was a great talker), the intrusion of business affairs, and the letters he received from all parts of the world—all of which were not simply answered but replied to only after a rough draft and a revision had been made. Then a final copy was written either by himself or typed by his always devoted sister Maria del Carmen. Finally, we must recall the composition of works of greater or lesser importance, works which were created between the hours devoted to *Atlántida*. Alongside the *Sonnet to Córdoba,* the *Homenajes,* the *Balada de Mallorca,* the transcriptions and arrangements undertaken for the Capella Classica, the adaptation of Pedrell's *Song of the Almogávares,* we can also cite unpublished scores—the incidental music for the *auto sacramental* by Calderón de la Barca, *El Gran Teatro del Mundo,* and for the comedy by Lope de Vega, *La Vuelta de Egipto.* Account must also be taken of the time-consuming preparations that are indispensible to every public performance, the various interviews, rehearsals, and obligations of all kinds which are the price of success. And naturally Falla could not help but devote to these different works and obligations the same sustained, minute, and rigorous attention which characterized his whole life.

201

Several days after the funeral service in Cádiz, the Spanish diplomatic pouch carried a pile of manuscript sheets covered with the fine writing of the deceased composer. These were delivered to Falla's brother Germán. There followed a time when the world of music pondered the fate of the work which only a few of Falla's closest friends had been privileged to glimpse. There was no answer to their questions. What, for instance, was the importance of Falla's work? It was known that the work was unfinished, but nobody knew to what extent it *had* been completed, nor was the silence of the heirs and of the Spanish government designed to put a stop to the legends that arose everywhere and soon gained wide currency. (It would serve no purpose to list these worthless rumors.) This silence was due to two principal causes: the embarrassment of the heirs in the face of this mass of pages which were wholly incomprehensible to them because they were ignorant of music; and the Spanish penchant for secrecy, for retiring within oneself, for inaction. Eight years went by before Germán and Maria del Carmen decided "to do something": they entrusted to Ernesto Halffter the manuscript, the responsibility of putting the score into some kind of order, and also, should it prove necessary, the responsibility of completing it.

Ernesto Halffter was first mentioned in these pages because he conducted the Orquesta Bética jointly with its founder, Falla. Born in Madrid in 1905, Halffter is generally considered a pupil of Falla, but it would be more exact to call him a disciple. Falla never had any pupils in the strict sense of the word, except perhaps in the difficult period of his beginnings as a musician. With his customary amiability, Falla had taken an interest in the young composer's works and had studied them closely in order to give him advice and encouragement. Halffter exhibited such extraordinary gifts as a composer that in 1923 Falla entrusted him with the direction of the Orquesta Bética de Cámara, which had been founded in 1922. Subsequently he often sought Halffter's assistance as an orchestra conductor and collaborator; Halffter orchestrated the *Seven Songs* and the *Fantasia Baetica*. He had also been director of the Seville Conservatory since 1934, the composer of works which had been performed to critical acclaim in many countries, notably the *Sinfonietta in D* and the ballet *Sonatine*. The friendship between the master and his young friend, and their exchange of letters, continued to the last month of Falla's life. Hence it was natural that Falla's brother and sister should have thought of Halffter as the logical person to complete *Atlántida*.

Before discussing the state of the score and what Halffter's task was to be, some comments about Verdaguer and his principal work are in order.

Jacinto Verdaguer (1845–1902) was a deeply religious Catalan poet who later became a monk. He had written the long poem *La Atlántida* shortly after finishing his university studies. There is a striking similarity in the ideas which, at an interval of forty years, were to concern these two men, Verdaguer and de Falla, never to meet on this earth but nevertheless joined together in close collaboration. They were both stirred by the same legends, the same historical exploits, and they shared the same strong feelings for their native land, translating these ideas according to the imperatives of their individual temperaments. Imbued with the spirit of the Platonic epic, and with a Franciscan spirit of compassion and charity toward all the suffering around him, Verdaguer conceived his work as a synthesis of expiation and redemption, uniting mythology and reality, legend and history, the poetry of the past and the misery and injustice of the present. The grandiose vistas and the bold aspirations described by Plato in his *Critias* slowly founder on evil and perversity; the people deserve the punishments meted out by Hercules at the command of the gods; the fabulous continent disappears in the depths of the ocean, not to reappear until the day of the redemptive discovery of a new world. Verdaguer was espousing a symbolic, poetic view of the eternal thrust toward justice and happiness.

Not surprisingly, this poem had a tremendous impact on the mind and imagination of Manuel de Falla, who since childhood had himself been enchanted with these same poetic, mystic legends. But Falla was to superimpose his ardent patriotism on Verdaguer's symbolism. For Falla *La Atlántida* was Cádiz, Christopher Columbus, the Spanish epic, the grandeur of the Golden Century. Thus an incomparable civilization, a new moral law replaced the ancient one. We have seen how the work gradually took shape in his mind from 1926 on and how, as he was translating the original, he was

203

gradually transforming the work, retaining and then developing further only those episodes that suited the expression of his views. Thus Christopher Columbus, the Christian hero, is charged with a mission parallel to that of the ancient Greek hero, but the latter punishes, the former redeems. Hercules frees the earth of the monsters of chaos; Columbus, by his discoveries, frees the earth of the monsters of ignorance. He defies the *non plus ultra* which the past had inscribed on the outermost edges of the earth and brings the light of faith beyond the seas. Through Columbus the land of Spain will be magnified; her power will derive not so much from the riches of the new Atlantis but from the spiritual strength, the boldness, the lofty conceptions that stir her sons to action.

Such is the overall plan of the *cantata scenica* as conceived by Falla from Verdaguer's poem. In 1928, he was planning to divide its text into two parts. In a letter addressed to his friend and future stage designer, José Maria Sert, he wrote: ". . . the first part is based entirely on passages from *La Atlántida* by Verdaguer, the second (Columbus) only drawn from this text. The title will be *Atlántida.*" We see that when the work was hardly begun Falla had decided to drop the article.[1]

Another letter to Sert, dated October, 1929, implies that at this time the plan had been distinctly enlarged, necessitating special documentation. Already in 1928, Falla was consulting the *Raccolta di Documenti e Studi Pubblicati dalla R. Commissione Colombiana nel IV Centenario della Scoperta dell'America,* Rome, 1892, and the *Historia del Almirante Cristobal Colón* by his son Hernando in the Madrid edition of 1892. From Seville he received the text of a lecture delivered at the Real Academia Sevillana de Buenas Letras on the *Libros y Autografos de Cristobal Colón,* including a description of the *Libro delle Profezie.* Since his own Bible did not contain these prophecies, he asked his brother Germán to send him another Bible, including the texts of Isaiah's verses in Latin![2]

---

[1] The letter cited above is taken from the collection of Enrique Franco, *La Grande Avventura di "Atlántida."* Milan, 1962. The dropping of the article did not fail to surprise some critics and particularly Verdaguer's compatriots. One of them, Manuel R. de Llauder, reporting on its first performance in Barcelona in *El Noticio Universal* of November 25, 1961, claims that he never had known of such an omission.

[2] E. Franco, *op. cit.,* p. 6.

All this research was conducted with the greatest secrecy, in keeping with Falla's usual custom and his dread of gossip, particularly the kind spread by the press. In his collection, E. Franco publishes extracts from letters of that same year; among others, there is one to Roland-Manuel, in which the musician announces his new work: "Thank God," Falla confided, "the work is coming along well, and in two months at the latest we will be able to talk about it freely. Until that day I beg you to *conservare il segreto*."[3]

Only after he had established the definitive text and composed some fragments of his work did Falla decide to sign a contract with Verdaguer's heirs. Thereupon, he empowered his friend and adviser Juan Gisbert Padró, a Barcelona industrialist,[4] to act on his behalf. The contract was signed on January 12, 1929; it stipulated that the work in hand was a "lyric and theatrical adaptation" of the poem by Jacinto Verdaguer.

Thus, from the beginning Manuel de Falla had thought in terms of the theater. Although he had more than once emphasized his desire to give the first performance of *Atlántida* at the monastery of Poblet because of its religious, historical, and artistic associations, we cannot doubt that he had conceived his work with the stage in mind. This is confirmed by an important letter to José Maria Sert, dated November 10, 1928, which we shall reproduce later.

We must now examine the task facing the disciple.

Germán de Falla had been in contact with Ernesto Halffter from 1948 on, but the latter set to work seriously only in 1954. The house of Ricordi did not officially sign a contract with him as the adapter and future editor of *Atlántida* until October, 1955. In 1956, Guido Valcarenghi, general manager of Ricordi in Milan, signed for the receipt "of five fascicles with original cover of the manuscript score including 98 sheets and 132 pages; these original items being the Prologue and Parts I and III, among which figured sixteen sheets of useful indications (sic)." A year later, Falla's niece, the daughter of Germán—who had died in the meantime—Maria Isabel de Falla, and her husband José Maria Garcia de Paredes handed over to Valcarenghi 55 sheets containing 81 pages of music in Falla's own hand.

[3] *Ibid.*
[4] Son of Maestro Miguel Gisbert, a colleague of Felipe Pedrell.

This included the second part of *Atlántida* as well as the definitive libretto.

As we know, the manuscript delivered by diplomatic pouch was in the form of sheets of paper on which was a fine notation. Some sheets—the least numerous group—carried a complete orchestration; others, the notation of a finished but not orchestrated composition; the greatest number offered only more or less summary indications, references, outlines which at times were barely marked out.

Halffter's first job was to arrange and classify these sheets in the order indicated by the libretto. After this first systematization, Falla's work assumed the following form:[5]

Original part complete, composed and orchestrated:

Prologue: "Atlantis Submerged." *"Hymnus Hispanicus"* (lacking some measures of the finale).

First Part: entirely composed, but with an almost total lack of instrumentation: "The Conflagration of the Pyrenees." "Pirene's Aria." "Hymn to Barcelona."

Second Part: incomplete and confused. Only outlines of various versions that needed to be selected, orchestrated, and completed in part. "Hercules and Geryon, the Three-headed Monster." "Hymn to Atlantis." "The Garden of the Hesperides." "The Game of the Pleiades." "The Atlanteans in the Temple of Neptune." "Hercules and the Atlanteans." "Death of Geryon and Anteus." *"Fretum Herculeum:* Calpe." "The Messenger Voices." "The Divine Voice." "The Submersion." "The Archangel." "The Tower of the Titans." "The Cataract." *"Non Plus Ultra."*

Third Part: extensively elaborated. Choruses and orchestration were complete in various parts. Elsewhere, some connective points were missing: "The Pilgrim." "Isabella's Dream." "The Caravels." *"La Salve en el Mar."* "The Night Supreme." "Finale."

Clearly an enormous labor, a crushing responsibility weighed upon the disciple's shoulders. It was not a question of finishing *Atlántida* as Alfano had completed Puccini's *Turandot,* that is to say, of completing a work which actually was finished up to a certain point, by utilizing given thematic material. The situation with

[5] E. Franco, *op. cit.,* p. 17.

respect to *Atlántida* was entirely different. It was Falla's usual pattern to interrupt the composition of one part in order to devote himself to another. For example, the date given on one page of the manuscript, July 8, 1946, in all probability the last written by Falla, refers to "Pirene's Aria," which belongs to the beginning of the work. As regards the second part, it was necessary to extract all the musical inferences from its scattered elements. Some of them had several versions, which meant difficult choices. Most of the choruses were completed but some included only the top voice; work on others, such as the chorus of the Titans, had been stopped after the first few measures. Numerous cross-references, some of them exceedingly enigmatic, notes that referred to other fragmentary reminders, some not even connected with this work, compounded the confusion.[6] Without a deep knowledge of Falla's style, of his musical ideas and attitudes, it would have been impossible for anyone to undertake a reconstruction of this kind, and we should not be surprised that it took Halffter eight years to complete his Herculean task.

Upon its conclusion Halffter read the following statement to the representatives of the international press gathered in the auditorium of the Milan publishers Ricordi on the morning of the dress rehearsal[7] of *Atlántida*. (It was published thus in the newspaper *La Stampa,* Milan):

"1. In *Atlántida* we note the permanence of musical elements which Falla considered as eternal and which are linked to the world of tonal music. Although he did not deny the cultural interest of dodecaphonic experiments, he considered "tone" to be the fundamental base of music.

"2. Contrary to prevalent opinion, the folklore elements in Falla are the point of departure from which the composer creates his themes by transforming them into a stylistically evolved form.[8] For example, in "Isabella's Dream" (third part) the inspiration

[6] No intimate of Falla had any information that could help the adapter because of the absolute secrecy with which the composer had enveloped his work. It is believed that the only persons who had ever been allowed to hear any passages were his future collaborator José Maria Sert and his friend and representative Juan Gisbert Padró.

[7] June 17, 1962.

[8] This confirms the thesis sustained in Chapter IV of the present work.

derives from the blending of two folk songs, one from Granada, the other from Catalonia. But the musical creation is exquisitely 'Falla-esque.'

"3. Falla based his last work on the modes of the great Spanish polyphonic age. An exemplar of Christian humility, a profoundly religious spirit, he abstained from writing any sacred music which might not possess the grandeur expressive of the mystic impulse . . . such as the marvelous chorus *"La Salve en el Mar"* based on the text by Alfonso the Wise, which, musically, is related to the style of the eleventh and twelfth centuries.

"4. It was Falla's desire that *Atlántida* should approximate the tradition of the mysteries and of the medieval *sacrarappresentazione,* which were continued for a longer time in Spain than elsewhere, and also of the celebrated *autos sacramentales* of the Golden Century. He wanted the performance to be both the folk and the religious interpretation of a spectacle in the church or on the square in front of it."

This last paragraph answers a fundamental question: how did Falla conceive his *cantata scenica* and the music which would illustrate it in view of the apparent contradiction between the terms *cantata* and *scenica* (staged)? The composer conceived it precisely as an *auto sacramental,* that is to say, the dramatic representation of a religious act in which the people join through their songs. Hence the chorus was to be the principal element, describing and commenting on the action and free to take part in it. The religious act was to be evoked by scenes "which must give the impression of the old stained glass of cathedrals." At first Falla had envisaged a movable stage setting. He had given up this idea in 1928, as we shall see in his letter to José Maria Sert. However, the minute details contained in this letter make us think that he had not completely abandoned the idea of movement on stage, which signified to Falla the presence of different characters whose function is to explain the action to the spectator. In the end, three principal soloists and several supernumeraries directly took part in the action: the leader of the chorus (*coryphaeus*) or commentator on the action, who is almost constantly on stage, a contralto, and a soprano, allegorical characters who in passing lend their feminine grace to two of the "stained glass" episodes.

The chorus certainly represents the principal "character" of the work, which inevitably was to lead Falla to a conception of notation in keeping with the mystical concerns that increasingly commanded his being, a conception very different from that of his previous work.

We know how profound was Falla's knowledge of the monumental polyphonic works of Spain's Golden Century, through Pedrell and his own studies, and how immense was his admiration for them; we must also recall that while on Majorca he interrupted his work on *Atlántida* several times in order to revise and transcribe motets from that great period. The *Balada de Mallorca* itself indicates the extent of his concern at that time with choral expression. The chorus was not only to occupy the most important place in *Atlántida,* but it was actually to be a double one. One chorus, the chorus of narration, remains immobile and invisible. It comments on the action, alternating with the *coryphaeus;* the second, the chorus of the action, sings and at the same time portrays the unfolding dramatic events. As for the notation, it is adjusted to the requirements of the scene being represented, homophonic or contrapuntal when the liturgical meaning demands it, very often vertical in the bravura and combat scenes. In short, in the choice of expression Falla was guided solely by the needs of the action under development at that moment. The wish "to represent," "to do something new" without a valid reason was always far removed from his mind. Equally far removed was the spirit of a "return to" anterior styles, which was so much in the air in 1928. His association with Moralès, Guerrero, Victoria, and Escobar, did not lead him to copy them. Rather, in all humility, he tried to rediscover something of that lofty Christian thought, that mystic exaltation which had guided their hands.

The same holds true with respect to the orchestra. Before *Atlántida* Falla's orchestra was generally reduced in size. Witness the Orquesta Bética de Cámara. It could be properly reinforced, as with the four horns, trombones, and percussion instruments for *The Three-Cornered Hat* and *Nights in the Gardens of Spain,* and also elaborated with the meticulous artistry of a master goldsmith. This sort of orchestra in *Master Peter's Puppet Show* and the instrumental arrangement in the harpsichord concerto are so many precious jewels, and many of Falla's admirers did not see any other way ahead for him save that. But the epic *Atlántida* required a wholly different kind of orchestra, and listeners at the first concert presentation in Barcelona were not a little surprised at the important orchestral apparatus that they beheld, an apparatus required by the Prologue, which had been completely orchestrated by Falla himself.

Naturally, this considerable and unexpected battery of instruments did not fail to spark controversies. Had it really been so conceived by the author? The existence of this original page of the score was to dispel all doubts. The Prologue revealed Atlantis submerged at the bottom of the sea. And so at the outset it was necessary to create a grandiose, terrifying, somewhat wild impression—hence the election of a sonorous approach. Naturally, this would not be constant. From the very first, the choral conception requires a particular instrumental accompaniment. To avoid drowning out the chorus with a thundering orchestral mass, the voices are often doubled instrumentally, which leads the composer to reduce his forces. At times the chorus is set off against the orchestra, and a search for balance becomes necessary. At other times the chorus occupies a preponderant place. The orchestra is then more or less on the second plan, and at other times it is completely suppressed because the chorus must sing a capella.

These were the new problems which Falla had posed for himself and, as it turned out, for his adapter. Thus Halffter not only had to adhere to his teacher's known style but also to assimilate the novel elements that had been added to it. It was another difficulty to be added to the already formidable difficulty presented by the amorphous state of a good third of the score. The years it took to complete this work, which required the patience of a Benedictine monk, did not seem excessive to those who have been able to take a look at the manuscript.

After this long and necessary preamble, it is time to proceed to the heart of the matter and study the music of *Atlántida,* attempting to extract as much as possible of the original from the reconstruction. However, a final observation is called for. After having heard and seen *Atlántida* in concert and on stage, it seems to this author that nothing would be more difficult than to pin down exactly its musical level. Even to analyze it on a purely technical plane is more feasible. Before all else we must never lose sight of the composer's aim and of the thought which guided him in creating his work, namely, to write music with a religious symbolism, beyond time, beyond the world. Therefore, if our reaction is surprise at a style which at times uses the purest, the most traditional diatonicism, at times the most archaic—and in consequence the most mysterious —modal, surprise at simple choral chords in the notation, which is more often vertical than contrapuntal, surprise at an orchestration now massive, now gossamer-light, surprise at the personal vision expressed in a foreign language, surprise at a recitative *appena accompagnato,* we would be failing to understand the musical thought that deliberately willed this simplicity, stripped of all useless ornament, austere, ascetic, removed from any so-called "artistic" view. It would be both useless and unjust to conclude that Falla was in a state of decline as a composer because we do not discern here the spirit of innovation that presided over the elaboration of *Master Peter's Puppet Show* or of the harpsichord concerto. Except in the Queen Isabella scene, Falla rejected the refinement and the charm that was at once descriptive, picturesque, and so profound in the former, as well as the strange sonorities and the instrumental coloring of the latter work. It is through the most frugal means that Falla arrives at the loftiest, the purest emotion, which alone was in keeping with the loftiness of this own mystic soul.

It should once more be asserted that *Atlántida* is an immense fresco, a legendary and poetical embodiment of his native land. Had there been world enough and time, Falla perhaps would have treated differently those passages that some critics find a trifle too sonorous. We will never know. But if the orchestral force had seemed necessary to him, one cannot see why Falla would have omitted it, nor just how this short-lived sonority would modify the value of the work.[9]

[9] It was curious to observe the opposing factions that were immediately formed among the first listeners or readers of *Atlántida,* one coterie loudly calling upon the composer to continue along the path indicated by his former works, the other reproaching him, no less vehemently, for doing just that. The first was most skeptical and attributed any novelty to the intervention of Half-

Technical Analysis

We shall first present the order of the scenes that was finally adopted:

Prologue: "Atlantis Submerged." *"Hymnus Hispanicus."*

First Part: "The Conflagration of the Pyrenees." "Pirene's Aria." "Hymn to Barcelona." "Hercules and Geryon, the Three-Headed Monster." "Hymn to Atlantis."

Second Part: "The Garden of the Hesperides." "The Game of the Pleiades." "Hercules and the Dragon." "Lamentation of the Pleiades." "The Atlanteans in the Temple of Neptune." "Hercules and the Atlanteans." "Death of Geryon and Anteus." *"Fretum Herculeum:* Calpe." "The Messenger Voices." "The Divine Voice." "The Submersion." "The Archangel." "The Tower of the Titans." "The Cataract." *"Non plus ultra."*

Third Part: "The Pilgrim—Prophetic Chorus—Seneca's Prophecy." "Isabella's Dream." "The Caravels." *"La Salve en el Mar." "The Night Supreme."* "Finale: (*De Reperta America—De Cristoforo Colombo Appulso—Laudum Celebratio*)."

The orchestral arrangement of the Prologue includes two flutes and piccolo, two oboes and English horn, two clarinets and bass clarinet, two bassoons and double-bassoon, four horns, four trumpets, three trombones and tuba, two pianos, two harps, numerous percussion instruments, and subdivided strings. This arrangement is Falla's. As we have seen, he orchestrated the entire Prologue, including the *Hymnus Hispanicus,* except for the very last measures. Here the problem was to portray a tempestuous sea, a half-submerged ship, then, little by little, the vision of Atlantis lying at the bottom of the ocean. Large fortissimo chords, arranged in syncopation through the whole gamut of the orchestra, vaguely recall the dissonances of the harpsichord concerto. Then there appear those diatonic scales of which Halffter was subsequently to make much use. The disturbing impression of a mysterious and terrifying world is created. The first chorus (p. 2)[10]—the chorus of narration—

fter; the second, no less skeptical, overwhelming the unhappy adapter with accusations that he was responsible for any return to the past. . . .

[10] Pages and numbers refer to the score for piano and voice as established by Halffter. (Ricordi Publishers and Proprietors, Milan, 1962)

from the beginning establishes the modal feeling that will prevail throughout a great part of the work. The notation is vertical, psalmodic, set off against the dissonances of the orchestra. The vision fades away; the orchestra gradually falls silent. The *coryphaeus* asks himself anxiously (p. 16): "Who will save Spain, moored like a gondola on the tempestuous sea?" Still written vertically, the chorus sings of the future greatness of Spain in simple tonal harmonies, based on fourths and fifths in the manner of the organum, the firm, powerful rhythm of a crowd on the march. The persistent orchestral accompaniment suggests bells, but in Falla's customary manner, the bell effect is achieved more by the flutes doubling the trumpets than by the bells themselves. The Prologue is terminated by a rather curious plagal cadence (fourth degree).

First Part

We know that this part was composed completely. Falla left only some indications for the orchestration. The *coryphaeus* tells the shipwrecked child, whom he holds by the hand, about Hercules' journey through the world, the recital barely moving against the background of kettledrums (p. 25). The chorus of narration portrays the "Conflagration of the Pyrenees" (p. 28), alternating harmonic and tonal effects with canonic imitation. At the appearance of Hercules (p. 42), the chorus sings a capella, uniquely syllabic and on two superposed fourths.

A brief chant for two voices (mezzo-soprano and baritone, p. 44) announces "Pirene's Aria."

This, the last page written by Falla and incontestably one of the most beautiful of the score, evokes the ambience of *Master Peter's Puppet Show*. Indeed, a similarity is to be expected between the archaic, modal atmosphere of the beginning of the aria and the harpsichord theme in the fourth scene (No. 62) of *Master Peter's Puppet Show*: "the Pyrenees." Be that as it may, Halffter sees in the principal theme a song of Granada which Falla was to utilize later for Isabella's dream, with a different rhythm but in the same Hypodorian mode. (The dream is in the key of B minor.) The great charm of this ecstatic, melancholy, and distant aria derives from its beautiful melodic line, from the suppleness of its rhythm in a very reduced am-

213

bitus, and from its modulations, which always come as a surprise. A very heavy-footed march (p. 50) is outlined at the moment when Pirene invokes the name of her father Tubal. Almost voiceless, it fades on a strange, very dissonant, indeed discordant chord, suggesting a future as mysterious as it is menacing (p. 50, last measure). The very light harmonic support was entirely composed by Falla. At the twenty-first measure of the manuscript we read the only instrumental indications that he has left: harp, piano. At the twenty-ninth: horns in F and pizzicati on the cellos. At the thirtieth measure the chorus joins the accompaniment on a pianissimo *"Ah"* in two superposed fourths. Halffter is to be congratulated for the discretion of his orchestration here.

In order to bury the Queen's ashes, Hercules builds a mausoleum by piling, one upon the other, enormous rock slabs wrested from the mountains. The chorus comments on his action in an old Catalan song that was popular throughout the Pyrenees (p. 55). The *coryphaeus* announces the *barcino,* the name which Hercules will give to the city that he promises to found: this is the "Hymn to Barcelona" (p. 62).

The chorus, divided into four and six parts, alternates between polyphonic and harmonic notation. Rhythmically very firm, it imposes the tonality of E major. On the manuscript it is a capella during the first ten measures of exposition of the two themes: one in rather ornamented triplets, the other in note against note chords. At the eleventh measure the instrumentation intervenes, doubling the chorus, but without a particular precision. Halffter has accomplished it with four horns and clarinets and bass clarinet on the one hand, flute, oboe, English horn, and horns on the other. The harmonic passages are strongly scanned.

Here ends the first part in the original version. Stage considerations led Halffter to include in it the next two scenes. The ensemble as a whole thus obtained a more satisfying balance.

"Hercules and Geryon" (p. 66). The arrival of Hercules on the way to Cádiz is announced by energetic, ringing sonorities, sustained by the kettledrums and drums. Falla notes here six horns and trumpets for veritable cascades of chords between which slide the rapid scales of the strings. The chorus salutes the Greek hero with its *"Evohé"* (p. 67). To characterize the three-headed monster (p. 71), Falla conceived of a second tenor who sings in tremolo and with *portandos*. He is framed by a baritone and a first tenor whose ironic barkings on syllables, letters, onomatopoeic words, and brief, more or less falsetto accents underline the principal voice. The accompaniment proceeds with rapid strokes and deliberately exaggerates the grotesque and rather terrifying aspect of this trio.

The vision of Atlantis appears to Hercules. The chorus of the action intones the "Hymn to Atlantis" (p. 80) and this (new) first part ends in a blaze of brilliance. The indications left by Falla enabled Halffter to build an exact reconstruction of the composer's thought. As in the "Hymn to Barcelona," the notation is at times syllabic, hymnic, but above all polyphonic. Two themes supply this double conception, alternating their rhythmic oppositions. But the "motet" concern obviously prevails, although the general effect is primarily powerful, heavy, and majestic, as is proper to a chorus of Titans. The orchestration, with its sonorous differentiations, is limited to supporting the voices.

Second Part

This is the least finished, the most confused section of the whole work. Halffter had to choose among several versions, most of them barely outlined, which he generally completed and orchestrated along the lines that seemed natural. Falla's work seems to have posed numerous problems which were very difficult to resolve and to have presented him with a conception that was wholly exterior, grandiose, excessive, monumental, spectacular, and, in reality, quite removed from its real nature. Furthermore, the order of scenes in the libretto could not but increase his difficulties, as exemplified in the fourth and fifth scenes: "The Atlanteans in the Temple of Neptune," and "Hercules and the Atlanteans," which are almost alike. Certain repetitions in the action obscured and complicated things further. After the tempest, for example, the sinking of the rocks of the Straits of Gibraltar and the disappearance of Atlantis, we again see the Titans building a kind of Tower of Babel and trying to scale the heights of the very heavens before finally disappearing into the cataracts of the ocean. Falla certainly considered these scenes necessary to the completion of his immense fresco, but they must have considerably slowed his task, already so slow and beset with such a variety of obstacles.

This second part brings a welcome relaxation after the vigorous accents of the "Hymn to Atlantis." At the beginning (p. 99) the *coryphaeus* narrates how Hercules discovered "The Garden of the Hesperides" (p. 104).

A brief prelude leads into the rhythm of a barcarole, which will accompany the game of the seven Pleiades, princesses of Atlantis and guardians of the golden fruits that symbolize its wealth and power (three sopranos: Maia, Aretuso, Celaeno; two mezzo-sopranos: Eriteia and Electra; two contraltos: Esperetusa and Alcyone). The chorus of narration (contraltos, then sopranos) first describes the marvelous garden where the Pleiades will be seen at play (p. 104). The Pleiades enter (p. 108); they dance and sing while playfully tossing the golden fruits, which they constantly admire. The notation is that of a double chorus which is set against alternately four and three voices, or five and two voices. We also note passages in which the united groups are formed with two plus two plus three voices (p. 121 ff.), each group singing in unison and their union generally producing sequences of fourths or fifths. Musically and scenically this scene is one of the most beguiling of the whole score. Based on a theme in the mode of A (Hypodorian), key of D, its gracious melodic contours and the suppleness of its barcarole rhythm (in 9/8) evoke a madrigal suffused with a mysterious atmosphere and a magic charm. The orchestral part, very light, very clear, is entrusted to the divided strings and to some woodwinds. We come upon polytonal effects (p. 126); a chord of B flat on a chord of B minor. As the game becomes more animated, a sort of lyric fever possesses the sopranos (p. 127), and it is communicated to the ensemble until the moment when the young girls catch sight of Hercules. There is a sudden stop, then a rest (p. 133). This is followed by a total change of the harmonic color. On a breathless rhythm and in three parts, the Pleiades announce "the warrior whose coming their father had foretold" (p. 134). They hide near the tree bearing the golden apples, which is guarded by a dragon. The *coryphaeus* narrates how Hercules slays the dragon, while the Pleiades intone a dirge in chorus in three voices, note against note, which rather singularly begins with the *"Ay!"* of the *polo,* a specifically Andalusian dirge (p. 137). This song then unfolds (p. 140) chromatically on the repetition of the same notes: E, D, E flat, D. The chanting of the chorus (p. 146), describing the transformation of the Pleiades into a constellation, terminates this tableau.

"The Atlanteans in the Temple of Neptune" then make their appearance (p. 148). "A temple of enormous dimensions . . ." (as Falla wrote to Sert), Atlanteans, Titans, Giants, and Cyclops are gathered together. All are listening in terror to the recital of the ravages perpetrated by Hercules. Large chords hammer the voices; the chorus is heavily scanned, note against note, with the exception of brief passages in fugal style (pp. 152, 157). Tonal superpositions create rough dissonances (p. 153). The orchestra plays *ostinato* (*sordo e monotono,* p. 155, No. 40). To simulate terror, the basses of the chorus rhythmically strike their mouths with the palms of their hands, thus producing a sort of chromatic trembling, while the tenors and the female performers sing with closed mouths (p. 160 ff.). Apparently, this idea was Falla's. This strange chorus ends with cries of utter desperation. The orchestral support is made of chromatic trills cut by the glissandos of the strings. The aim of these unique descriptive effects is to evoke the disordered agitation of the Atlanteans, while the Pleiades, from the height of heaven, again intone their dirge (p. 166).

In the following scene, "Hercules and the Atlanteans" (p. 173), the *coryphaeus,* then the chorus, describe the struggle of Hercules against his enemies and his victorious return to Cádiz, where the monster Geryon still reigns over the city "of ivory and mother-of-pearl" (p. 179 ff.). The effects of the preceding scene continue until the defeat and death of the monster (p. 184).

But the struggles and labors of Hercules are not yet over.

"Fretum Herculeum: Calpe" (p. 188). This scene contains one of the most beautiful of the narrations assigned to the *coryphaeus.* The solemn melodic line, broad and supple, closely weds the syllables and vigorously underlines the grandeur of the Herculean exploit—the breaking asunder of the mountains, which lets in the masses of water that engulf the doomed continent. But a last warning

is given to its guilty inhabitants by the "Messenger Voices" (p. 192).

Falla must have tackled this scene and the two following ones—"The Divine Voice" and "The Archangel"—only after long meditations, searchings, hesitations, and torments. His deep faith, his mysticism did not allow him to deal with such subjects except with the greatest respect, as indicated in the memoirs of José Maria Pemán. Pemán states that for Falla the Divine Voice had to be sung by the innocent voices of children, because "only children are not unworthy of interpreting the voice of God."[11] At that time (1934) a Catalan impresario, who had already contacted Falla in connection with the performance planned for the monastery of Poblet, was the innocent cause of a fit of holy wrath that swept over the composer. Falla wanted the Orfeo Catalá to fall to its knees upon hearing the voice of God, but nonetheless to continue to sing. The impresario objected to this unexpected requirement:

"Come, come, Don Manuel, singers cannot project a voice from the knees! It's impossible!"

Falla's eyes blazed with fury:

"But how can one not fall to his knees if one hears the voice of God?"

These concerns are reflected in the manuscript sheets of the different versions, heavily erased, bearing only some notations with references and reminders which obliged the adapter to complete some measures here and there. For example, only the voice of the Archangel existed on p. 222, although Falla had expressly mentioned two contraltos and a tenor. On the other hand, the pedal-like choral support was indicated. Elsewhere, the chorus of Titans included only four completed measures, followed only by the top line.

In spite of everything, Falla's thought is perceptible, and the prudence and respect of his disciple have succeeded in preserving the sublimity of this extraordinarily simple polyphony, so moving in its purity, which recalls the spirit of Monteverdi. Consequently, there is very little orchestral support for the mysterious voices which predict the end of Atlantis (p. 192). It is then that we hear the voices of children singing *Sanctus* three times on simple chords of B

---

[11] José Maria Pemán, *op. cit.,* p. 165.

major, which are miraculously superposed on those of the chorus (p. 195).

"*Dominus Dixit*" announces the chorus (p. 196). Subtle, murmured dissonances create a supernatural atmosphere on which floats the *Vox Divina,* a simple romance expressed by the children's voices (p. 198). When we hear this part, we think of Victoria's *soave austero.* The modal effect is underlined by the intrusion of an E flat in the key of F, the use of certain intervals and the non-resolution of the leading tone. Lightly accompanied (violins and flutes in unison), these ensembles are often treated a capella.[12] "*Aixi diu Jehovah*" (thus spoke God) resumes the *coryphaeus* (p. 207), who announces the vision of Hercules contemplating the tempestuous seas (p. 208, No. 77). A total change of character follows. The chorus, very dissonant, *staccato e marcatissimo,* narrates how Hercules cleaves the mountain in two with massive blows of his mighty club. Save for p. 209, the notation is generally syllabic. The terror of the onlookers before the yawning abyss is expressed by cries that increase in intensity until the end of the scene. At the last measure (p. 218) a rapid descent running along the interval of an eleventh evokes "the towers which threatened the heavens and which now embrace the earth." It is "The Submersion" (p. 219).

The Titans rebel during the submersion of the once proud continent. An archangel appears brandishing a flaming sword. In the absence of any indication, Halffter chose to double the melody in unison on the pedal of the chorus arranged in four octaves (p. 222). We have seen previously that the chorus of the Titans which follows (p. 224) in "The Tower of the Titans" included only the upper voice and four completely written measures, which Halffter drew on in order to complete and harmonize the ensemble. This scene, duplicating "The Atlanteans in the Temple of Neptune" (p. 148 ff.), recalls the same chromaticisms, the same effects of terror, cries, and "lugubrious and horrible" howlings (p. 227), *portandos,* and *glissandos* with closed mouth, but with greater intensity. Three soloists,

---

[12] According to Halffter, a note by Falla concerning this passage contains a fugued fragment based on the song of Salinas *Retraida está la Infanta* (second scene of *Master Peter's Puppet Show*). If he did not use it, he at least preserved its atmosphere.

challenging each other and describing the action, are set off against a double chorus specifically entrusted with these various cries (p. 226). The orchestra's only role here is to furnish padding, consisting of very dissonant chords, arpeggios, scales in rapid passages, and other artifices. The effects continue, even more accentuated, with blunt oppositions which go from fortissimo to *pianissimo subito,* like a crowd in the grip of panic. The Tower of the Titans collapses; all are swallowed up in the abysses of the ocean. But the voice of the archangel is heard again. These last two scenes, "The Tower of the Titans" and "The Cataract," are so similar to each other, in addition to their common resemblance to the "Atlanteans in the Temple of Hercules" and the scene of Hercules' struggle, that we can consider them as different versions of the same idea. In any case, it is good that they were kept, if not on the stage, at least in the score.

The last scene of the second part reveals the pillar on which Hercules, with the point of his sword, engraved the words *Non plus ultra* (p. 264).

Here the chorus of narration (with closed mouths) and the orchestra resume the dissonant, strange, grandiose, and wild chords of the Prologue (p. 265), which symbolize Atlantis and her catastrophe, in short, the very subject of the *cantata scenica.* Then, *mormorato,* on a few repeated chords, the chorus announces that all that remains of the accursed continent is a whirling abyss whose waters will slowly subside.

Third Part

As we have seen, the manuscript sheets of the third part are in a rather finished state of composition, in some points actually complete. Elsewhere they do present indications sufficiently precise— save at the extreme end—to enable the adapter to terminate the work with a good deal of certitude. This third part contains the most beautiful, the noblest pages of the score, not surprising since Falla's mind was most decided concerning this part of the subject. We also know that he rearranged Verdaguer's text in order to conclude his work on an act glorifying his native land, on an act of faith in and love for his country. But it is also an act of religious faith, as is proved by the last pages of the score: *La Salve en el Mar,* the

Hosanna the immense *Hallelujah,* texts which could not but exalt the inspiration of the musician and believer to its peak.

There is no *coryphaeus* in this third part. The shipwrecked child has become a man, but he has not forgotten the beautiful story that the old man told him, and the aim of his life is to give to his country the land that was wrested from it in the fabled past. His name is Christopher Columbus. He walks pensively in the twilight, not far from the stone pillars which bear the name of Hercules, and he thinks he hears mysterious voices calling to him from all corners of the horizon: "Christoferens! Christoferens!" Other voices sing a distant prophecy. Bells ring; their tone is profound and sonorous.

Venient annis saecula seris, quibus Oceanus vincula rerum laxet et ingens pateat tellus.

These words are arranged on a fourth (E–A) held by the divided basses, but the composer noted the accompaniment in counterpoint, which the chorus then takes up again (p. 266, No. 4). This is a chorus of deep feeling, marked by a purity and a simplicity of expression that is altogether Palestrinian in effect. Very slowly it describes the pensive walk of "The Pilgrim" (p. 267) in search of the star which will guide him to Queen Isabella. The Queen herself is thinking of the distant islands that a dove has revealed to her. Seated in a court of the Alhambra in Granada, she describes her dream to her ladies-in-waiting as she embroiders a precious cloak of blue velvet, which symbolizes the richness of Spain, situated on the sea that is bordered with marvelous lands predestined for glory.

"Isabella's Dream" (p. 274). These pages are a delight. They are the gems of the score, jewels which Falla delicately carved as he had already carved and mounted the precious song of Salinas in the "mounting" of *Master Peter's Puppet Show*: "Melisendra." The manuscript here is so nearly complete that, happily, we possess Falla's own complete thought. Here we discover the Falla who liked to imagine Isabella of Parma playing the spinet in the delightful Tocador de la Reina of the Arab palace.

The orchestral prelude, entirely composed by Falla, is marked *pomposo e gagliardo*. Actually, it is a somewhat solemn dance executed by the Queen's ladies and pages. It is preceded by a few arpeggios on the harp (doubtlessly replacing a lute), the only instrumental indication contained in the manuscript. A theme in 3/2 time—*marcato ma dolce*—cut by stops on half notes (in 2/2) provides the desired rhythm. The notation, very contrapuntal, in the spirit of a madrigal in four voices, remains clear and airy, and Halffter's orchestration—two harps, woodwind, no violins—is a model of discretion. The diffused modality is treated with a masterful hand, and the cadences are without a leading note or a dominant, the conclusion being effected on a resounding chord in G major.

"The Romance" (p. 276). It is preceded by the open-voice recital of a lady-in-waiting, a contralto, to which the voice of a page responds, accompanied by several chords on the harp. The Queen sings (p. 277, No. 17): "A dove was dreaming as dawn was breaking. . . ."

The romance utilizes a Catalan folk theme, the initial melodic phrase of the song *Bon Caçador: "una matinada fresca,"* but elaborated, modified with an art and a delicacy that transform it into a completely Fallaesque melody. This is the result every time this composer employs a theme derived from folklore. The Catalan critic Manuel R. de Llauder, to whom we owe the above information, sees in the phrase endings an Andalusian *giro,* Falla's tribute to both of the provinces from which he came, both very dear to him. The irregular rhythm confers upon Isabella's romance the nostalgic languor of a *guarija,* and the part-ternary, part-binary lilt of the melodic line rests upon the more accentuated divisions of the accompaniment.[13] Naturally, the modal feeling announced by the prelude continues in the "Dream." The key of G with a C sharp (Hypolydian) predominates and gives the passage its strange color. As regards the orchestration, the notes left by Falla are fairly explicit. At No. 18, p. 278, Falla prescribes oboe, clarinet, and pizzicati on the strings. At No. 19 (8 measures later), horn, two solo violins, harp. Three measures farther on, a tutti of violins. At No. 20, a *"harpe brève."* On a separate sheet, Falla had mentioned a harpsichord, a bagpipe, and a *"petit violin!"*

This admirable melody, a veritable anthology by itself, ends

[13] A song of the islands, the rhythm of the *guarija* must have especially impressed Falla here.

222

on a short passage for the chorus of action (the Queen's ladies-in-waiting), who marvel at the triumphal light enveloping Isabella's head like a halo (p. 285). The vision is slowly transformed into an apotheosis of the Queen, King Ferdinand, and Christopher Columbus, whose name the children repeat: *"Christophorus: haec dixit Dominus"* (God hath said these things, p. 287, No. 21), to which the chorus responds in a chant, note against note: *"Affer filios meos de longinquo, et filias meas ab extremis terrae"* (Bear my sons from afar, and my daughters from the ends of the earth, p. 289).

An orchestral prelude based on the original accompaniment of the scene of the caravels (p. 293 ff.) prepares for the heroic, very external effect that Falla desired, according to his manuscript notes. It is a song of valor and glory, in which the people shout their faith in the bold enterprise of the seafarer and his crew. Calls from the brass instruments were inserted here; they were, however, required by the rhythms and shadings noted by the composer. The misunderstanding of some critics, who saw this as a "storm for a Metro-Goldwyn-Mayer film," their sadness at observing "a certain weakening of the master" can only be explained by their real incomprehension of the stage requirements of this scene, to which the following scene furnishes a contrast all the more striking; Falla's *La Salve en el Mar* (p. 300).

This is a great masterpiece, the high point of the score; these are the most beautiful pages Falla ever wrote, indeed the most beautiful written by anyone since the beginning of the twentieth century. "Music beyond time, beyond the world," as was said before, a music which is the unique expression of a soul whose purity reaches across the centuries to join that of times forever lost. We hesitate to analyze such a musical idea for fear of robbing it of its freshness. Technically, it is perfect. We have only to listen to it, to let our hearts and minds drink it in. We cannot cease admiring the counterpoint, for it has an airy subtlety but also a sureness which has no peer except in the loftiest productions of the Renaissance.

Here Falla utilizes a Gregorian fragment extracted from the *Cantigas del Rey Alfonso el Sabio*[14] and entrusts it to one bass

[14] According to M. R. de Llauder, this Gregorian theme became part of Catalan folklore.

part and to two tenor parts, on which he superposes the voices of the children, thereby creating an impression of sublime religiosity.

There are few instrumental indications on the manuscript, except for a tremolo in the extreme bass on D, E flat, or a sequence of triplets around the same notes. Blank measures with the indication "orchestra" in the abbreviation, prove Falla's intention to complete them. Halffter assigned the tremolo to the bass strings and doubled the chorus with light touches from the woodwinds.

The baritones sing a psalmody—pianissimo and in unison —(p. 306): *Liberator meus de gentibus iracundis,* and "The Night Supreme" (p. 307), which precedes the departure of the caravels, begins.

On the theme of the prophetic chorus (cf. p. 269, No. 4), the chorus of narration tells how Christopher Columbus passes the night in lonely vigil. Then it intones a *Dies sanctificatus* (p. 309, *coro mistico*), simple and moving in expression, in which two fugatos are separated by a *Factus est Dominus* a capella, followed by the "Finale" (p. 312):

> *De reperta America*
> *De Christoforo Colombo appulso*
> *Laudum celebratio*

These few lines in Latin immediately suggest the atmosphere that will prevail in the "Finale." The "Voices of the Empyrean" join the "Voices of the Earth" to proclaim the triumph of Christopher Columbus and the grandeur of the homeland. The hispanic Cathedral appears, and the heroes arise from their tombs.

The "Finale" opens on an orchestral prelude of a descriptive, picturesque character which has particularly disconcerted critics. The caravels discover the New World, its birds, its palm trees, its exotic flowers. The harmonic setting and the instrumental touches at times evoke Debussy, at times Ravel's *Lever du Jour*. For this prelude, Falla had noted bird calls, which we find again on p. 313, at No. 60, and at the fifth measure of No. 61, p. 314. One is moved by the date of this notation—2-13-41—when Falla was living in Argentina. He had also procured an Inca theme, not surprisingly under the circumstances, and included it on p. 314, second measure, and p. 315, first measure. At the bottom of one fragment he noted: Catalan; at the bottom of another: Granada.

But we must clearly recognize that the indications left behind by Falla for this prelude as well as for the choruses that follow are rather imprecise. Thus, the choruses open with the *Hosanna* (p. 321, No. 66), for which there existed only the accompaniment in half notes on two staves, meant for the strings. It is followed solely (p. 322, No. 68) by the entry of the children. Another sheet included effects in quarter notes for a flute; rapid scales in quavers cutting the stave[15] further down. The *Laudate* (p. 327) was merely sketched, and the two choruses that had been envisioned remained in the state of chords in whole notes and half notes. On another sheet a passage in counterpoint in three parts with a flat in the key signature preceded the entrance of the children. There are several versions of *Adoremus Te,* with references indicating the harmonic arrangements in four parts. Under these conditions we can understand the enormous task Halffter faced in order to put this "Finale" in working order and still not violate Falla's wishes.

Beginning with three parts—two for bass, one for tenor—the *Hosanna* increases to seven parts, in addition to the added children (p. 323, No. 68), and even up to ten parts. The notation is generally vertical, at times very dissonant. We note curious superpositions: voices divided into two groups, that is, a trio of soloists set off against the ensemble of the others; in this way the sonority is considerably softened. The modulations are often very sudden, which makes us think that Falla deliberately must have written fragments of different themes, planning to weld them together later. The shadings are violently set off against each other. After the pianissimo of the *Adoremus Te* in C flat (p. 329), we pass, almost without transition, to the *Glorificamus Te* in A major in full voice (p. 331). Falla had consulted Dante's *La Vita Nuova* for this *Hosanna*!

The immense final *Hallelujah* opens after a chord of E flat

[15] This padding is quite unexpected from Falla; we find no example of it in his previous works. But we see (from the manuscript) that he himself suggested it to his pupil, who has been unjustly reproached. However, might it not be possible that in this "suggestion" Falla was noting down a special effect to be realized later in another way?

(p. 336, No. 74); it is extensively elaborated, written in a very free contrapuntal style, creating striking dissonances that confer an intense life upon this beautiful passage. At the beginning Falla noted: *Cantos Cataluña,* and it does indeed have a folklore flavor. The contrapuntal lines are at times cut by "hallelujahs" strongly scanned, in tutti, on groups of quavers (p. 337). As for the orchestral realization, it could only follow the choral notation, which it simply doubles. It is obviously very exterior and deploys its brass, its tremolos, and its percussive instruments without great discretion. But the importance of the choruses, the shading, which is almost constantly fortissimo, and, above all, this "Finale" celebrating the glory of the ancestors required a sonorous setting. Falla himself could not easily have done otherwise.

After a rest on a chord of G sharp, we pass to the verse *Pleni sunt coeli* (p. 341, No. 77), which contains a *Sanctus* based on the notes of a carillon of San Francisco (p. 342). At this moment the notation becomes exclusively vertical; the "hallelujahs" are scanned note against note; the values broaden considerably, and the *cantata scenica* ends with a last *Gloria*; it is held by the clarity, the purity of an immense fortissimo chord in C major.

The question inevitably arises: Was it really necessary to complete *Atlántida?* The great majority of the critics who heard the first performances in Barcelona and in Milan agreed that it was indeed necessary. The general view at once ranked some of the music among the most beautiful, and the loftiest expressions ever created.

If these passages were deprived of their context, even an imperfect context, they would lose a part of their meaning and purpose. At any rate, the score was too nearly completed to condemn it to the obscurity of the shelves of a library. As regards Halffter's contribution, we have seen that the original conception, a work based on choruses and recitatives, left only a secondary role to the orchestrator. On the other hand, in the central part in which Halffter had to undertake a real job of reconstruction, he was so imbued with Falla's spirit and so respectful of his friend that he was incapable of abandoning Falla's point of view. Only a comparison between the original manuscript and the complete score reveals that they are not one and the same. At a performance, the joinings and the unity of the whole work are such that it is impossible to discover a fault, to find anything out of place. In the final analysis, isn't this what really matters?

It was alleged—during the long silence after Falla's death and before the resurrection of *Atlántida*—that in his will the composer, under the influence of the extreme mysticism of his last years, had condemned all his works, particularly those for the theater. In addition to the fact that the right to produce his works after his death belonged to the public, to posterity, and, in a very real sense, to the publisher-proprietors, it was neither possible nor conceivable to leave the world of music in ignorance of a score to which, as we know, Falla attached the greatest importance, for it was the aim of his whole life, conceived and written with such faith and hope.

To conclude, we shall cite the opinion of a critic who can hardly be considered partial to the work. In response to the question posed above, Jacques Lonchampt wrote in *Le Monde* on December 16, 1961: "After the performance in Barcelona, I reply 'yes' without hesitation. Despite its imperfections, the work is so beautiful and so profound; it opens such vast perspectives on the development of the genius and the creativity of Falla that we do not even have the right to reject that work in which he has put the greatest enthusiasm, as he himself said in 1927."

Ricordi in Milan, the proprietors of Falla's works after the *Homenajes,* decided that the first stage performance of *Atlántida* would take place at La Scala. However, in order to conform with Falla's vow, and with the request of his heirs and those of the poet, and doubtless with public opinion, the Spanish government arranged for two concert performances of part of the work to be given at the Teatro del Liceo in Barcelona, Verdaguer's native city. These took place on November 24 and 26, 1961, and were followed, on November 30, by a third in Cádiz, Falla's native city. On the stage of the Liceo—where a stationary, very simple setting suggested the "hispanic Cathedral"—were the soloists Victoria de los Angeles, soprano, Raimundo Torres, baritone, four Catalan choral groups,[16] and the

[16] Capilla Clasica Polifonica of the F.A.D.; Coral Sant Jordi; Chor Madrigal; Escolania del Sagrado Corazon (P. P. Jésuitas).

Orquesta Municipal of Barcelona directed by its eminent conductor Eduardo Toldrá, who was actually crowning his musical career, for he died very soon after this event. The evening was memorable. Spain sent her most representative sons, and the international press was on hand; the emotions of all present reached a climax when the conductor, responding to the acclamations of the crowd, on its feet at the end of the performance, raised aloft the pages of Falla's score.

Spanish and foreign newspapers were unanimous in stressing the importance of the event, as well as the remarkable features of the work. In Barcelona's *El Noticio Universal* for November 25, 1961, the critic Manuel L. de Llauder wrote:

"In the construction of his posthumous work, Manuel de Falla had wedded simplicity to architechtonics, placing this union in the service of the lyric-dramatic intensity of the text, along with great mastery in the use of liturgical sonorities. This coincides in a certain way with the system employed by Stravinsky in his *Symphony of Psalms* and his *Mass*."

In *La Prensa*[17] F. Baratech recognized that the "great merit of Maestro Ernesto Halffter, Falla's disciple and collaborator, lies in his successful accomplishment of the task of assembling and reconstructing the fragments of *Atlántida,* to the point that we do not distinguish the part written by the eminent Gaditanian composer from the part by Halffter."

La Vanguardia, editorially[18] expressed its pleasure that "the Chief of State," through his vigorous insistence, had succeeded in obtaining for Barcelona the premiere of *Atlántida*. This was because of Verdaguer himself, because of Falla, who was fond of the city, the language in which the immortal verses were written, and, of course, because of Falla's repeatedly expressed wish that its first performance be held there.

Two of France's most eminent critics must also be quoted:

Clarendon: "Falla gives me the feeling that he is a prophet rising from his tomb after fifteen years—fifteen years of research, interpretations, experiments, discussions—to tell us: 'Behold the

[17] November 25, 1961.
[18] November 26, 1961.

truth, behold the music in which the image of the human adventure is but the reflection of the divine plan'!"[19]

Claude Rostand: "When the echo of the last chord dies away, we have the impression of having heard one of the most beautiful things in music, and during the performance we have constantly been saying to ourselves: 'How simple it is'!"[20]

On June 18, 1962, the curtain of La Scala rose on the Prologue and the three parts of *Atlántida*. This time, two women soloists shared the "Death of Pirene" and the "Isabella's Dream," Giulietta Simionato and Teresa Stratas respectively; the baritone Lino Puglisi sang the role of the *coryphaeus*. The secondary characters, mimes, dancers, the choruses of action and narration (led by the famous choir-master Norberto Mola), and the La Scala orchestra were under the baton of the young American conductor Thomas Schippers, who bore the official—and envied—title of *Maestro concertatore e direttore*. The décor and costumes were executed by the painter Nicola Benois, and the production was staged by Margherita Wallmann.

The atmosphere of the evening was different from that of the concert in Barcelona. On the one hand, the time—the end of the season at La Scala—was badly chosen; on the other the Italian public did not have the same nationalist reasons for enthusiasm as did the Spaniards. Nevertheless, the local and international press—and there was even more of the latter than at Barcelona—on the whole was full of praise for both Falla and his adapter; it was unanimous in its praise for the *fact* that this work had been concluded and performed. The only criticisms were directed at the staging.

Before turning to the press notices, one ought to learn more about that letter, referred to earlier in this chapter, which Manuel de Falla wrote to José Maria Sert:

Granada, November 10, 1928

My Dear Sert,

. . . This idea just occurred to me—but at this distance what we can do is of little use . . . and I shall not be coming

[19] *Le Figaro,* November 27, 1961.
[20] *Le Figaro Littéraire,* December 9, 1961.

to Paris before the end of May. Since I received your letter I have prepared these notes to supplement, although only in part, those that I had already written. I consider it indispensable that you be familiar with music that I am led to write and that we exchange impressions on my scenic "intentions." Can we not anticipate things somewhat in another way? Would you be able to come toward the end of the year or at the beginning of next year? (January is the best "moment" of the year in Granada!) I assure you that if it were not for the lack of time of which this work is the cause, I would go to Paris to spare you this trip. But . . . it is impossible.

Well, to return to the staging: Each day I see with greater clarity and conviction that the tableaux must be *motionless;* we must abandon the first project of the mobile tableau. It must be nothing like that. But what can be done is to divide the (principal) action of a tableau into two or more parts (when the dramatic situation requires it), separating the tableaux by tulle curtains which would obscure one while it faded away, and then, inversely, would be raised, revealing the *second* part of the tableau. The *tableaux* must *also* give the impression of the old stained glass windows of a cathedral, *but much more distinct and wholly transparent. . . .* The result of my recent visit to old Italian cathedrals has been *definitively* to reveal to me what up to now I sensed only approximately and as if in a hidden desire. I don't know whether I am making myself clear. . . .

But let us go back to the matter at hand: With respect to the Prologue it is already understood that the rising curtain will reveal Atlas supporting the firmament and Atlantis submerged (walls, arches, towers of different heights). Read the following strophes. (The pages that I indicate *always* correspond to those of the last edition of the poem, published by the Librarie de Catalogne.)

Page 27: "Behold the sea. . . ."

Page 28: "Behold the Titans, whose kingdom is boundless. . . . Their king is Atlas . . ." (but with the following variant that I consider necessary):

"He whom the sons of Greece imagine as a great mountain, his head crowned with stars—crouching, he effortlessly bears the machinery of the skies."

Further, on the same page: "One night the Giants bellowed: 'Oh, Atlantis, where art thou?' "

And after (p. 29): " 'And thou, who saved thee?—The omnipotent one.—What dost thou with thy riches?' "

Thus ends the Prologue.

I still have some doubts about the scene "The Conflagration of the Pyrenees," which I shall deal with subsequently, and which probably will be the first one of this first part. (The work, I remind you, will include two parts.) You understand that what I see as regards décor, costumes, etc., is of value only as an *indication,* but it seems to me to be useful to have you see how *I* see the scenes when I compose the music.

Gades. First, huge silver columns with neither base nor capital, on one side only, supporting a stronghold or a rampart also of silver. Three-headed Geryon (The Old Man of the Sea) is among the columns with his two-headed dog. Geryon appears crouching in front of Hercules (Alcides [*sic*]), who advances threateningly as he raises his club. In the background the Gaditanian harbor with numerous red and black, wide or pot-bellied ships. Some have a bronze prow and fly a purple flag. A silver wall encloses a part of the harbor. Afternoon sunlight.

Characters: Geryon ("That loathsome image of fraud"— Dante, *Inferno,* XVII.)

Of his three heads, the one in the middle is like a . . . .[21] One of the other two heads is bent, the face swollen with rage, eyes agitated. The third head, wholly red, looks backward with its serpent-like expression. The light shines on the three heads "like a kind of crown of gold" (*Ap.* IX). His hands are clawed, hairy, as are his arms right up to the armpits, and his shoulders, chest, and sides are covered with shields lashed together.

"Tartars or Turks never made cloth with more colors or groundwork and pattern, nor were such webs laid on the loom of Arachne" (Dante, *id.*).

[21] Word illegible.

Hercules. Greek helmet of thick leather, with plumes of horsehair in the center of it. A belt of tough vegetable fibers which, on the left side, supports a quiver full of arrows. A short tunic of dark metallic material, over which a lionskin is thrown. A huge bow is slung over his shoulder; his club is at his right. Thick sandals tied with fibers.

"The Garden of the Hesperides" (p. 45 to 49 of the poem). The seven daughters of Hespedes (the Pleiades). Songs and games. Dress: something like the Athena of Phidias (Dresden).

Alcides, entering the orchard in order to affix a branch to his helmet as a crest. The dragon. Lamentation of the daughters of Hespedes. Voice of Atlas. End of the *Canto de las Hesperides*.

The Temple of Neptune (Interior). Immense in breadth and height. The walls are of rock. The vaulted roof is made of ivory, inlaid with silver and gilded copper. There is an enormous statue of Neptune, whose head almost touches the ceiling. As for the exterior (used subsequently), its walls are covered with tin. The crenelations will appear gold in the reflections of the fire.

Atlanteans, surrounding the idol. Titans. Earthquake. A flash of lightning encircles Neptune's head. Mournful phantoms flit by like shadows. The Atlanteans gather in a secret meeting. They hear the clamor of their sisters.

Atlanteans and Cyclops tearing down, bit by bit, the pillars of the temple as they prepare to struggle against Alcides. Clamor of the Hesperides: "Alas. Behold the warrior whom our father had foretold. He comes," etc.

In disorder there appear other Titans—the oldest ones—brandishing weapons fashioned of stone and bone. Through the atrium of the temple we see Hercules, carrying the branch of the sacred tree. All hurl themselves on the hero, but Alcides, brandishing his terrible club, opens a pathway through them, toward the road to Gades, where he will plant the shoot of the orange tree.

"*Fretum Herculeum:* Calpe." Hercules cleaves the mountain in two with one blow of his club, letting the sea flow in.

"The Archangel—The Divine Word" (chorus): "The stars

and the planets seem to stop to hear the new, the most exalted word of God the omnipotent One."

The chosen strophes (pp. 68–69):

1. Giving, by the heart, to the earth.
2. For him, of the spacious dome.
3. Him against me. . . .
4. Oh! every threshold. . . .
5. Never more shall the continents be joined. . . .
6. Why do you splash me with mud? . . . .
7. But quick to efface it . . . .
8. I, I wish to mix them. . . .

The two strophes, then, end the "song"—*Gibraltar,* etc. The narrator will recite or sing them. During the preceding chorus ("The Divine Word"), we see Alcides prostrate "like a tree bending. . . ."

Hirsute, suddenly inflamed, terminating his work of destruction, he passes through the accursed land almost to the sea. At the beginning of the scene ("Calpe") the setting sun illumines the mountain; at the end the sky is dark and . . . "Dantesque. . . ."

"The Song of the Hesperides," who, as if stricken with madness, rush forward to meet Alcides—"God or mortal, whoever thou art, who submergeth my country," etc. "But no! Take me not away!" etc. (pp. 85–88).

The voice of Atlas (each time preceding the farewells of Hesperis to her daughters, p. 77). "Because you are mine, my daughters . . . ," and the two following strophes.

"The Submersion of Atlantis." Hercules, struggling with Anteus, smothers him between his arms by raising him off the earth. During this time, the Atlanteans, despairing of reaching Gades and fleeing the ocean's flood, try to storm the heavens. With tree trunks and even bushes that they carry up onto the mountain, they form a Cyclopean mound. They climb upon each other's backs; they reverse the clouds; those in the highest position raise their giant arms to reach the star-studded dome of the firmament.

The human fortress gives way, crashing down in a horrifying

cascade, while the Archangel, sheathing his endless sword, ascends again to the heavens. And Hercules, in the distance (far upstage) erects two columns of rocks. With his sword, he inscribes on them: *Non plus ultra*.

Thus ends the first part.

Second (and last) part:

Voice of the Empyrean: Christoferens!

"The Pilgrim." Columbus (in a coarse gray tunic like a Franciscan monk's, but with the traditional cap) is walking with a dragging step along a rugged uphill path, strewn with black crosses; the path is on different levels. An opening almost in the center of this path provides a glimpse of the Atlantic between the Pillars of Hercules (*Non plus ultra*) in the distant horizon. Through the amber columns the setting sun illumines the ocean and the earth with a magnificent light.

Prophetic chorus: *"Venient annis saecula seris,"* etc. (Seneca, *Medea*)

"Messager del Altissim? tu vinerias a relligar, colonna d'Isaias," etc.

"Isabella's Dream" (p. 148, etc.). Romance sung by a child's voice. Will this be a tableau? From the point of view of the physical design, could it not be a supplement to the Prologue ("Atlantis Submerged")?

We see the Queen embroidering the edges of her cloak, representing an immense and luminous sea, from the center of which rise the new islands. Above soars the symbolic dove, which drops the ring of the Queen, as she watches it.

"The Night Supreme." The prow of the Admiral's ship. Sails swelled by the wind. . . . Clear and starry sky, in which a few sea birds are flying. A faint flame seems to rise in the distance.

Columbus. His shoulders near the prow lantern, which faintly shines on him; he leans over the edge of the vessel. He raises his head and seems to be scrutinizing eagerly the immensity of the sky above him and of the sea around him.

Coro Mistico: "Credidi, propter quod locutus sum," etc. (*Psalms*, 115). *"Non timebo millia populi"* (*id.*, III, 6). *"Ecce Deus, salvator meus"* (*Isaiah*, XII, 2). Hymn: *"Ave Maria Stella."*

Prophetic voices: *"Qui sunt isti, qui ut nubes velant et quasi columbas,"* etc. *"Me enim insulae expectant,"* etc. (*Isaiah,* LX, 8–9).

"The Discovery." The Land of America. Splendid forests (very tall palm trees?) on the coast. In the background the prows of the three caravels with their captains (great beards, rich armor and clothing) and their noblemen. All are on their knees in an attitude of worship. On the ship in the center—the *Santa Maria*—Columbus, dressed in the uniform of an admiral, standing as though transfigured, with his arms crossed over his breast. At his side an ensign kneels holding aloft the royal banner of Ferdinand and Isabella.

A thick cloud envelops the vision. Then, gradually, the cloud dissolves, disclosing an immense cathedral. The trees (palm trees?) of the forest have been transformed into tall columns, but the ships have remained, occupying the background and keeping the same position. The tombs of the temple (the hispanic Cathedral) have opened; there emerge, alive once more, the Iberic heroes, the captains, the seafarers, the saints and heroes of a glorious history.

"Voice of the Empyrean, Voice of the Earth": *"Hosanna in excelsis. Benedictus qui venit in nomine Domini. Hosanna in Altissimis,"* etc.

I end now for today, dear Sert, three days after beginning this letter. When you have read these notes (which I pass on to you in absolute secrecy) tell me what you think and how they relate to your work. But I can assure you that they correspond exactly to mine. Once more, I believe that it is indispensable that we see each other in order both to establish everything and so that you may hear what I have succeeded in doing (?) which is enough, yet, nevertheless, *much* remains to be done.

This letter, whose indications were religiously and scrupulously followed at the first performance, reveals the difficulties facing the designer and the director. They thought they had resolved them by the use of an unchanging framework—the arches of a cathedral with great lofty columns—within which the tableaux would be projected and the soloists and the chorus of action would move. Some tableaux did succeed in poetically evoking the miniatures of an ancient manuscript as though the audience were turning the old pages. But others seemed unendurably heavy.

In this strict adherence to Falla's wishes, perhaps those responsible for the staging forgot that his ideas dated from a time when concepts of staging were very different from today's. Since Falla's time there have been the Wagners at Bayreuth, futurism, the bare stage, abstractionism. . . . Tastes have changed, as have methods of staging. But the real question is, of course, elsewhere. If the stage representation shocked some people, it did not modify their opinion as to the value of the work. Claude Rostand in *Le Figaro Littéraire*[22] sharply criticized the sets and all the more so because he felt that what was at stake was the "song of a man who has something important—very important—to say and who says it in a vocabulary and a style of radiant beauty." And Marcel Schneider (*Combat*), who also did not like the staging, saw in Falla "one of the greatest polyphonists of this century, the worthy successor of Cabezon and Victoria."[23] As for Clarendon, he concluded his second article in *Le Figaro* by writing: "What a work! It is not a Gospel, but a Summa. It is not a search for a new world of sonority, but a return to the purest sources of tradition. On the condition of having genius, one can indeed make something new with the oldest materials, and if one is called Christopher Columbus, one can discover virgin lands in the old tonal universe! It is a beautiful thing that Falla reminds young composers of this truth and that he ended his life not in a pyrotechnical display, but in peaceful contemplation."[24]

Of course, representatives of the Italian press came to the Milan performance from all corners of the peninsula. These are but a few of the opinions they expressed:

Massimo Mila in *Espresso*[25] wrote: "The 'Finale' contains, in the prophetic chorus, the galliard and the romance of Isabella, the *Salve en el Mar,* and the 'Night Supreme,' the most beautiful things of

[22] June 28, 1962.
[23] June 20, 1962.
[24] June 19, 1962.
[25] July 1, 1962.

the whole work and in fact the most beautiful things of all the music of our century."

In *La Epoca*[26] Giulio Confalonieri wrote: "A work that is constantly interesting, marked by an immense will and by an exemplary austerity, made solitary by its faith, its enthusiasm, its piety. . . . The heroic episodes, principally the episodes of Alcides and some of Columbus seem obtained by exterior means. . . . On the other hand, aspects like the scene of the Hesperides, the romance of Queen Isabella, and the prayer of Columbus' sailors demonstrate a powerful and ingenuous capacity to create in music."

Giorgio Striglia in the *Corriere Mercantile*[27] wrote: ". . . The part of the choruses, by far the most important, certainly represents the noblest, loftiest, and most inspired work modern music has produced."

In *Il Resto del Carlino* of Bologna[28] Lionello Levi commented: "Falla forsakes Andalusian and Castilian Gypsies, guitars, and castanets; he escapes from those nights and those gardens of Spain so suffused with mystery and sensuality . . . in order to go back to the spirit of the Palestrinian sixteenth century and the treasures of Spanish polyphony."

Finally, in *L'Europeo,*[29] at the conclusion of an article full of praise, Eugenio Gara especially singled out the chorus as "the real protagonist of an *Atlántida* that runs no risk of being submerged!"

And so this New Atlantis was finally revealed to the world. Now it is for posterity to judge the work which its author dedicated as follows:

> "To Cádiz, my native city,
> And to Barcelona, Seville, and Granada,
> To whom I am also bound
> By the debt of profound gratitude."

(signed)
Manuel de Falla.

[26] July 1, 1962.
[27] June 21, 1962.
[28] June 21, 1962.
[29] July 1, 1962.

Bibliography

Alfonso X el Sabio, *Codice de los Cantares y Loores de la Virgen Santa Maria*. Better known under the title *Las Cantigas de Santa Maria* (thirteenth century).

Aubry (G. J.), *Music and Peoples*. London, 1922.

Barbieri, *Cancionero de los Siglos* XV y XVI. Madrid, 1890.

Borrow (G.), *The Bible in Spain*.

Bottineau (Y.), *Espagne*.

Campodonico (L.), *M. de F.* Paris, 1959.

Casella (A.), *Le Piano*. Ricordi Americana, 1942.

Chase (G.), *The Music of Spain*. New York, 1941.

Chase (G.), *The Book of Modern Composers*. New York, 1942.

Collet (H.), *Essor de la Musique Espagnole au XXᵉ Siècle*. Paris, 1929.

Collet (H.), *Le Mysticisme Musical Espagnol au XVIᵉ Siècle*. Paris, n.d.

Combarieu (J.), *Histoire de la Musique*. Paris, 1942.

Dieulafoy, *Espagne et Portugal*. Paris, 1926.

Dumas (A.), *Voyage en Espagne*.

Gautier (T.), *Voyage en Espagne (Tra los Montes)*. Paris, 1878.

Golea (A.), *Esthétique de la Musique Contemporaine*. Paris, 1954.

Grove's Dictionary of Music and Musicians. See art. Falla by J. B. Trend.

Hilaire (G.), *Cantaores Famosos. Initiation Flamenca*. Paris, n.d.

Irving (W.), *L'Alhambra*.

Lavignac (A.), *Encyclopédie de la Musique et Dictionnaire du Conservatoire*.

First part, see articles:

Mitjana (R.), *Musique en Espagne*, p. 2003.

Laparra (R.), *Musique et Danse Populaire en Espagne*, p. 2353.

Second part:

Pirro (A.), *L'art des organistes*, p. 1198.

Pujol (E.), *La Guitare*, p. 1997.

Gigout (E.), *Musique Liturgique,* p. 2327.

Pierné (G.) and Woollet (H.), *Histoire de l'Orchestration,* p. 2657.

Gérold (T.), *Monodie et Lied,* p. 2788.

Tiersot (T.), *La Chanson Populaire en Europe,* p. 2904.

Bernay (Mme.), *La Danse,* p. 3423.

Laplane (G.), *Albéniz.* Geneva, 1956.

Larrieu (R.) and Thomas (R.), *Histoire Illustrée de la Littérature Espagnole.* Paris, 1952.

Levinson (A.), *La Argentina, Essai sur la Danse Espagnole.* Paris, 1928.

Lorca (F. Garcia), *Romancero Gitano.* Paris, 1954–1955.

Lucas (L.), *L'Acoustique Nouvelle.* Paris, 1854.

Matos (M. Garcia), *Cancionero Popular de la Provincia de Madrid.* (Ed. critica de M. Schneider y J. Roméu. Figueras.)

Matos (M. Garcia), *Folklore en Falla,* in *Música,* I, II. Madrid, 1953.

Matos (M. Garcia), *Lirica Popular de la Alta Extremadura.* Madrid, 1944.

Moreaux (S.), *Bartók.* Paris, 1955.

Neville (E.), *La Musique Espagnole,* in *L'Esprit Nouveau,* No. 18.

Pahissa (J.), *Vida y Obra de M. de F.* Buenos Aires, 1947.

Pannain (G.), *Modern Composers.* London, 1932.

Pedrell (F.), *Por Nuestra Música.* Translated by A. G. Bertal. Barcelona, 1893.

Pedrell (F.), *El Cancionero Popular Español.* Barcelona, n.d.

Pedrell (F.), *Hispaniae Scholae Musica Sacra.*

Pedrell (F.), *Organografia Musical Antigua Espanola.* Madrid.

Pedrell (F.), *Estudia Sobre Folklore Musical.* Paris, 1909.

Peman (J. M.), *Cien Articulos.* Madrid, 1957.

Pomès (M.), *Lorca, Poète de la Tradition Profonde.*

Pujol (E.), *Escuole Razonada,* with a preface by M. de F.

Robersart (Countess de), *Lettres d'Espagne.* Paris, 1929.

Roiter (F.), *Andalousie.* Lausanne, 1957.

Roland-Manuel, *M. de F.,* Paris, 1930.

Sagardia (A.), *M. de F.* Madrid, 1946.

Salazar (A.), *Música Moderna,* in *Cahiers d'Art,* No. 10.

Salazar (A.), *La Música Contemporánea en España.* Madrid, 1930.

Salazar (A.), *Música y Músicos de Hoy*. Madrid, 1928.

Salazar (A.), *Sinfonia y Ballet*. Madrid, 1928.

Salazar (A.), *La Música Actual en Europa y Sus Problemas*. Madrid, 1935.

Samazeuilh (G.), *Musiciens de Mon Temps*. Paris, 1947.

Sanz (G.), *Instrucción de Música Sobre la Guitarra Española*. Zaragoza, 1874.

Schonberg (J. L.), *Grenade et le Miracle Andalou*. Paris.

Sermet (J.), *Espagne du Sud*. Paris-Grenoble, 1953.

Silva (P. Andrade da), *Anthologie du Cante Flamenco*. Paris, Madrid, 1954.

Sopena (F.), *Escritos Sobre Música y Músicos*. Madrid, 1947.

Terrasse (H.), *Islam d'Espagne*. Paris, 1958.

Thomas (J. M.), *M. de F. en la Isla*. Mallorca, 1947.

T'Serstevens (A.), *Itinéraire Espagnol*. Paris, 1951.

Trend (J. B.), *M. de F. and Spanish Music*. New York, 1929.

Unamuno (M. de), *Entorno al Casticismo (Essence de l'Espagne)*. Paris.

Vallas (L.), *Debussy et Son Temps*. Paris, 1958.

Verdaguer (J.), *La Atlántida*. Translated by A. Savine. Paris, 1911.

Villar (R.), *Falla y Su Concierto de Cámara*. Madrid, 1932.

Articles on Manuel de Falla published in *La Revue Musicale*, Paris. Issues of November, December, 1920; June, October, 1921; April, November, December, 1922; February, March, August, December, 1923; January, 1926; July, 1927; April, 1928; July, 1930; May, 1931; February, 1932; April, 1934; May, June, 1936; February, 1940; July, 1945; January–February, 1947.

OTHER PUBLICATIONS

Musical Times, vol. 58, April, 1917. *The Chesterian,* vol. XXI, October, 1923. *Excelsior,* May 31, 1925. *Revue Pleyel,* October, 1925. *Musical Quarterly,* vol. XXIX, October, 1926. *Musique,* September 15, 1929. *New York Times,* November 23, 1930. *Music and Letters,* 1942, p. 133. *A B C,* Madrid, August 6, 1944. *Música,* Madrid, January, June, October, December, 1953.

PRINCIPAL WRITINGS OF MANUEL DE FALLA

La Musique Française Contemporaine (Preface to the book by G. J. Aubry), *Revista Músical Hispano-Americana,* July, 1916.

Claude Debussy et l'Espagne, in *La Revue Musicale,* December, 1920.

Felipe Pedrell, ibid., February, 1923.

Notes on Richard Wagner, for the Fiftieth Anniversary of His Death, Revue Cruz y Rayas, Madrid, September, 1933.

Notes sur Ravel, in *La Revue Musicale,* March, 1939.

Published without the name of its author: *El Cante Jondo,* Granada, 1922.

The Works of Manuel de Falla

Title	Genre	Date of Composition	Date of Publication	First Performance and Interpreters	Text	Dedication
Childhood compositions Scores unpublished or lost:						
Piece	Cello and piano					Sr. Viniegra
Quartet (Andante and Scherzo)	Strings and piano					
Quintet	Strings, flute, and piano				From *Mireio* (Mistral)	
Vals Capricho	Piano	About 1900	Union Musical Española, Madrid, 1940			
Serenata Andaluza	Piano	About 1900	Union Musical Española, Madrid, 1940			
Nocturno	Piano	About 1900	Union Musical Española, Madrid, 1940			
Tus Ojillos Negros	Voice and piano	About 1900	Union Musical Española, Madrid, 1940		C. de Castro	Sr. and Sra. de Alta Villa
La Casa de Tócame Roque	*Zarzuela*	1900–1902	Unpublished			
Limosna de Amor	*Zarzuela* In collaboration with A. Vivès	1900–1902	Unpublished			
El Corneta de Ordenes		1900–1902	Unpublished		J. Veyán	

242

Title	Form	Date	Publication	First performance	Text	Dedication
La Cruz de Malta	In collaboration with A. Vivès Zarzuela	1900–1902	Unpublished			E. Dugi
Los Amores de la Iñès		1902	Unpublished	Teatro Comico, Madrid, April 12, 1902		
Allegro de Concert	Piano	1902	Unpublished	May 4, 1905, the composer		
La Vida Breve	Opera in two acts and three scenes	1904–1905	M. Eschig, Paris, 1913	Casino Municipal, Nice, April 1, 1913 (Falconnet, conductor)	C. Fernández Shaw. Adaptation by P. Milliet	Mme. A. Adiny-Milliet and to the memory of C. F. Shaw
Four Spanish Pieces: Aragonesa, Cubana, Montañesa, Andaluza	Piano	1906	1909	Société Nationale de Musique, Paris, March 27, 1909, R. Viñes		I. Albéniz
Three Songs: The Doves, Chinoiserie, Séguidille	Voice and piano	1909	Rouart-Lerolle, Paris, 1910	Late 1910, Société Musicale Indépendante, Paris, Mme. A. Adiny-Milliet, the composer	T. Gautier (La Comédie de la Mort)	Mmes. A. Adiny-Milliet, R. Brooks, C. Debussy
Seven Spanish Songs: El Paño Moruno, Seguidilla Murciana, Asturiana, Jota, Nana, Canción, Polo	Voice and piano	1914–1915	M. Eschig, Paris	Ateneo, Madrid, January 14, 1915 L. Vela and the composer	Popular texts	Mme. I. Godebska
Oración de las Madres que Tienen a Sus Hijos en Brazos	Voice and piano	December, 1914	Unpublished	Sociedad Nacional de Música, Madrid, February 8, 1915, J. Revillo and the composer	Gregorio Martínez Sierra	
Incidental music for Othello		1915	Unpublished	Teatro Novedades, Barcelona, 1915	Shakespeare	
El Amor Brujo	Gypsy ballet	1914–1915	J. W. Chester, London, 1921	First version: Teatro Lara, Madrid, April 5, 1915 (Moreno Ballesteros, conductor)	Gregorio Martínez Sierra	

243

The Works of Manuel de Falla

Title	Genre	Date of Composition	Date of Publication	First Performance and Interpreters	Text	Dedication
				Second version (concert): Sociedad Nacional de Música, Madrid, March 28, 1916 (B. Pérez-Casas, conductor)		
Nights in the Gardens of Spain	Piano and orchestra	1911–1915	M. Eschig, Paris, 1922	Teatro Real, Madrid, April 9, 1916 (J. Cubiles, soloist; F. Arbós, conductor)		R. Viñes
El Corregidor y la Molinera	Pantomime in two scenes	1916–1917		Teatro Eslava, Madrid, April 7, 1917 (J. Turina, conductor)	Gregorio Martínez Sierra	
(first version of The Three-Cornered Hat)	Ballet in two scenes	1918–1919	J. W. Chester, London, 1921	Alhambra Theatre, London, July 22, 1919 (Ballet Russe; L. Massine, choreographer; E. Ansermet, conductor)	(from P. A. de Alarcón)	L. Matos
Fuego Fatuo	Opera in three acts	1919	Unpublished	Never performed	Gregorio Martínez Sierra	
Fantasia Baetica	Piano	1919	J. W. Chester, London, 1922	New York, 1920, A. Rubinstein		A. Rubinstein
Homenaje (to Claude Debussy)	Guitar	1920	La Revue Musicale, December 1, 1920	Société Musicale Indépendante, Paris, January 24, 1921 (Mme. M. L. Casadesus, harp-lutist)		

Title	Medium	Date	Publisher	Premiere	Text	Dedication
Master Peter's Puppet Show	Marionette play with music	1919–1922	J. W. Chester, London, 1924	Concert: Teatro San Fernando, Seville, March 23, 1923 (Orquesta Bética conducted by the composer) Staged: at the home of the Princess de Polignac, Paris, June 25, 1923 (V. Golschmann, conductor)	M. de Cervantes (Adaptation by M. de Falla)	To the glory of Miguel de Cervantes and to Princess E. de Polignac
Psyché	Mezzo-soprano and five instruments	1924	J. W. Chester, London, 1926	Barcelona, December, 1924 (C. Badia)	G. J. Aubry	Mme. Alvar
Harpsichord Concerto	Harpsichord and five instruments	1923–1926	M. Eschig, Paris, 1928	Associación de Música de Cámara, Barcelona, November 5, 1926 (W. Landowska, soloist; composer, conductor)		W. Landowska
Sonnet to Córdoba	Voice and piano	1927	Oxford University Press, London, 1932	Salle Pleyel, Paris, May 14, 1927 (M. Greslé)	Luis de Góngora	Sra. E. de Errazuriz
Balada de Mallorca	Mixed a capella chorus (based on the Ballade in F Major, Op. 38, of Chopin)	1933	Unpublished	Monastery of Valldemosa, Majorca, May 21, 1933	J. Verdaguer	Capella Classica Mallorca

The Works of Manuel de Falla

Title	Genre	Date of Composition	Date of Publication	First Performance and Interpreters	Text	Dedication
Hommage pour le Tombeau de P. Dukas	Piano	1935	*La Revue Musicale*, May–June, 1936			
Fanfare on the Name of E. F. Arbós	Orchestra	1933–1934		Teatro Calderón, Madrid, April, 1934 (E. F. Arbós, conductor)		
Homenajes: E. F. Arbós, C. Debussy, P. Dukas, F. Pedrell	Orchestra	1920–1938	Ricordi, Milan, 1953	Teatro Colón, Buenos Aires, November 18, 1939 (composer, conductor)		
Atlántida	*Cantata scenica* (completed by Ernesto Halffter)	1926–1946 (Incomplete at death)	Ricordi, Milan, 1962	Concert: Teatro del Liceo, Barcelona, November 24, 1961 (E. Toldrá, conductor) Staged: Teatro alla Scala, Milan, June 18, 1962 (T. Schippers, conductor)	J. Verdaguer	To Cádiz, Barcelona, and Seville

TRANSCRIPTIONS

Ave Maria for mixed chorus
Sanctus (Victoria) for mixed chorus
Amfiparnaso (Vecchi) for mixed chorus
Hymn for unison men's chorus (with accompaniment), based on the
  Song of the Almogávares by F. Pedrell
Reorchestration of the Overture to *The Barber of Seville* (Rossini)

246

INDEX

Abd-er-Rahman II, 26
Adiny-Milliet, Ada, 50–51
Aguilar y Tejera, A., 125
Agustina, 77
Alarcón, Pedro Antonio de, 14, 93, 108
Albaïcin, Maria del, 77
Albéniz, Enriqueta, 181
Albéniz, Isaac, 6, 12, 16, 18, 28, 37, 38, 45, 46, 48, 51, 53, 110, 122, 148, 153, 181, 195
Albornoz, S., 163
Alfano, Franco, 206
Alfonso X (the Wise), 3, 10, 27, 158, 182, 208
Alfonso XIII, 6
Alonso, Damaso, 170
Altermann, Jean-Pierre, 64, 115, 116, 184
Alvar, Madame, 153, 155
Alvarez, Antonio Machado, 122, 146, 170
Alvira, J. M., 71
Alzamora, Vicente, 181
Angeles, Victoria de los, 227
Ansermet, Ernest, 108
Antequera, Tomas de, 40
Arbós, Enrique Fernandez, 78, 85, 92, 178, 182, 187, 188
Arezzo, Guido d', 24
Argentina, La; see Antonia Mercé
Astruc, G., 63
Aubin, Tony, 187
Aubry, G. J., 65, 127, 130, 133, 138, 153
Averroës, 26

Baccarisas, G., 172
Bach, Johann Sebastian, 8, 31, 47, 137, 167, 176, 200

Badia, C., 155
Balaguer, Victor, 29
Balakirev, Mili, 22
Ballesteros, Moreno, 77
Banville, Théodore de, 20
Baratech, F., 228
Barbieri, Francesco Aseajo, 14, 15, 23, 28, 121
Barios, Angel, 118
Barraine, Elsa, 187
Barrientos, Maria, 172
Bartók, Béla, 42, 43, 114, 158, 176
Baudelaire, Charles, 50
Beaumarchais, Caron de, 112, 113
Beethoven, Ludwig van, 7, 8, 31, 50, 103, 137, 177
Bellini, Vincenzo, 7, 13
Benois, Nicola, 229
Bizet, Georges, 52, 112, 113
Bleriot, L., 52
Boabdil (Mohammed XI), 40
Bonneau, 167
Bordas, 49
Borodin, Aleksandr, 89
Bret, Gustave, 176
Bretón, Tomás, 14, 15, 32, 33, 47
Breva, Juan, 27, 41
Broca, Enrico, 8, 11
Brohly, Madame, 62
Brooks, Madame R., 51
Bruckner, Anton, 158
Buffano, 140

Cabezon, Antonio de, 24, 25, 236
Cabezon, Felix-Antoine de, 129
Cabrera, Geronimo de, 196
Calderón de la Barca, Pedro, 10, 13, 173, 201, 236
Calleja, R., 100
Calvo, J., 71

Campo, Conrado del, 67
Campodonico, Luis, 65, 151, 193, 195
Caplet, André, 65
Caracol, Manolo, 146
Carré, Albert, 53, 62, 63, 64, 113
Carré, Marguerite, 62, 63, 64
Casadesus, Marie-Louise, 115
Casals, Pablo, 12, 178
Casella, Alfredo, 111, 150
Castro, Cristóbal de, 17
Castro, Guillen de, 14
Castro, Juan José, 192, 195
Cervantes, Maria, 32
Cervantes, Miguel de, 119, 120, 123, 126, 135, 138, 175
Chabrier, Alexis Emmanuel, 45, 51
Charlemagne, 28
Charles III, 146
Charles V, 27, 40
Charpentier, Gustave, 57
Chase, Gilbert, 43, 56, 89, 110
Chavarri, Lopez, 172
Chester, J. W., 79, 84, 96, 108, 109, 124, 153, 156
Chicote, Enrique, 13, 16–17
Chopin, Frédéric, 7, 17, 18, 31, 92, 112, 113, 178, 179, 180, 183
Chueca, 14, 118, 197
Cione, Andrea di (Orcagna), 191
Clarendon (B. Gavoty), 228, 236
Clark, Edward, 92
Coeuroy, André, 65
Collet, Henri, 24, 52, 63, 86, 87, 168, 184
Confalonieri, Guilio, 237
Coolidge, Mrs. Elizabeth Sprague, 150
Cordova y Ona, S., 130
Cortot, Alfred, 183
Couffon, Claude, 143
Couperin, François, 160
Cristóbal, Juan, 117
Cruque, 167
Cruz, Ramon de la, 14
Cubiles, José, 85

Dante, 225, 231
Debussy, Claude, 36, 38, 45, 47, 48, 49, 50, 51, 52, 53, 54, 57, 65, 68, 74, 86, 87, 92, 112, 113, 114, 115, 148, 154, 158, 160, 162, 182, 187, 189, 190, 198, 224
Debussy, Madame Claude, 51, 167
Delage, Maurice, 49, 51
Dethomas, Maxime, 140
Devriès, David, 55
Diaghilev, Sergei, 93, 94, 101, 102, 103, 108, 111, 113, 118, 148
Diego, Gerardo, 19, 170, 172
Dieulafoy, Marcel, 27
Djebel Al Tarik, 3
Donizetti, Gaetano, 7
Dugi, Emilio, 15
Dukas, Paul, 33, 47–48, 49, 51, 52, 54, 68, 112, 114, 182, 187, 190
Dumas, Alexandre, 23, 42, 87
Durand, J., 49, 187

Elgar, Sir Edward, 173
Encina, Juan del, 195
Errazuriz, Eugenia de, 172
Eschig, Max, 54, 56, 63, 73, 86, 92, 169, 172
Escobar, 195, 209
Escudero, V., 77, 84
Esplà, O., 195
Espoz y Mina, 5
Euclid, 20
Eugene, St. (of Seville), 26
Eximeno, 23

Falla, German de, 6, 202, 204, 205
Falla, Isabel de, 205
Falla, Maria del Carmen de, 6, 53, 111, 113, 115, 176, 178, 195, 200, 201, 202
Farnese, Isabella, 153
Fauré, Gabriel, 33
Fernández, B., 70
Fiesole, Giovanni da, 37
Fleury, Louis, 155

Fra Angelico; *see* Giovanni da Fiesole
Francell, F., 62
Franck, César, 158
Franco, Enrique, 204, 205, 206
Franco, Generalissimo Francisco, 5

Galluzo, Eloisa, 8
Gara, Eugenia, 237
Gauthier, André, 53, 193
Gautier, Théophile, 4, 23, 42, 50, 51, 75, 86, 96, 116, 129
Gentien, 53
Gheusi, P. B., 140
Gisbert, Miguel, 205
Glinka, Mikhail Ivanovich, 22, 23, 146
Godeau, 167
Godebska, Ida, 73
Godebska, Misia, 49, 64
Godebski, Cyprian, 49, 64
Goléa, A., 73, 74
Gomez de la Serna, Ramon, 73
Góngora, Luis de, 28, 153, 155, 169, 170
Goossens, Eugene, 84, 114
Gorgora, 170
Gorostidi, Juan, 14
Gortazar, Juan Carlos, 34
Gounod, Charles, 9
Goya, Francisco de, 95, 96, 167
Granados, Carmen, 140, 172
Granados, Enrique, 12, 18, 28, 74, 195
Greco, El, 85
Gregory, St., 26
Grenville, Lilian, 55, 63
Gresle, Madeleine, 167
Grieg, Edvard, 7, 8, 18
Guerrero, Francisco, 24, 195, 209
Guillen, 170
Guridi, 67
Guzman, Fernand Perez de, 28
Guzman el Bueno (Alonso Perez de Guzman), 174

Hadrian, 109
Halffter, Ernesto, 74, 112, 137, 138, 178, 195, 202, 203, 205, 206, 207, 210, 211, 212, 214, 215, 219, 224, 225, 226, 228
Halffter, Rudolfo, 155
Haydn, Joseph, 7, 137
Hernández, Isidore, 69, 70, 105, 124
Hidalgo, Juan, 13
Hilaire, Georges, 41, 84, 90, 102, 104, 145, 146, 149
Honegger, Arthur, 158, 176
Hurtado, José, 70

Imperio, Pastora, 75, 77, 80, 85
Indy, Vincent d', 33–34, 48, 50, 68
Inzenga, José, 44, 68, 70, 71, 72
Isabella of Parma, 129
Istel, Edgar, 30, 62

Jammes, Francis, 86
Janacopulos, Vera, 169
Jankélévitch, V., 65, 73, 86, 92, 105, 111
Jerez, Chato de, 40
Jimenez, Geronimo, 101, 118
John of the Cross, St., 117
Juliana, Tio Luis el de la, 146
Juncá, Joaquin, 184
Juvenal, 11

Kochansky, 34
Koechlin, Charles, 84
Krein, Julien, 187

Lahowska, Aga, 95
Lalo, Pierre, 59, 64, 112
Landowska, Wanda, 124, 129, 153, 157, 166, 167
Lanz, Hermenegildo, 122
Laparra, Raoul, 39, 71, 72, 73, 79, 82, 104
Laplane, Gabriel, 23, 29
Larrieu, R., 28
Laserna, Blas de, 14
Laskine, Lily, 155

Lecera, Duchess of, 116, 117
Leoncavallo, Ruggiero, 58
Levi, Lionello, 237
Liebich, Franz, 65
Liszt, Franz, 23, 31, 92
Llauder, Manuel R. de, 204, 22, 223, 228
Lledo, 138
Llobet, Miguel, 113, 187
Longchampt, Jacques, 227
Lopez, Rafael, 67
Lorca, Federico Garcia, 5, 11, 41, 42, 73, 76, 118, 122, 143, 149, 150, 159, 170, 194
Lotti, Cosmo, 13
Lucas, Louis, 20, 21, 68, 83, 161, 164
Lull, Ramon, 29
Luna, Pablo, 67
Lyon, Gustave, 167

Madariaga, Salvador de, 139
Maimonides, 26
Malats, Joaquin, 32
Malipiero, G. Francesco, 114, 138, 150
Maria Christina, Queen, 12
Marin, Francisco Rodriguez, 70, 97, 98, 140
Marshall, Frank, 32–33, 195
Martial, 11
Massenet, Jules, 58
Massine, Léonide, 102, 108
Matos, Leopoldo, 94
Matos, Manuel Garcia, 43, 44, 69, 70, 71, 72, 96, 97, 98, 100, 104, 107, 120, 121, 122, 123, 124, 125, 127, 131, 146, 147
Mauclair, Camille, 193
Mayreder, Rosa, 93
Meana, Paco, 67, 77
Mejorana, Rosario la, 75
Mendoza, Iñigo López de, 28
Mercanton, J., 145
Mercé, Antonia, 77, 84, 140, 172, 180

Mérimée, Prosper, 23, 40, 42, 84, 112, 113
Messager, André, 54, 61
Messiaen, Olivier, 21, 187
Mickiewicz, Adam, 179
Mila, Massimo, 236
Milan, Luis, 172
Miles, Napier, 139
Milhaud, Darius, 124, 158
Milliet, Paul, 53, 54, 63, 73
Miranne, J., 55
Miresky, 49
Mistral, Frédéric, 9
Mitjana, Rafael, 13, 38
Mola, Norberto, 229
Molina, Tirso de, 14
Montesino, 122
Monteverdi, Claudio, 137, 218
Montherlant, Henry Millon de, 42
Montoya, Roque (Jarrito), 40
Mora, Pilar, 32, 33
Moragos, Rafael, 74
Moralès, Cristóbal, 24, 25, 195, 209
Moreux, Sergei, 42
Morphy, Count de, 12, 121
Moyse, 167
Mozart, Wolfgang Amadeus, 7
Muñoz, Eduardo, 67
Murciano, Francisco Rodriguez, 147

Nakamura, Mademoiselle, 74
Navas, F. Garcia, 100, 102
Nin, Joaquin, 70, 92, 168
Núñez Robres, Lazaro, 107

Ocon, E., 72
Odero, Alejandro, 8
Ohana, Maurice, 124
Orcagna; see Andrea di Cione
Ortiz, Manuel Angeles, 122
Ortiz y Cussó, 18, 31, 32, 149
Otano, R. P., 193

Padró, Juan Gisbert, 205, 207
Padro, Loreto, 16
Pahissa, Jaime, 2, 15, 17, 30, 34, 42,

52, 58, 62, 64, 68, 71, 80, 83, 90, 93, 95, 98, 101, 105, 112, 115, 118, 122, 150, 157, 159, 163, 166, 171, 173, 174, 180, 191, 192, 195, 196, 197, 198, 199

Paredes, José Maria Garcia de, 205

Paredes, Maria Isabel de Falla Garcia de, 85

Pareja, Ramos de, 24

Parnac, Valentin, 73, 87

Parodi, Clemente, 6

Pasquier, J., 167

Pedrell, Felipe, 12, 22–23, 24, 25, 26, 27, 28, 29, 30, 31, 38, 42, 68, 70, 71, 74, 97, 121, 122, 125, 128, 134, 144, 147, 149, 164, 172, 182, 183, 188, 191, 193, 201

Peines, Niña de los, 40

Pellicer, José, 32

Pemán, José Maria, 4, 174, 175, 218

Pennela, 112

Pérez-Casas, Bartolomé, 22, 28, 33, 43, 78, 139

Pergolesi, Giovanni Battista, 113, 165, 166

Petit, Raymond, 155

Philip II, 25, 27, 89

Philip IV, 4, 13

Philip V, 14, 153

Picasso, Pablo, 95, 97, 102, 108

Pidal, José Menendez, 200

Pierné, Gabriel, 187

Pla, José, 85

Plato, 3, 203

Plutarch, 20

Polignac, Princess Edmond de, 112, 119, 122, 135, 138, 139, 150

Pomès, Mathilde, 118, 143, 170

Prunières, Henri, 111, 114, 167

Puccini, Giacomo, 54, 58, 158, 206

Puglisi, Lino, 229

Pujol, Emilio, 115, 121, 172

Purcell, Henry, 139

Quintero, Joaquin, 54

Quintero, Serafín Alvarez, 54

Quirell, 9

Rameau, Jean Philippe, 20

Ravel, Maurice, 22, 33, 46, 48, 49, 50, 66, 73, 74, 86, 92, 114, 148, 154, 155, 176, 224

Redondo, Niño R., 138

Régnier, Henri de, 139

Reinhardt, Max, 173

Respighi, Ottorino, 141

Revillo, Josefina, 74

Ricordi, Giovanni, 189, 192

Ricordi, House of, 53, 205, 207, 212, 227

Ricordi, Tito, 53, 54

Rieti, V., 150

Rimski-Korsakov, Nikolai, 23, 44

Rios, Vincente de los, 116

Roda, Cecilio de, 18, 120, 125, 127, 134

Rodrigo, Joaquin, 38, 187, 195, 200

Roiter, F., 145

Rojas, Fernando de, 29, 191

Rojas, Vito, 14, 77

Roland-Manuel, 21, 48, 64, 68, 92, 117, 138, 152, 158, 163, 168, 205

Romero, Segismundo, 150, 159, 196, 197

Ropartz, Guy, 187

Rossini, Gioacchino, 13, 168, 180

Rostand, Claude, 229, 236

Rouart-Lerolle, 51

Roussel, Albert, 114

Rubinstein, Artur, 92, 109, 111, 178, 199

Ruhlmann, Franz, 62, 63

Ruiz, Juan, 28

Ruiz-Azna, Valentin, 193, 195

Rusiñol, Santiago, 85, 86, 150

S., T. A. de, 46, 90, 91

Sagardia, Angel, 16, 17, 18, 20, 36, 43, 74, 85, 94, 142, 155, 172, 195

Saint-Saëns, Camille, 8, 31
Salazar, Adolfo, 22, 28, 30, 42, 78, 109, 137, 158, 161, 162
Salinas, 121, 127, 128, 131, 134, 158, 170
Salvador, Miguel, 78
Samazeuilh, Gustave, 49, 92
Sanchez, F. Garcia, 184
Sanchez, Gaspar, 184
San Martin, Melchor de Almagro, 36, 37, 41
Sanz, Gaspar, 158
Satie, Erik, 114, 118
Scarlatti, Domenico, 96, 105, 137, 148, 160, 165, 167
Schindeler, 138
Schippers, Thomas, 229
Schloezer, B. de, 138–39
Schmitt, Florent, 48, 66, 114, 187
Schneider, Marcel, 236
Schönberg, Arnold, 21, 158, 166
Schumann, Robert, 31
Segovia, Andrès, 141–42
Segura, 138
Segura, Dr. José, 141–42
Seneca, 109
Sermet, Jean, 4
Serrano, Arturo, 67
Sert, José Maria, 64, 139, 141, 173, 185, 204, 205, 207, 208, 217, 229, 235
Shaw, Carlos Fernández, 31–32, 62, 63
Sibelius, Jean, 158
Sierra, Gregorio Martinez, 67, 74, 75, 78, 93, 108, 112
Silva, Andrade da, 41
Simionato, Giulietta, 229
Simo, Vincente Torro, 200
Sopeña, Federico, 142
Stratas, Teresa, 229
Strauss, Richard, 158, 181
Stravinsky, Igor, 49, 84, 113, 114, 118, 122, 138, 139, 147, 158, 162, 169, 228

Streliski, 55
Striglia, Georgio, 237
Sunyol, Padre (of Montserrat), 80

Tansman, Alfred, 178
Tarrega, 113
Thomas, Juan Maria, 113, 152, 176, 177, 178, 180, 182, 183, 184, 185, 200
Thomas, R., 28
Tiersot, Julien, 39, 70, 71, 82, 104
Toldrá, Eduardo, 228
Torrès, Eduardo, 137
Torrès, Raimondo, 227
Tragó, José, 11, 12, 18, 31, 32, 177
Trajan, 109
Trend, J. B., 70, 89, 138, 171
T'Serstevens, A., 6, 89
Turina, Joaquin, 36, 48, 67, 74, 78, 195

Unamuno, Miguel de, 170

Valcarenghi, Guido, 205
Valéry, Paul, 139
Vallas, Léon, 148
Vallin, Ninon, 140, 172, 173
Van Loo, Esther, 30
Vasquez, J., 161
Vaughan Williams, Ralph, 139
Vecchi, Orazio, 183
Vega, Lope de, 13, 42, 201
Vegue y Goldric, Angel, 124
Vela, Luisa, 67, 68
Velázquez, Diego, 167
Verdaguer, Jacinto, 1, 173, 174, 175, 179, 185, 203, 204, 205, 220, 227, 228
Verdi, Giuseppi, 13, 158, 183
Verdu, José, 69
Veyán, Jackson, 15
Vich y Manrique, Bishop, 181–82
Victoria, Tomás Luis de, 24, 141, 165, 178, 195, 200, 209, 219, 236
Vieuille, 62
Vigneau, 62

Villalonga, 24, 183
Villar, Rogelio, 43
Viñes, Pepe, 35, 48
Viñes, Ricardo, 35, 47, 48, 92, 173
Viniegra, Salvador, 8, 9, 12
Vivaldi, Antonio, 137
Vivès, Amadeo, 15, 28, 77, 87, 197
Vix, Genevieve, 51
Voga, H. H., 146
Vuillermoz, Émile, 115, 116, 168

Wagner, Richard, 8, 57, 236
Wallman, Margherita, 229
Wiener, Jean, 138, 139
Wolf, Hugo, 93
Wolff, Albert, 140

Ximenez, F. Cardinal, 89

Ziryab, 26
Zuloaga, Ignacio de, 95, 140
Zurbarán, Francisco de, 8

Demarquez

Manuel de Falla.